D0824234

Praise for *The Road to Omaha*

"McGee intricately relates the action on the field and the myriad personalities of the coaches and players—from the super stud and future mil-
lionaire to the son-of-a-dairy-farmer-turned-championship-hero. . . .
[An] entertaining read."   —*Publishers Weekly*

"For less than the price of dinner at one of Omaha's famed steakhouses
you can submerge yourself in the festival-like atmosphere of the
CWS. . . . Each chapter weaves the history and pomp into a day's action
at Rosenblatt Stadium."   —*BaseballAmerica.com*

ALSO BY RYAN McGEE

ESPN Ultimate NASCAR

THE ROAD TO OMAHA

HITS, HOPES, AND HISTORY
at the
COLLEGE WORLD SERIES

by Ryan McGee

THOMAS DUNNE BOOKS | ST. MARTIN'S GRIFFIN | NEW YORK

THOMAS DUNNE BOOKS.
An imprint of St. Martin's Press.

THE ROAD TO OMAHA. Copyright © 2009, 2010 by Ryan McGee. All rights reserved. Printed in
the United States of America. For information, address St. Martin's Press, 175 Fifth Avenue,
New York, N.Y. 10010.

www.thomasdunnebooks.com
www.stmartins.com

Book design by Rich Arnold

The Library of Congress has cataloged the hardcover edition as follows:

McGee, Ryan.
    The road to Omaha : hits, hopes, and history at the College World Series / Ryan
McGee.—1st ed.
        p. cm.

    1. College World Series (Baseball) (2008)   2. California State University, Fresno—
Baseball.   I. Title.
    GV878.3.M37 2009
    796.357'63—dc22

                                                                            2009003789

ISBN 978-0-312-62802-4 (trade paperback)

First St. Martin's Griffin Edition: May 2010

To the Little Sioux Four:
Josh Fennen, Aaron Eilerts, Sam Thomsen, and Ben Petrzilka

CONTENTS

PROLOGUE: THE ARRIVAL

At 1:00 A.M. on Thursday morning, June 12, 2008, the red Arrow bus turned right off of Interstate 80, climbing up the off-ramp of Exit 454. This was the last exit in Omaha, the final stop in Nebraska before the big highway leapfrogged the Missouri River and landed in Council Bluffs, Iowa en route to all points east.

Seconds earlier, the Fresno State University Bulldogs baseball team had been a typical bunch of chattering college students, carrying on about breaking balls, video games, and girls. Then someone spotted the big green road sign that read, EXIT 454, 13TH STREET SOUTH, STADIUM.

In an instant, they fell silent.

Bus driver Chris Clark chuckled as his suddenly serious passengers scrambled for the windows, glancing into the rearview mirror as he thought to himself, *Gets them every time.*

"There it is!" Someone shouted it from the left side of the aisle, causing everyone to jump up and cram into the shouter's half of the bus. As the trees whipped by, the big black left-field scoreboard began rising into view, topped by the light-traced letters of a semicircle sign, a beacon calling out to baseball fans as if it were their mother ship.

ROSENBLATT. HOME OF THE NCAA MEN'S COLLEGE WORLD SERIES.

The image hardly seemed real. Like every college baseball team, the Bulldogs had talked about Rosenblatt, read about Rosenblatt, seen it on

TV, and set it up on a pedestal as the ultimate goal of the season and of their college careers.

Now there it was, and in thirty-six hours they would be one of only eight teams allowed to stand on that field as participants in the 2008 College World Series (CWS).

As they pulled into the parking lot the experience became even more dreamlike. The stadium even had a kind of aural glow about it, a halo provided by the nighttime bank of lights coming off the field and into the rainy night. A hardball mirage in the middle of the gridiron-crazy Great Plains.

Down on that field were a handful of stadium security team members sitting on folding chairs, keeping an eye on the diamond while fighting to stay awake. When asked if they heard voices in the outfield or saw spirits in the grandstands during those long nights, the sentries admitted that they did feel a presence. "It's not a voice or a ghost or anything like that," said one police officer. "But there's something in there with you at night. I keep expecting Shoeless Joe Jackson and Moonlight Graham to come walking in across the outfield."

Joe never played at Rosenblatt, but Joba did, the baby-faced ace of the Nebraska Cornhuskers long before he was Mr. Chamberlain, toast of Yankee Stadium. Moonlight Graham never sat in the Rosenblatt dugout, but Rice University head coach Wayne Graham had and would again in 2008, his seemingly annual return to unleash yet another missile-throwing Rice Owl pitching staff on an unfortunate opponent. The ghosts of the dugouts still talk about his army of Texas-grown arms that hurled their way to the school's first NCAA championship in 2003 by mowing down an all-star team of traditional baseball powerhouses.

That same mound was once the launching pad for a kid named Dave Winfield, who struck out twenty-nine batters for Minnesota in two days in the summer of '73. Eight years later Frank Viola of St. John's strode to that same pile of dirt, the survivor of a legendary regional slugfest with Yale's Ron Darling, carrying dual shutouts into the eleventh and twelfth innings, Darling yielding no hits, before St. John's won in the twelfth. The clash was so moving that Hall of Famer Smoky Joe Wood, a man who pitched against Christy Mathewson and who was a teammate of Cy Young, said a better game had never been thrown in all of baseball.

In 1983, a fresh-faced Texan named Roger Clemens toed that same rubber, joined by college pal and future Red Sox teammate Calvin Schiraldi. The Rocket may have been leaner than his more-recognized future Fenway and Yankee personas, but as he won the Series clincher he was certainly no less intimidating at twenty-one than he was at thirty-one or forty-one.

That same year, Arizona State's Barry Bonds roamed the Rosenblatt outfield along with Oklahoma State man-child Pete Incaviglia—Inky—who drew a crowd of thousands just to watch him take batting practice. And Michigan infielders Chris Sabo and Barry Larkin were in the formative years of a relationship that would win them a World Series with the Cincinnati Reds seven years later.

As their careers moved on past Omaha, each athlete became more famous on much bigger stages for his play, his earnings, and in some cases his flaws. But here at Rosenblatt they were all still kids playing a kids' game.

It's the kind of game that still leaves people shaking their heads in disbelief when they stand over at first base. That's where the entire '82 Miami Hurricanes baseball team (including the batgirls) should have been awarded an Oscar nomination for their ability to sell a hidden ball trick so masterful that it has its own nickname—the Grand Illusion. That same corner of the diamond is where Oklahoma State's Robin Ventura's fifty-eight-game hit streak died, where North Carolina's hopes for the 2006 title went wide right, and where Louisiana State University's Warren Morris suddenly leapt into the air, realizing that he hadn't slapped a game-tying hit, but rather he had won the national championship with a two-run homer.

Second base was once the domain of Arizona State's Bob Horner, who played at Rosenblatt one day and who was on the field with the Atlanta Braves the next. In 1951, a Popeye look-alike named Don Zimmer manned that same second bag, breaking in the dirt that would later be kicked around and dived into by the likes of California's Jeff Kent and LSU's Todd Walker.

Round the horn at shortstop and third they still play the infield in and guard the line just like Georgia Tech's Nomar Garciaparra, University of Southern California's Roy Smalley, Long Beach State's Jason Giambi, and Minnesota's Paul Molitor.

Since 1950, they came to Omaha by van, train, and plane. In the old days they stayed in local university dormitories and rode in bouncy yellow school buses. Over the years the dorm rooms became hotel suites and the bats went from ash to alloy, but while the rest of the collegiate sports world became buried under money, the College World Series and its comfy old blue home managed to preserve its sense of innocence and wonder. The administrators and event coordinators could have made more cash if they'd wanted to, just as the student-athletes could've copped an attitude if they'd so desired. Instead, everyone was kept in line by the ghosts of Rosenblatt . . .

. . . By the memories of Arizona State's longtime coach Jim Brock, who hacked and coughed his way through the first game of the 1994 Series. It was obvious that the two-time CWS championship coach was dying, but he guided his Sun Devils to a win over Miami, only to be flown back home to Arizona, where he succumbed to cancer eight days later, less than forty-eight hours after his team was eliminated in the semifinals.

. . . Kept on task by the image of Cal State Fullerton's Mark Kotsay sending ball after ball into the gap and into the stands, smacking two homers against Southern Cal to win the 1995 title. By Minnesota's Jerry Kindall, who legged out a triple in '56 to become the first (and as of 2008, the only) player to hit for the cycle, then returned to coach Arizona to three titles. And by the Bando brothers, Sal and Chris, who each led separate Arizona State teams to championships a dozen years apart.

For every future big league superstar there were hundreds of young Rosenblatt heroes of whom most people had likely never heard, boys who went on to become school principals, insurance salesmen, and car dealers. Like Fritz Fisher, who pitched eleven innings and cracked a game-tying triple to lead Michigan to the '62 title, then became a bank vice president in Toledo. Or freshman pitcher Brett Laxton, forced to start the '93 CWS championship game because the LSU Tigers were out of pitchers and who responded by striking out sixteen Wichita State batters to win the title and to earn the first championship game shutout in thirty-three years.

Seven years later Tiger Brad Cresse, who was 1-for-12 in the 2000 College World Series, stroked a left-field hit that won the championship in the bottom of the ninth. The image of that winning run being scored, of LSU's Ryan Theriot sliding across home, popping up to his feet and tossing his helmet into the Rosenblatt grandstands, is a vision that screams out from every level of CWS experience.

Pure, unhinged, uncorrupted, refuse-to-sellout joy.

It was the search for that joy that brought Fresno State to the doorstep of Rosenblatt Stadium in the middle of the wet night. They knew that no one was going to let them into the stadium to walk around and to try conjuring up those ghosts in person. They also didn't care. They'd found the holy ground and they merely wanted to look upon it in person. They'd get to walk on its grass soon enough.

Just like their seven opponents, the ones sound asleep in their Omaha hotel rooms, the Bulldogs had earned the right to come and to commune with the spirits of Rosenblatt, those remembered and forgotten.

And who knew? Perhaps they would be able to add their names to the roll call of College World Series greats and moments. Texas . . . Southern Cal . . . LSU . . . and Fresno freaking State.

Why not?

ONE

THE BLATT

Friday, June 13, 2008
Opening Ceremonies

At 3:00 P.M. on Friday, June 13, 2008, the eight head coaches of the NCAA Division I Men's College World Series strolled one by one into the Hall of Fame Room of Omaha's Johnny Rosenblatt Stadium. On the field their teams were being rotated through a continuous gauntlet of batting practice, team photos, media interviews, and mandatory all-hands-on-deck autograph sessions. Tomorrow the games would begin. Today was about acclimation, atmosphere, and smiles.

The eight men greeted one another, smiled, shook hands, and took their seats. No one ever actually enjoyed these press conferences, but on a day like today it didn't feel like the hassle that it usually was. Scattered throughout the United States were 278 other coaches who were sitting at home dreaming of being so inconvenienced.

Since June 14, 1950, every first day of the College World Series looked and felt just like this one.

Omaha, Nebraska.

Rosenblatt Stadium.

Eight teams.

Two weeks.

Double elimination.

One champion.

God bless America.

Every coach knew what was at stake and what had to be done. Their teams had been divided into two four-team double-elimination brackets. Lose twice and you were out. The winners of those two brackets would get a clean slate, erasing any losses from their record, and face off in a best-of-three series for the national championship.

Now they were just anxious to get on with it.

Six hours earlier, Florida State was the first team to hit the field, the much-hyped Seminole sluggers taking their turn in the day's heavily regimented National Collegiate Athletic Association (NCAA) schedule. Then every hour on the hour until 5:00 P.M. the remaining seven schools made their rounds—Stanford, Miami, Georgia, Rice, Fresno State, North Carolina, and LSU. Team photo, ten minutes of stretching, fifty minutes of hitting and fielding, twenty-minute presentation on the dangers of sports wagering, one half hour of autographs, barbecue dinner at 7:00, opening ceremonies at 9:00, fireworks at 9:40, don't be late.

What happened if they were?

"We've never really had to worry about that," said NCAA official Damani Leech, surprised that someone even dared to ask the question. "Nobody ever is."

As one team hit away, the next in line entered the ballpark through one of the bullpen tunnels down each foul line. It was the exact same stroll through the exact same tunnel that had been walked by Zimmer, Winfield, and Mike Mussina. At the top of that tunnel waited the same Omaha sunshine that once washed over the not-yet-inflated shoulders of Bonds, Clemens, Rafael Palmeiro, and Jason Giambi. Long before their names became identifiable to so many as symbols of everything wrong with the game, they were innocent kids experiencing the same initial reaction to their new surroundings as these, the innocents of 2008.

"Holy . . ."

Unfailingly, as each first-time CWS participant spilled onto the field, he would simultaneously drop both his equipment bag and his jaw, awed by the sight of the ballpark known lovingly as The Blatt, the home of college baseball's best since the Truman administration. A typical twenty-year-old collegian's entire baseball life had been played out in front of crowds of dozens, hundreds if he was lucky. Even a baseball-addicted school such as the University of Miami was lucky to draw a sellout crowd of 5,000.

Rosenblatt seats 24,000.

"Dude," one Stanford player said to a teammate, "it looks so much bigger than it does on TV."

Above those slack-jawed players, scattered throughout the red, yellow, and blue seats were already several thousand of those fans, each section of the stadium providing its own Norman Rockwell painting. Fathers and sons, mothers and daughters, grandparents and grandchildren, school groups, youth baseball teams, and at least a dozen folks who looked as though they had slept beneath the bleachers since the final out of the 2007 Series, waiting fifty weeks for their next CWS fix.

Some were attending the College World Series for the first time. Others were arriving for their tenth, twenty-fifth, or fiftieth. And holding with CWS tradition they had all entered the park to watch the day's opening ceremonies for the very reasonable price of free.

Just beyond the left-field wall a pillar of smoke rose from the trees lining Bob Gibson Boulevard, a thick white cloud produced by a small city's worth of purple-and-gold-clad LSU fans. They waved and threw strands of Mardi Gras beads to the conga line of cars that crawled by, slowly snaking its way along the two-lane road, gawking at the tent-sized GEAUX TIGERS flags and rounding the block around The Blatt searching for a parking spot. The stop-and-go traffic, mostly stop at this point, crept left onto Thirteenth Street, the main conduit from downtown Omaha to the nearly sixty-year-old ballpark. Overhead stood a massive fiberglass gorilla, adorned with a banner reading, WELCOME CWS FANS, FROM KING KONG BURGERS, PHILLIES, STEAKS, AND GYROS.

A few blocks north, the marquis at Chop's Bowling Alley flashed in giant red letters:

CLOSED TODAY. GONE TO SERIES.

The fortunate fans who'd found a place to stow their cars were already strolling the uphill climb of Thirteenth Street to buy T-shirts and caps and consume cold beverages, from the throat-sharpening brews of Starsky's Beer Garden to free bottles of fan-labeled "Jesus Water" handed out by a Christian group known as the Ninth Inning Ministry.

They stood in line at Zesto, a self-proclaimed "nationally known" ice cream stand, they shot baskets and threw strikes in the NCAA's interactive Fan Fest, and they filed in and out of the neighboring Henry Doorly Zoo to see the tigers and owls before going inside the ballpark to see the Tigers and the Owls.

"It's like going to the state fair," said one red-faced girl as she attempted to slurp down some Zesto strawberry soft serve before the sun got to it first. "But it's even better because there's baseball."

Inside The Blatt, the grown-ups felt more than a little like the young slurper. And why not? The sky was cloudless, the temperature perfect, and Top 40 hits blared through the concourse, occasionally punctuated by the sounds of . . . what was that? Organ music? Did they still play that at ballparks?

The batting cage was sprawled out over home plate like a dark green opera clamshell. From deep within it came the repetitive, unmistakably metallic sound that has become the instant audible signature of June in Omaha.

Tink.

Tink.

Tink.

Four hundred feet away, the bleacher creatures leaned over the outfield wall, screaming each and every time a ball came sailing their way off the barrel of the aluminum bats, which happened much more often than not. Those same fans bellowed even louder when a smash fell short and the unfortunate fielding player was faced with Rosenblatt's eternal on-field decision: Do I throw this ball back in for more BP or do I be a hero and toss it into the stands?

In the concourse, the twenty-five-man Miami Hurricane roster was seated at a ridiculously long line of tables and each player was handed a Sharpie marker. As fans began to work their way down the line to collect autographs, the Canes began to bang out a hip-hop beat on the tabletop. Before long the fans joined in with handclaps and foot stomps. Even the concessionaires got into the act, rat-a-tat-tatting with their tongs on the side of the hot-dog cookers.

On the top step of the third-base dugout, LeRoy Swedlund's sixty-one-year-old grin managed to out-gleam his mirrored sunglasses, spectacles that reflected the spectacle around him. Swedlund had earned the right to stand here as a representative of the Omaha Rotary Club. Standing alongside was fellow Rotarian Jim Stewart, who first attended the College World Series as a preteen batboy in the 1950s.

As long as anyone in Omaha could remember, the eight participating College World Series teams had been assigned hosts from local civic organizations and service clubs, from the Lions Club to Kiwanis to Offutt Air Force Base. Prior to the event, they sold books of general admission tickets to raise money for their favorite charities. Once the Series began, anything a team desired—Gatorade, donuts, dinner reservations, Band-Aids, whatever—they only had to ask their designated hosts and it would materialize. There is no greater symbol of the relationship between the event and the town than the one between the teams and their host.

During the mayhem that followed Cal State Fullerton's title-clinching victory in 2004, catcher Kurt Suzuki became so mobbed by fans that he couldn't make his way through the parking lot to attend the team celebration across the street. So Optimist Club ambassador Fred Uhe threw the 200-pounder on his back and gave him a piggyback ride through the masses.

Six years earlier, Long Beach State starting pitcher Mike Gallo stood frozen in the clubhouse, refusing to take the mound until he'd scarfed down his ritualistic pregame snack of precisely one orange and one apple. A heady 49er coach placed a call to Concord Club member and financial adviser Terry Devlin, who sprinted out of his office, raced through a local grocery store, and produced the produce in the nick of time.

Free tickets.

Organ music.

Jesus water.

Piggyback rides.

Good luck finding any of the above at the Final Four or the Bowl Championship Series (BCS) title game.

So far Swedlund and Stewart's assignment of looking after Rice University had happily lacked such drama. The Owls were making their seventh trip to Rosenblatt in twelve years, so they had the Series routine down pat. But just in case, the Rotarians would be at their beck and call from the moment they'd landed on Thursday until they loaded up and went back home to Houston, either the elated owners of their second CWS championship trophy or a crushed bunch of college kids.

Either way, standing in the dugout with the sun on your face beat the hell out of working in the electronic document imaging business, which is what Rotarian host LeRoy Swedlund did before what he called "semiretiring."

"I don't throw the word 'perfect' around very much," he said as Owl assistant coach Mike Taylor walked by and slapped him on the shoulder. "But you know what this is right here? This is the perfect day. No winner or losers today. Just perfect weather, good old-fashioned baseball, and smiles all the way around."

The perfect day. Back in the Hall of Fame Room, Mike Batesole was missing it.

As the eight head coaches began addressing the assembled media types, the forty-four-year-old skipper of the Fresno State Bulldogs put on a brave face, but was already feeling the pinch of being in charge of the what-the-hell-are-these-guys-doing-here team of the 2008 tournament. Who else would have a damn mandatory head coach's press conference scheduled at the exact same time of his team's first session of batting practice?

As Batesole had taken his seat at the far left side of the NCAA's trademark high-and-long, blue-and-white table, he was greeted by Mike Martin of Florida State, who was bringing his thirteenth team to Rosenblatt and ninth in the last eighteen seasons. To Martin's left sat Mark Marquess of Stanford, who had recruited Batesole as a player out of high school and who was here for his fourteenth CWS; then Jim Morris, practically a citizen of Omaha after eleven trips in his first fifteen seasons at the University of Miami. And so it went, all the way down to the far end of the table. In all, the seven coaches joining him on the stage had participated in fifty-nine editions of the College World Series, four of them as both a player and a coach.

When Batesole walked into The Blatt a few minutes earlier, it was for the very first time.

Twenty-four years earlier he'd nearly made it here it as a shortstop at Oral Roberts University, but twice his teams fell one game short of clinching a CWS berth, losing to superpowers Oklahoma State and Wichita State.

In 1996, his first season as an NCAA Division I head coach, he took upstart Cal State Northridge, a program he'd saved from execution by a budget-conscious administration, and once again stood on the brink of Omaha. The Matadors stunned Marquess and his Stanford team on their home field, but ran out of steam in their seventieth game of the season, falling to Martin's Seminoles. Yet again, he'd come up one game shy.

Batesole turned the sting of those losses into motivation, vowing not to attend his sport's penultimate event until he had earned it. Every time he received his invitation to the American College Baseball Coaches Association meetings that coincided with the Series he gave away the CWS-emblazoned freebies that came with the invite and threw what was left in the trash.

Now, finally, he was here. Rosenblatt f'ing Stadium. And here he was, stuck in a press conference, sitting behind a microphone under blinding TV lights while his team was out there, *tinking* out big flies and bigger smiles in the sunshine.

In truth, the Hall of Fame Room was merely a large, generic rectangular conference room, buried behind the first-base concourse. Because of the stadium's full-time tenant, the Class AAA Omaha Royals of the Pacific Coast League, it was decorated with the jerseys and mementoes of the greatest names in Kansas City Royals history. Sadly, that history boiled down to only three men—George Brett, Frank White, and manager Dick Howser. And as with all things pertaining to the Royals, everything in the Hall of Fame Room remained frozen in time, its calendar permanently stuck on October 27, 1985, the night the big club earned its lone World Series title as well as its last real moment of relevance in the baseball world.

"Why is all this Royals crap in here?" one out-of-town writer asked another, pointing to the three framed jerseys, along with a fourth, number 1/16, belonging to Omaha icon Warren Buffett, annual contender for richest man on planet Earth and coowner of the O Royals.

"I'm not sure," his colleague replied. "I think there used to be a minor-league team here that had something to do with Kansas City. And the other jersey must be Jimmy Buffett's. Is he from Omaha or something?"

For the next hour, the coaches went through the routine of the pre-Series presser. Each coach gave an opening statement and Batesole was allowed to deliver his first so that he could be dismissed early and get back to his team.

He cracked jokes about pitcher Justin Wilson's wild ways, saying, "He makes me go through a pack of Marlboros every time he starts a game."

He thanked Rice head coach Wayne Graham for leaving the Western Athletic Conference for Conference USA, opening the door for schools like Fresno to finally have a chance to win the league's baseball championship. "We played Rice about fifty times when they were in our conference and I don't think we scored a run against them."

He even hearkened back to the Omaha-or-bust game against Arizona State in Tempe, a contest his team won in extra innings just five days earlier: "They hit fifty balls out of the park in batting practice. We're still working on our first bucket from the start of the season."

The room of college baseball scribes was more than a little stunned. Batesole wasn't exactly known for his witty rapport with the media . . . or for that matter, anyone else. Oh well, they thought collectively as he was excused to join his team on the field, he can be as funny as he wants. Fresno won't be here more than two games anyway.

With Batesole gone, the questions to the seven remaining coaches began in rapid-fire succession. They were asked about individual players, about the sudden increase in parity across the 286 schools playing Division I baseball, and about recent NCAA rules changes regarding shortening the season, tightening schedules, and potentially reducing the number of baseball scholarships.

North Carolina coach Mike Fox was asked about the pressure of bringing back a team for the third consecutive year ("I'd rather have that problem than not"). Mark Marquess and LSU head coach Paul Mainieri were asked about the relief of getting their storied programs back to Omaha after unusually long absences (Mainieri: "I'll guess they'll let me keep my job a little longer"). Fox, Morris, and Martin were asked to explain how their league, the Atlantic Coast Conference, had managed not to win a College World Series since, of all schools, Wake Forest had taken the crown in

1955 (Morris, conveniently forgetting his twelve seasons at Georgia Tech: "It's not our fault, Miami joined the ACC just five years ago").

Then the entire group was asked to address the difficulty of earning a trip to Omaha. Every year began with fall practice and a fifty-game regular season, followed by each school's respective conference tournament. Surviving those three stages meant earning a berth in the NCAA's grueling double-elimination bracket. Like college basketball's much more famous tournament, baseball began its postseason with sixty-four teams. The first round was referred to as the Regionals, sixteen separate four-team double-elimination tournaments. The sixteen regional winners move on to the Super Regionals, eight two-team best-of-three weekends to determine the eight invitees to Omaha.

March might be Madness, but it used up an entire month to determine the Final Four. The crucible of baseball's Regional and Super Regional rounds were compressed into two hit-and-run weekends.

Seventy-two-year-old Graham growled at being asked to describe the rigors of the baseball season to stand among the Omaha Eight. "It feels like a vampire got a hold of you and left you with just enough blood to live."

For a half hour everyone chatted, laughed, and yawned. Georgia head coach David Perno, despite having his team here for its third CWS in the last five seasons, wasn't asked a single question that didn't begin with, "This is for all the coaches . . ."

Over that first thirty minutes, the media danced around the elephant in the room, the one prominently illustrated with blueprints and architectural drawings, mounted on giant foam-board posters and displayed on a line of easels along the right-hand side of the Hall of Fame Room. A room, it turns out, that had just been earmarked for a bulldozing.

"This question is for all the coaches. How do you feel about this week's announcement that Rosenblatt Stadium will be replaced by a new ballpark in 2011?"

That announcement had been made only three days earlier at an outdoor press conference attended by NCAA officials, Omaha municipal brass, and most of the media members in attendance at this press conference. The ribbon-cutting ceremony was held on the approximate future location of the new home plate, in parking lots C and E adjacent to the still-new Qwest Center arena and convention center, right smack in the center of downtown Omaha.

The proclamation had long been expected, yet was no less shocking to hear aloud. The College World Series would be moving to its brand-new $140-million downtown state-of-the-art home in three years. A full three miles north of The Blatt, Zesto, Starsky's, the zoo, and the ice cream girl's beloved state-fair atmosphere.

"I've been coming here about as long as I can remember," said Stanford head coach Mark Marquess, who first came to Omaha in 1967 as the Cardinal first baseman. "Over the years I've seen Rosenblatt grow from a little minor-league park up on this hill into what it is today. Listen, change is good. But what makes this event great is what hasn't changed. The commitment from the city of Omaha. What I've always seen in those stands. The ten-year-old kids begging for autographs and then returning as adults to watch their kids do the same. When we stop seeing that, then we've got problems. . . ."

"I'll tell you this," Mike Martin added quickly. "I'm glad I'm not the one who had to make that decision."

"That decision" produced a nearly decade-long debate that at times decayed into good old-fashioned cheap-shot nastiness. The Battle of the Blatt had proved to be one of the longest, most vocal, and divisive public squabbles in Omaha history.

No small achievement by any stretch of the imagination.

The city of Omaha was originally devised as nothing more than a real-estate scheme. Residents of Council Bluffs, Iowa, were desperate to ensure that the long dreamed-of Transcontinental Railroad would someday run through their town. So on July 4, 1854, a group of enterprising locals crossed the Missouri River into the still-new Nebraska Territory and proclaimed their plans to build said town. They then frantically rowed back into Iowa, scared off by a party of Indians who had stopped to watch the drunken white people propose toasts to their own genius. Eleven years and six days later, the first rails of the Union Pacific Railroad were spiked in Omaha City.

The years in between were a constant bloody tug-of-war between those who owned land and those who wanted to. A group of particularly ruthless bastards was known as the Claim Club, known to repeatedly dunk landowners into the frozen waters of the Missouri until, on the verge of an iced-over death, they finally agreed to sign over what was rightfully theirs.

Soon Omaha was declared the capital of the territory, but only after a series of backhanded political moves designed to slant the newly formed House of Representatives in the city's favor. The reaction was a giant, chair-throwing, nose-breaking bunkhouse stampede of a brawl on the House floor, a throw-down that involved, among others, J. Sterling Morton, founder of both Morton Salt and Arbor Day. For the better part of the next half-century, Omaha slugged its way through fights between cowboys and Indians, cowboys and cowboys, railroad men and Indians, and pretty much anyone who dared to walk its streets.

When Omahans weren't dragging one another around by the hair, they were dragging each other into court. They sued over land claims and business deals gone bad. A group of local prostitutes even tried to sue to get their well-deserved earnings from an unruly client whom they claimed was blackmailing them. He also happened to be the sheriff of nearby Lincoln.

Wrote one Kansas City paper: "It requires but little, if any, stretch of the imagination to regard Omaha as a cesspool of iniquity, for it is given up to lawlessness and is overrun with a horde of fugitives from justice and dangerous men of all kinds who carry things with a high hand and a loose rein . . . If you want to find a rogue's rookery, go to Omaha."

Nearly a century and a half later, the iron-necked personality of Omaha's citizenry had become more subtle. But if the situation called for it, they still had the ability to tap back into their venomous Wild West ancestry.

Just ask Mike Fahey.

"You know where it's the worst? You should go with me to the grocery store." As the city's forty-ninth mayor admitted it, he pulled his lips tight against his teeth and glanced down at the long conference table in front of him, looking more than a little exhausted. "The older ladies love to corner me at the grocery store and tell me everything I'm doing wrong."

Just a few days earlier the sixty-four-year-old mayor stood with NCAA

President Myles Brand in the Qwest Center parking lot, just a few blocks north of his office on Farnam Street, and made the new stadium announcement. The two men also unveiled an agreement that would keep the College World Series in Omaha until 2035, a major departure from the typical short-term contracts of the past. And it was certainly a different path for the NCAA, who had publicly entertained the idea of moving the event from city to city as it did with the Final Four, Frozen Four, and nearly every major collegiate championship.

But no tax-paying, Omaha-loving citizen seemed to care about the new long-term guarantee. They only cared that their beloved stadium was going to be flattened.

Since Mayor Fahey's election in 2001, no single issue had galvanized the city like the future of The Blatt. As early as 2004, he was being booed during civic appearances, already a victim of rumors that the NCAA was pressuring the city to raze the ballpark. Bumper stickers and yard signs began springing up around Omaha, declaring SAVE ROSENBLATT and accompanied by a TV ad campaign starring Kevin Costner, who declared that the old ballpark was a "field of dreams."

The worst of it all came during three public forums held over one sadistic week in March 2008. As citizens strolled to the microphone to ask questions of His Honor, there was little honor in the darts they threw his way.

At Lauritzen Gardens seventy-one-year-old Al Italia pointed his finger at the mayor and declared, "Rosenblatt is Omaha. Rosenblatt is the College World Series. Rosenblatt is the tradition of baseball in Omaha!" A freshman at Westside High School drew a standing ovation when he wondered aloud why the mayor couldn't push his plan back five years to raise more private money. Declared another attendee, "There's more holes in this plan than Swiss cheese!" In the middle of it all, an Omaha citizen named Gregory Lyons fired up a Web site and filed an affidavit seeking to have the mayor recalled.

Had the Missouri been iced over, Mayor Mike Fahey most certainly would have received a dunking from the Claim Club.

But what the citizenry hadn't fully understood was that a new ballpark wasn't merely an option. It was *the* option. Two years earlier, the NCAA and the city had agreed in principal to a $26 million Rosenblatt renovation plan, merely the next stanza of a constant reconstruction process started in 1992. That plan had resulted in thousands more seats, a new press box, a total makeover of the playing field, and a brand-new 27-by-57-foot video board. In all, the additions had already cost the city nearly $50 million.

Turns out, it wasn't enough.

On March 12, 2007, Omaha received a proposal from the NCAA titled "New Stadium," with a subtle hint that without a new facility the College World Series might go shopping for a new home, or implement a traditional Final Four–style rotation that would take it from city to city.

So Mayor Fahey and the city made the only move available to them. They pushed ahead with a plan to fund and build a new ballpark. "As painful as it is to think you might be remembered as the mayor who tore down Rosenblatt," Fahey said with a sigh, "it would be worse to become the mayor that lost the College World Series."

As the eight coaches answered questions about leaving Rosenblatt, Fahey stepped off the elevator on the third floor of the downtown municipal building. Just as they did every morning, he and his staff strolled down a long hallway toward his office, walking past the portraits of the forty-eight mayors that preceded him. On one end hung the scowl of Jesse Lowe, Omaha's first mayor and a man with a Lincolnesque beard who looked as though he certainly could have held his own during one of those State House brouhahas. From portrait to portrait, each previous mayor sported his own intimidating frown, most garnished by some sort of overgrown facial hair.

Then there was mayor number thirty-one, sporting a smile so big the photo seemed as if it had its own spotlight, the portrait of John R. Rosenblatt, founding father of The Blatt.

As a kid, Johnny Rosenblatt was obsessed with baseball, earning two letters as outfielder at Omaha's Technical High, but was forced to turn down the University of Iowa's scholarship offer because he had to earn money for his family. During the summers he was known to play in as many as six sandlot games a day, switching uniforms for a series of local semipro teams, including the Murphy-Did-Its, the Carter Lake Ball Club, and the Omaha Buffaloes of the Western League (even though he sometimes had to use the name Johnny Ross to slip in past the occasional anti-Semite).

In 1927, barely one year out of high school, Rosenblatt played along-side Lou Gehrig and against Babe Ruth, when the two Yankee sluggers came to O Town to participate in an exhibition game between Rosen-blatt's Omaha Prints and the rival Omaha Brown Parks. (After the game, Ruth was presented with an egg that had just been laid by a local namesake hen known as the Babe Ruth of Poultry, inscribed "From the Queen of Eggs to the King of Swat.") In a game against barnstorming Negro Leaguers, Rosenblatt faced Satchel Paige, who quickly put the kid two strikes down then shouted, "Now I'm going to strike you out!"—which he promptly did.

Eventually the kid was hired by Roberts Dairy, who needed some per-sonality in the factory sales department and a glove up the middle on the factory ballclub. Rosenblatt soon rose to the job of sales director and quickly began leveraging his newfound clout to sell his city to baseball's minor leagues. But to do his wooing he needed a ballpark, so he and friend Eddie Jellen cobbled together supporters to found the unoriginally titled Original Stadium Committee. Even after Jellen died in World War II, Rosenblatt continued his push for the park.

Residents living around the existing Fontenelle Park stadium north of downtown rejected the idea of expansion because of the lights and the noise (in retrospect not exactly the greatest move). So Rosenblatt hand-picked a south-side hilltop location for a new stadium at the corner of Thirteenth Street and Deer Park. Like Mayor Fahey, salesman Rosenblatt took his lumps from the public, but he eventually broke ground with a handful of local contractors, even managing to sidestep a national coal strike by traveling to Gary, Indiana, to bring in the steel needed for con-struction.

Municipal Stadium was dedicated on October 17, 1949, complete with an exhibition game of Nebraska-born professional ballplayers, including Philadelphia outfielder and future Hall of Famer Richie Ashburn. Unfor-tunately, few local sports fans noticed because down the road in Lincoln, Frank Leahy's Notre Dame Fighting Irish was putting a hurting on their beloved Nebraska Cornhusker football squad.

Omaha was then, as it still is, a football town first.

That didn't matter to Johnny Rosenblatt, who'd been elected to the Omaha City Council and had dangled his new stadium to convince the St. Louis Cardinals to send their Class A ballclub back from Iowa (in their first game he promptly began the local tradition of "hitting out" the first pitch of the season instead of throwing it out).

He'd also successfully hosted the American Legion's 1949 Junior World Series. Soon he—along with Ed Pettis, secretary-treasurer of locally owned Brandeis Department Store, and Morris Jacobs, coowner of Bozell-Jacobs Advertising—leveraged the success of the Junior World Series to convince the NCAA to move their struggling baseball championship to Municipal Stadium the following summer. It didn't hurt that Rosenblatt and his team of diplomats had agreed to share all profits 50/50 and would also pay off any financial losses the NCAA might incur from the event.

By 1954, Rosenblatt was mayor and by '64 the ballpark was renamed Johnny Rosenblatt Stadium. Even as Parkinson's disease began to prematurely rob him of his trademark ebullience, nothing brought a bigger grin to Rosenblatt's face than knowing that minor-league ball and college baseball's biggest event was being played in his stadium, the building that people told him was a bad idea and now had his name over the door.

"It weighs on me every day," Mayor Fahey admitted less than a week after the groundbreaking ceremony that ensured Rosenblatt's stadium would be flattened. As he talked, guests sat outside his office in a waiting area, flipping through magazines and newspapers on the table before them. Among those papers was a glossy brochure touting the benefits of the new downtown ballpark. It featured some slick artist's renderings and trumpeted amenities such as an open 360-degree walk-around concourse, twenty-eight luxury suites, party decks, and much, much better parking.

Sitting beside the sales pitch was a local independent newspaper topped by the headline: IT'S TIME FOR MAYOR FAHEY TO RETIRE.

"Sometimes," he said with a shake of the head, "it takes sacrifices in the present day to preserve the future. Listen, I used to live right next to Rosenblatt. Believe me. I'm going to miss it, too."

But for now, on this perfect Friday, Johnny Rosenblatt Stadium was still there. Still there for three more editions of the College World Series and still there sitting atop that handpicked hill and packed with more than enough Johnny Rosenblatt–like smiles to offset the mayor's permanently furrowed brow.

As the day's final batting-practice session wrapped up, the fans filed outside to grab another brat, another can of pop, and to watch the still-snaking traffic inch its way around the block. In the south parking lot the rock band Candlebox prepared to hit the stage for a free concert, flanked by a giant banquet tent where the eight teams would eat dinner together in college baseball's largest cookout. Dr. Sam Phillips and a group of fellow Omaha physical therapists known as "Last Year's Champions" had fired up the smokers nearly twenty-four hours earlier and had ribs, chicken, brisket, and "plenty of sides if you are into that that sort of thing" slow-cooked and ready to serve.

But before brisket, there was business. The coaches, finally finished with their media conference, met in the press-box cafeteria with their athletic directors, NCAA officials, ESPN producers, and stadium-operations directors to discuss the protocol for the two-week event.

"Above all, let's respect the teams after they have been eliminated," stated Larry Templeton, outgoing Mississippi State athletic director (A.D.) and chairman of the NCAA Baseball Committee. "It is important that we stay on schedule and that we clear out the dugouts and locker rooms for the teams coming in for the day's next game. But remember that a loss is a loss and we need to give these student-athletes their space and let them deal with that before we start trying to push them out of here. Now let's go eat some barbecue. . . ."

Later that evening, beneath a perfect three-tiered Nebraska sunset and in front of a perfect capacity crowd, each team was introduced as they marched in from center field, dressed in knit shirts and ball caps, lined up behind their school's flag as if they were arriving for the Olympic Games. They took their seats on the field, lined neatly in rows of five, four teams per baseline, with underdog Fresno State taking its place alongside five-time College World Series champion LSU and North Carolina, the two-time defending runner-up.

At precisely 9:40 P.M., the first fireworks cluster left its cannon, setting off a show so spectacular that the cars rumbling by on I-80 began pulling over onto the shoulder to watch, and the merchants on Thirteenth Street strolled out of their storefronts to stand on the front stoop and snap pictures.

Next door, zoo director Daniel Morris watched his animals as they paused, looked skyward to see what the ruckus was all about, and then stopped eating to take it in. Used to be, the explosions would freak them out, but they had grown as the event and the pyrotechnic display had grown with them. Now they were used to it and Morris could relax and watch it himself.

No city politics.

No demolition crews.

No charge for admission.

Yes sir, the perfect day.

Play ball.

TWO

THE PICK

Somewhere in Iowa, Dave and Linda Burns weren't lost, but they were close.

One day earlier the two sixty-nine-year-old retirees had left their home in Akron, Ohio, cramming two weeks' worth of supplies into their compact car and heading due west to Nebraska. They cruised south of Chicago, jumping onto Interstate 80, the modern highway that traces one of America's tried-and-true westward trails. The roaring road traces a path that was followed by the California Trail, the Mormon Pioneer Trail, the Pony Express, and the coveted Transcontinental Railroad.

In eight days they would celebrate their fiftieth wedding anniversary and they would do it from their box seats at Rosenblatt Stadium. Over the winter their daughter Jenny, one of five grown children, had asked her parents what kind of a party they wanted for their big day.

"We don't want a party," her mother said plainly. "We want to go to the College World Series."

Dave Burns was a baseball man and as a result Linda had become a baseball woman. His entire adult life was spent splitting time between the job he had to do (working as a purchasing agent at a machine shop) and the job he wanted to do—coaching baseball. He coached youth league teams, F and E league teams, fall ball, and served as an assistant at Akron's Kenmore High School, winning championships everywhere they would have him.

Dave's father had coached him as a kid, Dave had coached his three sons, and now his kids coached their kids. These days the Burns grandparents spent their time driving from ballgame to ballgame to support the next generation, from Akron all the way down to Atlanta to see grandson Dustin, who hoped to catch the eye of Coach Dave Perno and his Georgia Bulldogs.

Despite all the thousands of games they'd attended during their lives together, all they wanted for their anniversary was, of course, to see more baseball.

"We'd wanted to go to the College World Series for nearly thirty years," Linda explained. "But with five kids we never had the time or the money to do it. When those same kids asked what we wanted, that's what we told them. All our friends said, 'There aren't any cruise ships in Omaha!' but we didn't want a cruise. We wanted to go to see the games, especially before they tore down Rosenblatt."

Jenny jumped on the Internet and then onto the phone. It's too early, a CWS ticket agent told her, but we'll get back to you. A few weeks later, she got the call she'd been waiting on. Two seats came open on the first-base side, given up by an Omaha Royals season-ticket holder. Jenny had requested tickets for only the final games of the tournament, but now the ticket office was dangling two seats available for all eleven days. "So I did it," the proud daughter said with a laugh. "And the reaction we got from Mom and Dad was priceless."

Now Mom and Dad were somewhere in Iowa, and for the first time during the trip the highway was grinding to a halt.

We might still make it, they told one another. The first pitch wasn't for a few more hours.

More than 130 miles away in downtown Omaha, Florida State's Buster Posey was beginning the morning of his first-ever CWS appearance with a scene that had become part of the soft-spoken catcher's weekly routine during this, the most prolific individual season in college baseball history.

Go to the ballpark and get a big hit.

Go to class and get a big grade.

Go to a ceremony and get a big award.

At 10:00 A.M., barely three hours before the first pitch of the first game of his first College World Series, the twenty-one-year-old catcher stood quietly in the downtown headquarters of the Omaha Chamber of Commerce, awaiting yet another of those big awards. Standing alongside were his fellow nominees, including Georgia shortstop Gordon Beckham, who would be taking the field at The Blatt for Game Two against Miami once Posey's Seminoles were finished with Stanford. Beckham and the other finalists, third baseman Brett Wallace of Arizona State and pitcher Aaron Crow of Missouri, had earned their nominations with very impressive numbers.

But Posey's stats were otherworldly.

The junior came to Omaha as the NCAA's season leader in six offensive categories, including batting average (.460), runs batted in (92), and, thanks to a stunning explosion in the NCAA tournament, tied for first in home runs (26). In the eight tourney games leading into Omaha he'd hit .417 with seven homers. In more than a century of college baseball only one man had managed to win the triple crown, Indiana's Mike Smith in 1968. With a good showing in Omaha, Posey could become the second.

In the midst of the tournament he was also taken fifth overall by the San Francisco Giants in the Major League Baseball First-Year Player Draft. In all, seven players participating in the 2008 College World Series were taken in the first round, including five of the first dozen picks. Among those players, Posey was chosen first. When his name—"Gerald P. Posey"—was announced by Commissioner Bud Selig, his teammates didn't react with typical college-aged jealousy. They rose to give Buster a standing ovation.

Oh by the way, he'd also played all nine positions in a single game against Savannah State. And, oh by the way, his college grade point average was just a few hundredths shy of a perfect 4.0.

During Friday's press conference in the Hall of Fame Room, six of the eight coaches had referred to "Buster" by first name only, as if he were Bono or Madonna. Three had declared him one of the best players, perhaps the best player, they'd ever seen. Friday night's edition of *Baseball Tonight* on ESPN suggested that fans should tune into the College World Series even if they didn't care a thing about it, just to watch Posey's swing. FSU Sports Information Director Jason Leturmy's list of daily interview requests had steadily increased as Omaha had grown closer, especially after Posey's selection in the draft in the middle of the Super Regional against Wichita State.

He was, quite simply, The Pick.

"You're kind of hoping he'll be a jerk when you meet him," said Beckham, taken eighth by the Chicago White Sox. "Then you realize he's a nice guy and you're like, dammit . . ."

The award on the line on this particular morning was the Dick Howser Trophy, the national player of the year as voted on by the Collegiate Baseball Writers Association. For Posey's coach, Mike Martin, this commendation was even more special than the higher profile Golden Spikes Award given away later in the summer. Why? Because of the man whose name it honored. Howser became Florida State's first baseball All-American in 1957 and '58, and later returned to become the Noles's head coach. He asked Martin to serve as his top assistant in 1979, and the following season Martin moved to the end of the bench when Howser left to manage the New York Yankees. Martin, along with the rest of the baseball world, had anguished when Howser was killed by a brain tumor eight years later, only three years after leading the Kansas City Royals to their World Series title.

Every game Martin coached at FSU, he did so on Mike Martin Field at Dick Howser Stadium, walking past a bronze bust of his old friend every time he entered the ballpark.

On Friday, unlike those dullard writers, Martin had glanced at his late friend's jersey hanging on the wall of the Hall of Fame Room and smiled. Now, one day later, when Posey's name was called out as the winner of the Howser Trophy, he was smiling again. Martin and Posey beamed, shook hands, accepted congratulations, and posed for photos.

But soon the coach cut the celebration short and herded his catcher out the door. It was time to get ready for a ballgame.

An hour later, Martin and the FSU team bus were rolling south toward The Blatt. As they neared the stadium, the sixty-four-year-old coach sat up in his seat and turned to watch the players behind him. This was his favorite part of every trip to Omaha, seeing the looks on the players' faces as they crested the hill of Tenth Street and the big blue ballpark rose into view. When he made the trip as a player in 1968, he was injured and relegated to being a base coach. The bitterness of not being able to play had kept him from pausing to savor the Series experience. Ever since, he made sure that none of his players made that same mistake.

This group reacted the same way all his other teams had, with a buzz of nervous excitement. On their clubhouse wall in Tallahassee there was a giant picture of Rosenblatt with the phrase, "It ends here." They'd seen that picture every day of their college careers, but this was way better.

Martin wasn't the only coach who knew the power of coming over that hill. For decades head coaches had dangled The Blatt in front of their players as the ultimate goal, including Fresno's late-night stop to start the 2008 Series. Former big-league third baseman Robin Ventura remembered his coach at Oklahoma State, Gary Ward, taking the Cowboys two hours out of the way during an early season trip to Iowa. The bus pulled into the parking lot at Rosenblatt and Ward walked his team out onto the frozen field. "This is it, gentlemen. This is where you want to be in June."

As Martin's team now reacted to the view, their coach gathered two quick visual notes about his familiar CWS surroundings. Traffic was already jammed up on every road around the stadium and the center-field flags were blowing out, pointing east into Iowa as stiff as if they were made from plywood.

"I've been keeping an eye on those flags for about forty years now," he said with a point. "When they're blowing in that direction, that means we're in for a wild afternoon. You have no idea what's going to happen."

Missing from all those cars that Martin had noticed was the red Ford Focus of Dave and Linda Burns. The happily married couple was still making their way through Iowa and growing increasingly impatient.

They were now headed north. The wrong direction.

Severe rains throughout the first two weeks of June had sacked the center of the Hawkeye State with record flooding and now more than thirty miles of I-80 were closed. So, with one eye on the detour signs and another on their watches, they left the well-traveled trail and said a little prayer for the victims of the devastation around them.

"It's okay," Linda told her husband. "We can still make the first pitch."

They'd traveled more than 500 miles and waited thirty years to get to The Blatt. A few more minutes in the car wasn't going to hurt.

If it had been up to Jackie Jensen, that's exactly how he would have traveled to the inaugural College World Series in 1947—by automobile. The University of California outfielder and pitcher feared no man on no field, athletic or otherwise.

What he hated was airplanes.

Some mistook the five feet eleven, 190-pound Oakland native's shyness for cockiness. He wasn't arrogant, but if he'd wanted to be he'd certainly earned the right. At barely twenty years of age he'd served in the Navy at the end of World War II and was on his way to becoming an All-American halfback. They called him the "Golden Boy of the Golden Bears" because of his curly blond locks, soft hands, and rocket right arm. During the previous football season the sophomore was a big-play machine, chunking out a 56-yard punt return versus Wisconsin, throwing a 47-yard touchdown pass versus Oregon and hauling in 56- and 29-yard TD receptions against Washington and UCLA. By 1949 he would be a Heisman Trophy finalist and husband to an Olympic diving silver medalist, Zoe Ann Olsen.

But man, did Jackie Jensen hate to fly. Unfortunately, in the spring of '47 he had no choice.

The Bears baseball squad had qualified for the newly formed NCAA Baseball Playoffs, a committee-selected field of eight collegiate teams that would participate in two separate four-team regional tournaments, one in Denver and the other in New Haven, Connecticut. The two regional winners would square off in a neutral site best-of-three engagement that the NCAA had ambitiously titled the College World Series.

As the Bears boarded a DC-6 for the western regional, the Golden Boy was none too happy about the idea of buzzing the whitewashed tips of the Rockies. His older teammates, nearly all of whom had served much lengthier stints in the war than Jensen, were plenty accustomed to dicey air travel. As their ride landed at the Oakland airport to pick up the team, it shut down its two outermost engines to save fuel as it taxied, standard operating procedure.

The Bears seized the opportunity to haze the gridiron hero.

"We shouted, 'Hey Jackie, this plane is broken!'" center fielder Lyle Palmer remembered, describing the scene as his team walked across the tarmac. "We kept going, 'What are we going to do? Only two of the four engines are working!' Well, he took off running. We had to chase him down and make him get on that airplane."

By the time Cal took to Merchants Field, Jensen's nerves were settled enough to take the mound and outduel the home team Denver Pioneers 3–2. The next day they defeated Texas and future NFL Hall of Famer Bobby Layne with a go-ahead run in the ninth to win 8–7. Cal coach Clint Evans nearly missed out on the clincher, not to mention the rest of his life, when stadium personnel tried to quick-dry the rainy outfield with a gasoline fire, an inferno that was started while the coach was still standing in center field.

"Clint ended up becoming one of my very dearest friends," Lyle Palmer said from his Bay Area home, chuckling as only an eighty-four-year-old can. "But when I played against him I thought he was a real son of a bitch. I always wondered if maybe they hadn't tried to set him on fire."

S.O.B. or not, it was the Cal coach who had first suggested the formation of the College World Series. He'd been impressed with the early success of the NCAA's eight-year-old basketball tournament and felt his sport deserved the same kind of high-profile event. Clint Evans first circulated the idea with fellow coaches and then made a formal proposal to the NCAA in January 1947. Only five months later he and his Bears were set to face off with the Yale Bulldogs for the first-ever NCAA baseball championship, played in . . . Kalamazoo, Michigan?

The campus of Western Michigan was chosen as the site of the first College World Series because the Broncos hadn't qualified for the national baseball tournament, thus making it a neutral site. Of course, it didn't hurt that WMU's head coach and athletic director, Judson Hyames, was also the chairman of the national playoffs. In fact, the ballpark where the Series was to be played was Hyames Field.

It was the kind of local political play of which the Nebraska Territory House of Representatives would have been proud.

The good news for Jackie Jensen was that the team took a train from Denver to get there.

Over two days, June 27–28, 1947, only 3,792 fans paid to watch the Cal-Yale matchup, some scared off by rainy weather, others by indifference. What they missed was the chance to see two future stars in action. Thanks to an eleven-run eighth inning, Cal took Game One by a score of 17–4, then sent the Golden Boy to the mound to seal the deal in Game Two. By the sixth inning, his overworked teenage arm began to tire, but the game's other big name had seen all he needed to identify the kid as a big-league talent.

"There was an air about Jensen," Yale first baseman George H. W. Bush recalled in 2001. The Eli team captain was known by his teammates as "Poppy" and known throughout college baseball for his defensive prowess, once described by a Raleigh, North Carolina, newspaper as "Yale's husky first sacker." "There are just some people who walk into the room or onto the field and you just know there's something different about them. Jackie Jensen had that quality. A lot of us in that Series were older, we'd come back from serving in the war, and he looked like a kid out there. But I knew there was something special about him."

The Bears survived a late Bulldog rally to win the first-ever CWS title, the second game ending when Bush struck out chasing a curveball from starter-turned-reliever Virgil Butler. The Cal team reboarded Jensen's beloved train and chugged back home to Berkeley, at one point steaming through Omaha's Union Station, just a mile and half north of where Johnny Rosenblatt's new stadium was under construction.

"To my knowledge, Jackie never got over that fear of flying," teammate Lyle Palmer recalled. "Years later when he came back to coach the team at Cal, he'd leave in his car and drive to UCLA and Arizona while the team flew in."

Aviaphobia aside, Bush's assessment of the blond-headed Californian was spot-on.

In 1948, Jensen finished fourth in the Heisman vote and left college to play baseball with the Oakland Oaks of the Pacific Coast League. Soon he and teammate Billy Martin had their contracts sold to the New York Yankees, where Jensen was the heir apparent to Joe DiMaggio until a guy named Mickey Mantle arrived. He eventually landed with Ted Williams's Boston Red Sox, winning the 1958 American League MVP, a Gold Glove in '59, and earning three All-Star appearances. (The team slipped sleeping pills into his preflight drinks and then hauled the unconscious outfielder onto planes.)

But when Jackie Jensen jogged onto the field at Kalamazoo, no one, Bush included, was ready to place the expectations of such a fantastic future on his teenage shoulders. Major League Baseball's First-Year Player Draft didn't yet exist. Neither did radar guns, Internet message boards, Blackberries, nor ESPN.

Today, by the time a player of Jensen's pedigree arrives in Omaha he has been the subject of constant exhaustive analysis since his preteen years. MLB scouting directors repeatedly claim that they don't start evaluating talent until a player's junior or senior year in high school, but that doesn't stop persistent parents and obsessive baseball fans from cranking out amateur scouting reports to manufacture buzz around The Next Big Thing. Since its inception in 1981, the back pages of *Baseball America* have been packed with ads for "training secrets the pros don't want you to know" and "instant exposure to college and pro scouts."

"Here's the thing about all of that," Coach Mike Martin said on the eve of the 2008 Series. "If a player is really, truly great then he doesn't need Web sites or reports to tell you how good he is or how good he's going to be. You know it as soon as you see him."

The Florida State skipper knows of what he speaks. In twenty-nine years as head coach of the Seminoles he has identified and produced more than forty All-Americans and seen nearly 200 of his players sign professional contracts, including Doug Mientkiewicz, famous for securing the final out of the curse-busting 2004 World Series for the Boston Red Sox, and two-sport phenom Deion "Prime Time" Sanders.

In 1995 and '96, Martin came to Omaha with outfielder J. D. Drew, considered by many at the time to be the best player in college baseball history. In '97, Drew batted .455 with 31 home runs, 100 runs batted in, and 32 stolen bases, numbers worthy of an MVP season in Major League Baseball, but posted in less than half as many games.

But in 2008, by his admission, Martin brought someone even better to The Blatt.

Buster.

In the spring of 2003, Martin's son and assistant coach, Mike Martin Jr., had one of those you-know-it-as-soon-as-you-see-him moments, sitting in the bleachers at Lee County High School in Leesburg, Georgia.

"The first time I saw Buster Posey I immediately called back to Tallahassee and told Dad he had to get up to Leesburg. We don't do that very often, if ever. If we convince a player to come to our campus, then he meets with the boss, the boss doesn't go out on the road to meet him. But I think he was hitting like .540, he was 10–1 as a pitcher, and his grade point average was better than a 3.9. Those are once-in-a-lifetime kind of numbers and once I saw him in person I knew they were legit. Dad needed to come close the deal on him before anybody else did, especially the big-league clubs."

A few weeks later, Dad came up into Georgia to watch Posey play in a regional tournament. He really liked the kid after seeing how he carried himself, how he swung the bat, and after spending some time with his family in the grandstand. Then Buster moved to the mound for the last inning and Martin got out his radar gun. The first pitch registered 92 miles per hour (mph).

Says the coach: "I went from like to love in one pitch."

During Posey's freshman year the Seminoles were in need of a shortstop, so that's where Buster played, hitting .346 and earning a spot on the Freshman All-American team. The following fall Martin needed a catcher, so Martin Jr. and associate head coach Jamey Shoupe suggesting trying Buster behind the plate. "I thought they were pulling my leg. But we set up the pitching machine and he took a few pitches and it looked like he'd been doing it all his life."

Had he?

"No, sir," Posey said quietly. "Never had."

For the next few months the kid lived in a catcher's crouch. He watched TV bent at the knees, read textbooks with his butt balanced an inch off the floor, and Memorexed the mechanics of that year's big-league postseason catchers, including Ivan Rodriguez of the Detroit Tigers, Joe Mauer of the Minnesota Twins, and Jorge Posada of the Yankees. The next year he hit .362, threw out 41 percent of potential base stealers, and was the youngest finalist ever named for the Johnny Bench Catcher of the Year Award.

However, unlike Drew and Jensen, Posey hadn't yet earned the right to play on college baseball's biggest stage.

Florida State's baseball program had long been enslaved by the same curse that once hindered its higher profile football squad. Mike Martin was every bit as charming as head football coach Bobby Bowden and equally in demand throughout the Sunshine State for speaking engagements, particularly among Christian organizations. Like Bowden, Martin ranked near the top of every major coaching category, among the top five coaches in all-time wins and in the top ten in winning percentage. When the Seminoles qualified for the 2008 NCAA tournament, it marked their twenty-ninth consecutive postseason appearance.

But entering the 2008 CWS, they were 0-for-28 when it came to turning one of those postseason appearances into a national title, unfairly labeling the proud program as "soft" and "statistically inflated." Just as Bowden had to endure for so many years, Martin was forced to publicly downplay the annual shin kick of disappointment, but those closest to him knew that, like his football friend, the lack of a ring was eating him up inside.

During Posey's first two years the Noles had failed to make it out of the first round of the NCAA tournament, including a stunning defeat at home in Tallahassee at the hands of Mississippi State. In 2008 they had nearly stumbled again, dropping the first game of both the Regional and Super Regional to Bucknell—*Bucknell?*—and Wichita State, forced to fight back with one loss hung around their necks like a noose, but surviving six elimination games at home to earn their first trip to Omaha since 2000.

"What a shame it would have been to not get Buster to Omaha," Coach Martin said the morning before Game One. "I don't know if I could have lived with myself knowing that he never got the chance to play on our biggest stage. In one of our regional games against Tulane, he came to the plate and all of the sudden I realized that the entire stadium—more than 6,000 people—were standing and chanting Buster's name. He'd hit two home runs already and now they were on their feet. All I could think was, man, what kind of pressure is this to put on a twenty-one-year-old kid?"

The following night, Posey was serenaded by a raucous group of FSU fans known as the Animals, a song they had written expressly for him, singing, "Bus-ter Pose-ee, he'll hit a home run . . . Bus-ter Pose-ee, he'll throw you out . . . Bus-ter Pose-ee, he'll strike you out, too!"

No one ever wrote a song about Jensen . . . or Drew . . . or Tim Wallach . . . or Fred Lynn . . . or any other superstar who had walked onto the field at Rosenblatt Stadium.

When Posey finally got off the bus at The Blatt, he made the same walk awaiting every CWS player, stars and no-names. The two team buses always parked side by side in Lot A, the massive south-side parking lot, dumping the squads out squarely in the middle of the thickest pack of fans. Every player, already in uniform and carrying his own equipment, had to weave through the crowded crossroads, where six different groups of people converged at once.

The line at the ticket office blended into the families seeking the shade of the trees along the first-base wall of the ballpark, who spilled into the rows of tailgaters that flowed all the way out to College World Series Boulevard, which surrounded the fans posing for photos in front of the Road to Omaha statue, who were bracketed by those standing in line at the front gate to have their bags checked by security, all of whom were bordered by local TV sports reporters lined up to for their midday live shots and the four booths of "Radio Row."

Two dozen Florida State players managed to quietly snake their way through the crowd in safe anonymity.

Not number 8.

"There he is!"

"Buster, can I have your autograph?"

"Buster, do you have a second for a quick interview?"

"Buster, are you going to hit a home run?"

No pressure, right?

During pregame batting practice, he waited for his turn in the cage as a pack of youngsters shouted "Buster! Buster!" from above the first-base dugout. With a smile he waved to the kids, leaning to his left to look around an ESPN camera that was permanently camped two feet from his face, and promised to come over and see them as soon as he was done hitting.

Then he went to work.

As he took his place in the righty side of the batter's box, he spit into his hands, rubbed his palms together, and then placed his right foot on the back chalk line, lined up evenly below his right shoulder. He took his left foot and swung it out toward the third-base dugout, placing it nearly a full step off of his left shoulder and opening his stance to face the pitcher. He held the bat out, samurai style, holding steady to lock in on the mound, all at once calming his soul while unnerving the poor soul sixty feet away. Then, simultaneously, his hands came up across his chest, his wrists breaking back to bring the knob of the bat above his right ear. After a couple of swishy practice strokes, the barrel of the multicolored Louisville Slugger TPX bat wagged up and down a little and then came to a rest over his right shoulder, pointing back and toward the ground at his eight o'clock. He coiled tight but remained loose all at the same time.

The kids kept shouting his name as the first pitch whizzed by. On the second, he shut them up.

The sound of the bat slapping the ball was more of a crack than the typical ping. The ball rose, then rose some more, eventually arcing into a descent that left it clanging off the red aluminum roof that stood ten feet over the top row of the left-field bleachers, some 425 feet away.

"Oooooohhhhh. . . ."

The children echoed the sound that came from every corner of Rosenblatt.

Then he did it again . . . and again . . . and again.

The Pick had arrived.

"There's always a guy," explained Ron Fraser, the former Miami head coach who came to Omaha twelve times with the Hurricanes. "There's always one guy who has the buzz around him. The one 'you can't miss no matter what because this guy is going to be in the big leagues' kind of guy. In 1983, we had all these ace players in the Series who'd just been drafted and they all ended up being great big leaguers. Chris Sabo was at Michigan. Dave Magadan was there with Alabama. Barry Bonds was with Arizona State. They were all in Omaha that year. But then Roger Clemens came walking in there with Texas. Even with all these other superstars there, there was something different about Clemens. You just looked at him and thought, *Shit*."

Before Clemens there was Russ Morman of Wichita State, Terry Fran-cona of Arizona, Bob Horner of Arizona State, and Dave Winfield of Minnesota. After Clemens came Pete Incaviglia of Oklahoma State, Ja-son Varitek of Georgia Tech, and FSU's J. D. Drew.

Like Posey, those future Major Leaguers came to Omaha with an unfair amount of attention and pressure that came with the scouting reports and urban legends. Unlike Posey, their pressure cookers were actually turned up in the middle of the biggest week of their baseball lives.

"You want to know where I was when I found out was drafted?" As Kyle Peterson told the story, the pitcher-turned-ESPN analyst pointed to the middle of the Rosenblatt playing field. The Omaha native left for Stanford in 1995, but came back home to play in the College World Series two of his three seasons with the Cardinal. "I was standing right there, behind the screen you see in back of second base. I was fielding throws from the outfield during batting practice before our first game of the Series in '97 against Auburn. Our sports information guy comes running out and says, 'You just got drafted by the Brewers!' I walked off the field and all my friends and family were standing there over the dugout cheering for me. It was the greatest moment. Then once it sunk in I was like, oh crap, I better pitch well this week."

The battle between college baseball coaches and the pros has been waged for nearly a century, with the big leagues taking full advantage of what they view as a second minor league system. In the 1950s and '60s, scouts would hang out all over The Blatt or by the team buses and hotels, contract offers in hand. Each time the NCAA tried to fend them off, the Majors merely laughed and did whatever they wanted. Following the '55 College World Series, the NCAA adopted a "College Player Rule" that stated pro scouts couldn't sign a player until after he'd earned his college degree. They ignored it. Over the next ten years, the NCAA would throw out more new policies and the pros would tunnel around them once again. Eventually, after the MLB First-Year-Player Draft was started in '65, everyone agreed that a college player couldn't be signed until after his ju-nior year, which meant that college coaches would have to recruit the best talent under the assumption that they'd be gone after three seasons.

"They don't care a thing about us," Mike Martin said from his FSU office a few weeks after the 2008 Series, simultaneously counseling a group of incoming freshman who might still choose to go pro and a group of rising seniors who wrestled with the same choice. "You'd think after all the talent we've provided them with over the years they would cut us some slack every now and then, but they don't."

Throughout the 1980s and '90s the MLB Draft coincided with the first days of the College World Series. The result was added stress and distraction when a player and his team needed it the least.

In 1998, Miami third baseman Pat Burrell was on deck awaiting his first at-bat in Game One of the CWS against West Coast powerhouse Long Beach State. As he stepped out of the circle and began striding to the plate he was called back by a Miami athletic department official. "Congratulations, Pat, you've been selected by the Phillies as the number-one overall pick. Now go get a hit."

Burrell knows that he reached first via a base on balls only because the box score told him so. In reality he doesn't remember a single pitch of the at-bat. All he could think about was his new life in Philadelphia. At least he wasn't alone. Four more teammates were drafted that same day and two the next. Morris has always believed that Draft Distraction was a big reason that the '98 team, which was ranked number one in the nation, lost two of three and went home early.

In 1989, the LSU Tigers came to Omaha for the third time in four years. During their first two visits they got acclimated to the CWS circus, winning one game in '86 and nearly reaching the finals in '87. When they returned in '89, they did so as the favorites, mainly because of the hype surrounding a six-foot, six-inch flamethrower from Denham Springs, Louisiana.

"I have never seen a college player receive the amount of attention that Ben McDonald did." Skip Bertman said it as he fiddled with his CWS championship ring, one of five that he earned during his eighteen years as head coach. "Not before and not since. By the time he got to Omaha his junior year he'd already won twenty-nine games in three years, he'd won a bunch of national player of the year awards, been named a two-time All-American, and won an Olympic gold medal. And as soon as we got to Rosenblatt, we had to set up a separate press conference for him because he'd been drafted number one overall by the Baltimore Orioles."

On top off all that, McDonald had pulled off a Paul Bunyan–like effort the previous weekend in the NCAA regional in College Station, Texas. LSU had to beat number-one-ranked Texas A&M twice in a row on the Aggies' home field to return to Omaha. Lose once and they were going back to Baton Rouge. Big Ben was the winning pitcher in the first game, played left field, and then returned to the mound in the eleventh inning of the second game to earn the save and to send the Tigers back to the Series.

"By the time he finally took the mound in Omaha he was just spent," Bertman remembered. "He had blisters all over his fingers from Texas A&M, we'd crisscrossed the country, and everywhere Ben went he had to answer questions about where he thought he was going to go in the draft. He lost the first game against Miami and then lost our third game against Texas. If I could have that over I wouldn't do that to him again. But I wanted him to succeed in Omaha so badly."

Instead, McDonald stands atop the CWS record book for most losses by a pitcher, losing all four of his appearances between 1987 and '89. After that fourth loss, his last collegiate start and an elimination game that sent the Tigers home, Bertman gave Big Ben the option not to participate in the postgame press conference, but McDonald insisted. When the writers asked him about never having won a game in Omaha, he answered in his soft, bayou drawl, "Well, maybe I can come back as a pro and do well in Omaha one day. It's a great place."

What a Buster-like thing to say. And the people of Omaha have never forgotten it. To this day, whenever McDonald comes to Omaha as an analyst for LSU Tiger Radio, they don't remember the losses or the unfulfilled potential. They love him because he loved them.

When the NCAA expanded the baseball tournament to sixty-four teams in 1999, the MLB Draft moved out of the College World Series and into the middle of the second-round Super Regionals. The timing was better, but still not perfect. Coaches would have preferred it to be moved to the beginning of the week, the Monday or Tuesday following the regional round instead of the Thursday or Friday that lands right in the middle of the Omaha-or-home round of sixteen.

Only one week prior to the 2008 College World Series, the Miami Hurricanes were locked in the middle innings of the first game of their

Super Regional with Arizona, the score knotted up at 3–3. Head coach Jim Morris was in his customary position, sitting on the home-plate end of the dugout, fully enthralled in the action unfolding on the field before him and delving into his three-ring binder full of strategy, searching for an edge, any edge, against the twelfth-ranked Wildcats.

That's when Cane slugger Yonder Alonso slid up beside Morris on the bench. Barely twenty-four hours earlier, the All-American first baseman had been drafted seventh overall by the Cincinnati Reds and the big club already had the big-hitter thinking about the big leagues.

"Hey, Coach . . ."

"Yeah."

"I was on the Internet this morning and did you hear about what the Reds are going to do? They want to fly me up there and introduce me to the fans before a home game and do a whole special ceremony about me being born in Cuba. They're going to bring in Tony Perez to give me my jersey and everything. Isn't that cool?"

"Yeah, Yonder, that's great. But I need you to be thinking about Arizona."

As Posey strode to the plate in the first inning of Game One, he wasn't thinking about playing catcher for the San Francisco Giants. He was thinking about playing catcher for the Florida State Seminoles, about finally giving Coach Martin that national championship, about ending the ACC's fifty-three-year streak without a CWS title, and about the first pitch he was going to see from Stanford ace Jeremy Bleich, who was finally beginning to hit his stride after an injury-hampered season.

He was also thinking about Stanford catcher Jason Castro, who'd been taken tenth overall by the Houston Astros. The two backstops had gotten to know one another very well over the last year. They were teammates in the Cape Cod League, where the nation's best college players go to play in the summertime. (Most end up humbled by having to trade in their aluminum bats for old-fashioned wood, but it hadn't affected these two.) They shared duties behind the plate for Yarmouth-Dennis until Castro suffered an arm injury. They'd also been in the same room at the same time for several of those awards ceremonies like the Posey party held earlier that morning. A few days later they would stand shoulder to shoulder in Wichita, each hoping to win the Johnny Bench Award.

In their pregame interviews, both catchers likened their styles to Boston Red Sox captain Jason Varitek, though their coaches leaned more toward using the better hitting-and-throwing comparisons of Ivan Rodriguez and yes, even Bench.

So far Castro had answered more questions about his name than about baseball. Not only did it rhyme with his new team, the Astros, but his hometown was Castro Valley, California, and Cuban dictator Fidel, the one Alonso's family had fled, was in the news with health problems. He also shared the name with a recent dreadlocked contestant on *American Idol.*

"Everyone thinks they are asking the name questions for the first time, like they're the first to figure it out. But you just smile and answer them anyway. And for the record, no, I'm not the guy from *American Idol.*"

Over the first eight innings of Game One the two teams played nearly straight up. Posey had one hit, as did Castro. Each team got a solid five frames from their starting pitchers. Stanford jumped out to an early 2–0 lead, but Florida State came back to tie it up 5–5 entering the ninth.

The Seminole offense wasn't just about Posey. They'd hit .354 as a team throughout the season, scoring nearly ten runs per game. In the postseason they'd hit .384 with more than thirteen runs per outing. But the comeback in the eighth had masked a familiar Omaha problem for FSU. They were leaving runners on base. A lot of runners. In the seventh they had the bases loaded with no outs. But freshman pitcher Drew Storen forced the Noles to pop up twice to the infield, and froze shortstop Tony Delmonico on a wicked fastball on the outside corner. Posey had the one hit, but had struck out twice already and left four runners stranded.

"We'd had some problems driving in runs," Martin said after the game. "But we were excited as we could be after tying it up in the eighth. Then the wheels came off."

One of those wheels ran squarely over Delmonico.

The junior shortstop was playing in his first CWS game, but making his third trip to the event. His father, Rod, was the head coach at Tennessee for eighteen years, bringing the Vols to Rosenblatt twice, in 1995 and 2001. Tony, still just a kid, was the batboy for both trips.

When Coach Rod was unexpectedly fired in '07, Mike Martin asked him to come back and rejoin the staff at Florida State where he'd once served as assistant head coach. Tony, Tennessee's starting shortstop, came with him. Now the two Delmonicos were back in Omaha together, excited to be in the same dugout for Father's Day weekend.

That excitement turned to horror as the marathon game ground toward the finish.

Posey left his position behind the plate and took to the mound, where he'd earned six saves as a closer during the regular season and hadn't given up an earned run. A position player leaving his post to take the mound in professional baseball is unheard of. In college ball it isn't uncommon, but the sight still sends a charge through the grandstand, especially when The Pick is the one doing double duty.

The longtime fans still buzz about Minnesota's Dave Winfield in 1973, when he started two games on the mound, striking out fifteen batters, and hit .364 with a home run against Georgia Southern that legend says landed in the lion's cage at the zoo. They marveled again in '85 at Mississippi State's Bobby Thigpen, who led the Bulldogs to Omaha as both an outfielder and the nation's top reliever. And in 2002, Texas freshman Huston Street (who was actually born on an avenue in Austin) started at third and earned four saves in four games as the Longhorns took the title.

Winfield and Street were both chosen as CWS Most Outstanding Player. Thigpen was not. After smacking a grand slam in the sixth inning of State's semifinal game against Miami, he gave up a two-run jack in the ninth to eventual MOP Greg Ellena.

"That's the nature of the job," said Thigpen, the eventual MLB record holder for single season saves. "Playing two positions, it's hard. But it was also the most fun I ever had playing ball. When people didn't know it was coming and as I would jog in from the outfield I would hear this murmur in the stands like, 'Wait a minute. What is this guy doing?'"

Posey's transition always caused an even bigger stir. He wasn't merely coming in from a position in the field. He had to go to the dugout and first take off all of his catcher's equipment.

Just before throwing his first pitch, the catcher-turned-closer looked over to Tony Delmonico and gave the shortstop a nod as to say, *Forget the strikeout. Forget that error you had in the seventh. Forget that I've only got one hit. We have the best offense in the world and we're going to win.*

Then, with Game One tied 5–5, The Pick got picked apart.

He inherited one runner at first and immediately faced left fielder Toby Gerhart, who also happened to be a running back on the Stanford football team. Gerhart smacked the second pitch from Posey hard into the ground, a super-high bouncer that third baseman Stuart Tapley had to wait on . . . and wait on . . . and wait on. By the time he hauled it in and made the throw to first, speedster Gerhart was already safe.

Two on, no outs. Up came Jason Castro.

Posey's first pitch to his former Cape Cod teammate was raked toward the bag at first, taking a strange hop and drawing an emphatic *foul ball* point from first base umpire Mike Conlin. It appeared to be fair, sending a cloud of chalk into the air. Florida State had caught a huge break. Three pitches later, to Conlin's relief, everyone forgot the missed call.

Jason Castro's grounder to shortstop Delmonico was classic fodder for a double play, perfectly placed to kill the Stanford rally.

As the grounder rolled toward Tony Delmonico, the runner from second, Cardinal leadoff man Cord Phelps, hesitated to leap and let the ball roll through his feet like croquet wickets. That hesitation was just enough to cause Delmonico to flinch. The ball looked as though it would roll flat to the ground, but leaped into the air at the last split second, hurdling the webbing of the shortstop's glove and glancing off his wrist. By the time he turned to pick it up, all three runners were standing on all three bags.

Error, shortstop. E-6. Bases loaded, still no outs.

The next batter was first baseman Brent Milleville. Mike Martin called in his infield, willing to concede a possible base hit for a chance to throw out the go-ahead run at home. The strategy didn't come into play as Milleville popped up for what should have been the final out of the inning. Instead it was a sacrifice fly and all three runners moved up.

Stanford 6, Florida State 5, one out.

Martin and Posey elected to intentionally walk the next batter, designated hitter Randy Molina, in the hopes of setting up the double play. It never happened. Center fielder Sean Ratliff lofted a soft single up the middle to drive in two more runs.

Stanford 8, Florida State 5, still one out.

Left fielder Joey August drew a four-pitch walk from The Pick, who was beginning to look exhausted. With the bases loaded, third baseman Zach Jones stepped into the righty side of the batter's box. He worked the count to three balls, one strike, forcefully trying to rack up Posey's pitch count.

The fifth pitch was slapped down hard on the dirt in front of the plate and scooted off across the grass toward shortstop. Tony Delmonico drifted to his left, already thinking about how he would scoop up the grounder and toss it to second and finally kick off that inning-ending double play.

He hopped left and pulled up his glove just above the ground in anticipation of another last-instant hop. This one stayed on the ground, rolling along the dirt just to the right and just below the shortstop's glove.

E-6. Again.

Stanford 10, Florida State 5, still one out.

When the top of the ninth finally ended, Stanford had scored eleven runs and led 16–5. Fittingly, the final batter of the game was Posey, who grounded into a 6–4–3 double play to end the game. The final line on The Pick: 1-for-4 with two strikeouts, one grounder into a double play, and four runners left on base with one-third of an inning pitched, two walks, two hits, and six runs, one earned.

As the team grabbed its bags and headed up the narrow stairway toward the outside parking lot, NCAA officials grabbed Posey and informed him that his number had come up for a random drug screening. After a pissy day, he now had to go piss in a cup. While he did his duty, Stanford coach Mark Marquess and the three Cardinal players selected for the postgame press conference said the name "Buster" no less than sixteen times. Even after a loss, The Pick was still The Story.

Meanwhile, Delmonico's Seminole teammates acted as if the shortstop was made of radioactive material. No one was mad. They just didn't know what to say. He'd had one of those nightmares that wake up every ballplayer in a cold sweat. One of those three-error-on-national-television-just-get-me-to-the-damn-bus sort of days.

It would have been easy for the kid to remind everyone that he was playing injured, that he was hobbling around at the toughest position on the field with a sprained ankle that was swollen like grapefruit and a lower left leg full of stitches. But to his credit he did not. He took his lumps and absorbed the stunned stares all around him.

Now he had to make the same crowded walk back to the bus that he'd made into the The Blatt six hours earlier. The fans made just enough room to let the Seminoles pass through, as Florida State fans shouted encouragement to the twenty-one-year-old junior. A pair of well-lubricated Miami loyalists attempted to do the opposite before they were silenced by a couple of elderly Omaha women. Delmonico heard none of it, or at least did a fine job of acting like he hadn't. He just kept walking.

As he stepped toward the door of the motor coach he was intercepted by Darren Cook, one of the team's service-club hosts from the Omaha Cosmopolitan Club.

"Don't sweat it, buddy," Cook said as he handed the infielder a cold bottle of water. "Have something to drink and something to eat here. Tomorrow we're going to have you guys down to the riverfront for the world's greatest steak fry. It'll be great."

At first the downtrodden player looked up confused. Then he met eyes with the forty-seven-year-old auto-parts salesman, who held out a brown-bag lunch and slapped the kid on the shoulder.

For the first time in a long time, Tony Delmonico smiled.

As the Seminole bus churned out of the south parking lot of The Blatt and headed back up Thirteenth Street, Dave and Linda Burns finally pulled their Ford into a parking spot on the other end of the stadium. As they climbed out of their car and stretched off the stiffness of the I-80 westward trail, they looked up at the hillside above them. There it was.

The welcome they had dreamed of, in tall white lettering that could be seen all the way back into Iowa, the same sign that had welcomed Fresno State three nights earlier.

ROSENBLATT. HOME OF THE NCAA MEN'S COLLEGE WORLD SERIES.

The couple made the walk up the hill to the front gate. They beamed at the bright blue steel and deep brick red of the entrance way and handed their tickets to a volunteer worker who welcomed them with a grin as big as their own. They walked to their seats, marveled at what a fantastic job their daughter had done getting them, then put those plastic chairs to good use.

They came to their feet and clapped as the number-one team in the land, the Miami Hurricanes, and the eighth-ranked Georgia Bulldogs hit the baselines for the national anthem before Game Two. Then they laughed as two eight-year-old boys behind them, dressed head-to-toe in UGA black and red, began to bark like not dogs, but Dawgs. As the anthem finished up, the sun began to set over the third-base grandstand.

It was exactly as they had imagined. Perfect.

The sky grew darker and the boys got louder, especially as the game rumbled into the top of the ninth inning, where the Bulldogs were at bat.

The Hurricanes were a perfect 45–0 when they carried a lead into the eighth inning, primarily due to the work of first-round draft pick Carlos Gutierrez, soon to be a member of the Minnesota Twins. The six-foot-three righty had recovered from Tommy John surgery, was converted from a starter to a closer, and had become accustomed to intimidating his opponents just by standing on the mound.

But Georgia was not shaken.

Catcher Bryce Massanari knew the best pitch to swing at would be the first one, a 93-mph fastball, and he lofted it into center field for a base hit. The catcher was lifted for a pinch runner, Matt Fuller, who was immediately moved into scoring position with a sacrifice bunt from center fielder Matt Cerione.

Facing the next batter, freshman Robbie O'Bryan, Carlos Gutierrez did a masterful job of multitasking. His middle infielders, committed to holding Fuller on second, played nearly behind the bag, meaning the infield gaps were extremely vulnerable, especially if someone made contact with one of the closer's signature low outside sliders. While concentrating on the batter, Gutierrez also repeatedly stepped off the mound to keep the runner in check.

Miami head coach Jim Morris had all the confidence in the world in his closer and had placed the game in the pitcher's right hand. The pitcher reinforced that confidence by not only holding the runner, but also striking out the batter. He pumped his fist at the accomplishment, but stopped when he felt the red rush down his spine that something didn't feel right.

The third-strike slider had dropped earlier than catcher Yasmani Grandal was prepared for. It skipped off his mitt and then the dirt below, quietly rolling between the catcher's feet, past the left foot of home-plate umpire Bill Speck.

Initially, no one but Grandal knew what was happening. Only when he suddenly started spinning around in search of the ball did Gutierrez start his panicked pointing. The Georgia bench stood and screamed to O'Bryan to run, who immediately started sprinting to first, and Fuller went from second to third. Instead of two outs with a man on second, there was one out with runner on the corners.

As soon as he arrived at first, O'Bryan was pulled by Georgia head coach Dave Perno for a second pinch runner, Steve Esmonde. Left fielder Lyle Allen watched the first 88-mph slider from Gutierrez, then cut at the second, slicing a quickly dying shot to left field, which took a wicked bounce at the feet of outfielder Adan Severino. If he had dived for the ball, he might have caught it. Then again, had he missed it would have rolled all the way to the fence. He took it on the hop.

Tie game, 4–4, men on first and second, one out.

Carlos Gutierrez was now officially rattled, looking toward Severino in left with his mouth hanging open. Now second baseman David Thoms dug in, totally focused despite the fact that his sister Julie's wedding was happening back in Georgia at that very moment. Gutierrez was anything but focused. He tossed an 84-mph slider across the right corner of the plate, which Thoms took a hard cut at, but barely stroked with the bottom of his bat. The ball bounced high and then skipped off the grass into Gutierrez's glove, a very nice defensive play as he ran off the mound fifteen feet to his right.

He scooped up the ball, double-clutched to calm his nerves and fired it to Yonder Alonso at first. At least he tried to. The throw sailed a good six feet to the left of Alonso's glove, banging off the tarp in foul territory and taking an agonizing slow roll into the right-field bullpen. Both runners scored and the hitter cruised into third.

Georgia 6, Miami 4. When senior third baseman Ryan Peisel drove in Thoms, his fourth RBI of the night, the Bulldogs took a 7–4 lead into the bottom of the ninth and trotted out their closer, Josh Fields. He threw fourteen pitches to record the three outs.

As the crowd cheered in delight a man in LSU Tiger gear ran through the stands tossing out strands of beads. Only one day in, the Sixty-second College World Series had begun with two upsets in two games. College baseball's top two teams were both 0–1. The unsung squads that no one expected to be here were both 1–0. There had been two games played in the 2008 College World Series and both had been decided in the ninth inning by mind-blowing rallies and heartbreakingly poor performances.

Dave and Linda had missed Game One, but so what? They wouldn't miss another pitch from this moment until a champion was crowned eleven days later.

Happy anniversary, baby.

THREE

THE UNDERDOG

Sunday, June 15
Game Three: Fresno State vs. Rice
Game Four: LSU vs. North Carolina

All along Tenth Street, the historic old churches of South Omaha were alive with celebration and song, giving thanks on what had started out rainy but was now a clear and sunny Sunday morning.

Most of the old stone buildings had been standing for more than a century, the spiritual and social centers of the neighborhoods known as Little Italy and Forest Hill. This was Omaha's original Gold Coast, the fulfillment of that promise made by the picnickers of 1854, where millionaires once took horse-drawn carriages to abandon the reckless abandon of downtown.

On this day the worshippers of Tenth Street thanked God for sparing their city from the tragic floods and violent storms that had ravaged their neighbors to the north and east. They asked Him to heal the hearts of the families of four young Boy Scouts who had been killed by a tornado during those storms.

They thanked the Lord for dads and granddads on this Father's Day.

And they thanked the Almighty for the healing powers of the great game of baseball.

At St. Frances Cabrini Catholic Church, a massive wooden sign posted in front of the old stone building announced WELCOMING COLLEGE WORLD SERIES FANS AND PLAYERS, with a golden bat and glove painted next to the cross, all displayed under the watchful eye of the Virgin Mary.

Just up the street a banner declared, DIETZ UNITED METHODIST CHURCH LOVES BASEBALL! Inside the 120-year-old church Reverend Stephanie

Ahlschwede welcomed out-of-town visitors, excused her Game Three ticket holders a few minutes early, and quietly, to herself, asked for a little divine intervention for her alma mater, the University of North Carolina, later that evening.

As the churches opened their doors at noon, the parishioners spilled out and turned their cars south onto Tenth Street, making the short drive to the day's second house of worship, Rosenblatt Stadium. Out of the pews and through the turnstiles came countless combinations of fathers and their children, all taking part in what has to be the grandest Father's Day celebration on planet Earth.

The tickets they used to enter the old ballpark had more than likely been handled, sorted, and sold by Eddie Sobczyk, CWS box-office manager. For the forty-seventh consecutive year . . . no, wait, maybe it was fifty consecutive years . . . Sobczyk sat behind the glass of The Blatt's box office, tucked into the first-base side of the ballpark's massive main entrance.

For the last thirty-one years son Mike had been by his side, making the drive in from Boston with his wife, son, and dog to help sell tickets. In 2007, he had to cut short a business trip to Chennai, India, frantically flying 7,600 miles to make it in time for his thirtieth consecutive Father's Day in the ticket booth with his old man. "Until someone else can prove otherwise, I'm going to say I hold the record for longest distance traveled to attend the College World Series."

For at least the last ten years, Jay Sobczyk, in 2008 a rising senior at the University of Connecticut, had been there to help *his* old man.

The Sobczyks' primary job each game morning was to sift through and redistribute a stack of newly arrived unused reserved seats, tickets returned by season ticket holders who couldn't use them or leftovers from a participating school's per-game allotment. Every morning of every CWS game, long before the sun had risen over the zoo, fans began lining up outside Sobczyk's window hoping to snatch up whatever came available. Late-arriving fans, a consistent sampling of regulars, and, of course, the scalpers.

Eddie liked to think they were stopping by just to see him.

"People ask me all the time if just once wouldn't I like to do something normal for Father's Day," the "eighty-something" said as he unconsciously printed and shuffled a stack of newly arrived seats. ("He likes to lie about his age," laughs Mike.) "I've been right here for about every Father's Day that I can remember. What's normal? This is normal to me. And where else would I want to be than with my son and my grandson?"

Bob Bruns didn't need any of Sobczyk's last-minute seats. The engineer from Holland, Michigan, had ordered his tickets months in advance. He and his two teenage sons, Jacob and Sam, made the nine-hour-plus drive on Friday, arriving at their Council Bluffs campground just in time to watch the opening-ceremony-fireworks show from their tent across the river.

Fifteen years earlier Bob gave his father and little brother CWS tickets as a Father's Day / Graduation present. For fifteen years he'd listened to their stories of "Man, you've got to go someday" and "It was the greatest trip ever." But back then his boys were still in diapers and as soon as they could run their summers were dominated by baseball. There was no time for Omaha.

Finally, in 2008, the schedule worked out. The longtime pitcher-catcher battery of Jacob and Sam finally had a break between their seasons at Holland Christian High School and their summer league, so their father ordered tickets and packed the camping gear. The three Bruns boys slept under the stars for two nights and went to both of Saturday's wild ninth-inning comeback games.

On Sunday morning they went over to Creighton University to see the school's ballpark, watched a couple hundred kids participate in the NCAA's free CWS baseball clinic, and then rode around downtown Omaha to kill time before the day's two games.

Bob played it cool with his two teenagers, but inside he kept thinking about what his dad and brother had said. They were right.

Greatest trip ever.

Even as Omaha has transformed itself into a homestead for big business (see the massive ConAgra Foods complex sitting nearly next door to the row of Tenth Street churches), its metro population of more than 800,000 residents have remained, at their core, blue collar.

Like the ticket-selling Sobczyks, Nebraskans are classically Midwestern, unfailingly polite hosts who welcome the eight teams of the College World Series with the honest intention of remaining neutral . . . unless, of course, their beloved Cornhuskers happen to make the trip up from Lincoln. When Nebraska doesn't make the cut (they made the CWS field only three times over its first sixty-two years), the good people of Omaha simply root for good games and good times.

But they've always been a sucker for The Underdog.

When Oregon State rolled into Rosenblatt in 2006, they figured to quietly vanish after two games, just as they'd done during their first-ever appearance the previous year. Coaches call it "two-and-'cue" as in two games, two losses, and then heading back home to fire up the barbecue for the remainder of summer.

The Beavers were blitzed by Miami in their first game 11–1. Then they beat Georgia, avenged the loss to the Hurricanes, and dismissed 2003 CWS champion Rice. The Omaha bandwagon was full steam ahead, powered by stories of Oregon State's blue-collar kids who spent nongame days applying for temporary Nebraska fishing licenses. When the Beavers came back from one game down to defeat North Carolina in the championship series, one writer referred to Rosenblatt as "Corvalis East."

The locals don't just love unexpected title runners, they worship them.

The 2008 field of eight offered only one underdog candidate among a bracket packed with perennial powers. A Cinderella so ugly, she was downright cute. And she had a foul mouth to boot.

"What the f . . . ?"

At 9:50 A.M., on the second floor of the Hilton Garden Inn, the last of the Fresno State Cinderellas, er, Bulldogs, were shuffling through the breakfast buffet in the Seavey Room, already in uniform and mere minutes away from loading onto the bus for their ride to The Blatt. You've never really had an omelet until you've eaten one with your cleats on.

The sprawling hotel conference space took its name from Webber Seavey, Omaha's first chief of police. Seavey patrolled the city's dusty streets during the final years of the nineteenth century. He was charged with the unenviable duty of maintaining some sort of order among the lawless likes of illiterate cattlemen, power-mad land barons, drunken

Indians, and the saltiest prostitutes on the plains. This very building, located at 1005 Dodge Street, had been the headquarters of the Omaha Police Department, where Seavey and his heirs screwed up their courage before stepping out onto the street to do battle with whiskey-embalmed lowlifes.

Bulldog relief pitcher Holden Sprague didn't care about any of that, not even as his younger sister Grace tried to give him a history lesson on what she had just read on the plaques in the hotel hallway. He just wanted a damn piece of toast.

"What the . . . *hell?* Did anyone else get this toaster to work?"

His irritation was understandable. Sprague, along with the rest of the Fresno State team, had been on the road for a solid month. What's more, they were tired of people acting like they didn't belong in Omaha in the first place. During the opening ceremonies Coach Mike Batesole overheard a CWS worker telling another, "Don't worry about these guys, they'll be gone in two games."

Even God seemed to have a problem with Fresno, bouncing around their Wednesday night charter flight like it was attached to bungee cords, victims of the same frightening storm that had claimed the lives of the four Boy Scouts. After a series of midair drops that the pilot rated "a nine on a scare scale of ten," they were forced to land in Lincoln, where they waited for their bus to arrive from Omaha and finally get them into town around one o'clock in the morning for the late-night bonding session with The Blatt.

What the . . . *hell?*

"Dude, watch your language," a teammate said to Sprague with a point to the young boy sitting at the table. "You're going to teach the kid here a whole new vocabulary he doesn't need to know yet."

Noah Mayne just snickered and ate his breakfast. Swear words were certainly nothing new at this late stage of the baseball season, so the nine-year-old just ate his cereal and giggled to his grandfather, surrounded by his Bulldog heroes and simply happy to be here.

Assistant coach Mike Mayne giggled back. If the kid was happy to be in Omaha, then the white-haired pitching coach was going to need a dictionary to find the words to describe his emotions. During a lifetime of coaching, from high school to junior college to now Fresno, he'd dreamed about reaching Rosenblatt in uniform. Now here he sat, in that uniform, eating breakfast and talking baseball with his grandson and his adopted sons for the 2008 season.

Noah Mayne could rattle off every Fresno State player's stats, strengths, and weaknesses quicker than any media member or university sports information director. He knew so much about the team that Sprague suggested perhaps he should suit up and sit on the bench for games. "We can give you Sean Bonesteele's uniform," the pitcher cracked, referring to his seldom-used bullpen mate. "Bonesteele doesn't need it. He's too busy searching for health food in the beef capital of the world. That should go well."

Mike Mayne laughed, had his coffee, and briefly talked to Sprague about his approach should he end up on the mound later that day. It was the perfect illustration of what he did as the team's elder spokesman. He had his fun, but politely got the youngsters to focus when it was time to, nudging their easily distracted minds back toward the task at hand and riffling through a half-century of coaching experience to prep them for game time.

When the coach woke up that morning he already knew that this was going to be the greatest of his sixty-two Father's Days. One year ago, he was happily retired, having traded in his cleats and clipboards to split time between a summer house in Cameron, Montana, a town so remote it barely earns a dot on the map, and the home he still kept back in San Jacinto, California. His love affair with the game had started as a baby-boomer child, and was nurtured during four years as a player at UC Riverside, seven years as a high school coach, and fifteen seasons at the end of the bench with Orange Coast College in Costa Mesa. He'd worked as a scout and roving instructor for the Seattle Mariners, given private lessons to hardball hopefuls, and even put in some time as a spring training catching instructor for the Oakland A's.

After the turn of the millennium, he and wife Patricia decided to slow things down, buying the place outside of Yellowstone National Park, and settling in to watch their oldest son Brent, Noah's father, finish out a solid fifteen-year career as a big-league catcher. But in the fall of 2007, the game called back Mike Mayne for one last trip around the bases. More accurately, a call was placed on behalf of the game by Fresno skipper Mike Batesole.

Twenty years earlier, when "Bates" was an infielder in the Dodgers organization, he and other local professionals would come over at Mayne's invitation to work out on his field at Orange Coast, guys like Darryl Strawberry, Eric Davis, and Mark McGwire. Mayne quickly noticed that most of the pros would do their thing and head home, but not Batesole. He'd hang around for hours, working with Mayne's junior-college kids, instinctively teaching them baseball fundamentals in the field and at the plate. Batesole's minor-league instructors recalled a similar scene at Dodgertown during spring training, when he would stay long after everyone else had hit the golf course, lingering around the batting cage to watch Kirk Gibson and Steve Sax take instruction from L.A. coaches.

"He hardly ever said a word that I can remember," said Tommy Lasorda, longtime Dodgers manager. "But you could tell he was studying everything. How the great ones worked so hard all the time, with the dedication that it takes to put in all the extra hours. Even the guys with so much talent you'd think they would just put it in cruise control, but he watched them work their butts off. And he soaked up everything our instructors said. It didn't get him to the big leagues as a player, but it sure has made him a great coach."

By 1988, Batesole's playing days were finished and he was on Mike Mayne's staff as an assistant, eventually moving on to stops at Cypress College and Cal State Northridge, due in no small part to calls of recommendation placed by Mayne, one of California's most respected baseball men. So when Batesole suddenly lost his pitching coach on the eve of the '08 season, he coaxed his mentor out of retirement to take the job.

"And here we are in Omaha," Mayne said during Friday's batting practice session, grinning through his white mustache and throwing his hands toward the heavens like an exaggerated shrug of the shoulders. "Who saw this coming?"

Honestly? No one did.

Batesole's Father's Day had started by answering questions about that very topic during an early-morning meeting with the team of ESPN broadcasters and producers. This was a mandatory game-morning stop for every head coach and sometimes a handful of his best players, a chance for that night's production team to gain some insight into the strategies and mind-sets for the game.

When the coach woke up in his third-floor hotel room, he roused up his two young sons, Kody and Korby, and told them they were going to take a little Father's Day walk. As the three Batesoles walked the three blocks down to ESPN's hotel (likely walking by Bob Bruns and his two boys), an early-morning thunderstorm started gathering overhead. Fresno State media relations director Steve Weakland suggested the coach and his kids might want to grab a car, but Batesole just shrugged off the clouds.

It certainly wasn't the darkest mess he'd had to endure this year.

The most anticipated team in Bulldog history had stumbled out of the 2008 starting gate as if they needed to be put down and out of their misery. They lost the first two games of the season to UC Davis, a team that was in its first season of NCAA Division I baseball. They lost twelve of their first twenty, including an embarrassing performance in their own home invitational tournament. In the search for a spark the pitchers began over-throwing and the hitters started trying to smash six-run homers. Batesole explained it all the same way to anyone who asked: "We were thinking about Omaha in March when we should have been thinking about March in March."

By season's end, third baseman Tommy Mendonca would lead the nation in strikeouts with an NCAA single-season record ninety-seven whiffs, mostly compiled during those desperate early days of spring. The lone bright spot was the staff pitching ace, junior Tanner Scheppers, a mid-to-high 90-mph hurler who racked up an 8–2 record in his first dozen starts, rocketing up draft boards across the Major Leagues. But even that light was snuffed out thanks to a season-ending shoulder injury in mid-spring.

By the time the Dogs reached mid-March, the stands at Beiden Field were emptying and the mood in the clubhouse was only marginally better than that aboard Captain Cook's HMS *Bounty*. Some around the program wondered aloud if the Scheppers injury hadn't been caused by overuse. Senior shortstop Todd Sandell, unhappy at losing his starting spot to freshman phenom Danny Muno, had a run-in with Batesole at the start of a big midseason series against Nevada and ended up with an empty locker. Some said he'd quit; others said he'd been told never to come back.

The conspiracy theories, preseason expectations, and all the questions about both settled into the Bulldog clubhouse like a cloud of tear gas.

Coach Batesole tried to loosen his team with laughter, inspiration, then anger. None of it worked. So he settled on the completely opposite approach, withdrawing quietly into what he could control: his stat books, strategies, and film study. He scrapped the big pregame speeches, stopped worrying about trying to find his team's motivation. Instead, he quietly went to his seven remaining seniors and suggested that they get their crap together. They did, calling a team meeting and making their teammates promise to stop whining, stop obsessing about stuff like the umpires, and stop sulking. It was time to focus.

"That was the turning point," admitted outfielder Steve Susdorf, who'd turned down $50,000 from the Detroit Tigers to return for his senior season. "Coach went around the room and asked every player to define his role on the team. If what we said was wrong, he corrected us and told us what our role actually was in his eyes. Everything suddenly became clear. Coach would worry about X's and O's and the team kind of became responsible for itself."

Some believed that Batesole was putting too much pressure on himself and his team. He'd done it before, especially when he first took the job at Fresno. There were even rumors of a nervous breakdown. Those closest to him, and there had never been many, had long worried that his inward intensity would one day do him in. Even his seemingly perfect family life as a teenager had been blown up for a while, when a disagreement with his father led him to temporarily move in with the family of high school teammate and future big-league all-star Lenny Dykstra.

Years later Batesole invited Dykstra out to see one of his practices at Cal State Northridge. Dykstra couldn't believe how hard his old buddy was on the college kids, at one point telling one of the players to "pack his shit and get out of here." When Dysktra questioned the tactics later that night, Batesole explained that everyone on the team had to buy into his plan, and once they did they'd be rewarded by winning. A few months later that Matador team, including the kid who'd been told to pack and leave, came to within a game of going to Omaha.

"Everything Bates does, he's all in," Dykstra said of his old friend. "Playing baseball, schoolwork, and now coaching baseball, and being a father and a family man. He's either going to do it perfectly or he's not going to mess with it. And he's going to do it his way. That approach might drive some people away, but if you stick with him, even when he pisses you off, then you're going to love the end result. Just ask his kids at Fresno."

Some thought Coach Batesole had pressed too hard at the start of the 2008 season, overexcited about the potential of his ballclub and squeezing them too hard to find it. Others thought he was simply playing the age-old coaching strategy of creating a last-resort motivation for one's players—unite them by giving them a common enemy in the coach.

When the late head coach Jim Brock was asked to describe his approach to his Arizona State clubhouse, an approach that led the Sun Devils to thirteen CWS trips and two championships (not to mention the only man to ever keep catankerous Barry Bonds somewhat in check), he said it was a deliberate three-step plan. "We would lose early in the season, I would terrorize them into winning, and then 'reward' them by leaving them alone."

Batesole sure seemed to be using the same blueprint.

Whatever the plan, if there even was one, by the time the Western Athletic Conference Tournament arrived at the end of May, Batesole had tightened his one-man inner circle so much that not even his three assistant coaches knew exactly what he was up to or when. He watched film and devised his offensive and defensive strategies. (*My starter is a lefty who lives on fastballs in the lower half of the strike zone . . . and the top of their lineup is loaded with right-handed slap hitters on a fast dry infield, so my infielders will start out playing deep and shifted toward the first base line.*) Assistants Matt Curtis and Pat Waer made sure those strategies were implemented, and Mayne became Team Dad, focusing on big-picture direction and serving as the listening board for the student-athletes.

As starting pitcher Justin Wilson so eloquently stated, "Losing sucks. When you're losing you'll do about anything to turn it around. And you know what? We did."

While no one was paying attention (Fresno spent the entire regular season outside *Baseball America's* top twenty-five poll), the Bulldogs quietly began to win ballgames, albeit uglier than their namesake animal. They sacrificed victories in their midweek nonconference games against the likes of Cal and Long Beach State in order to save their strength for their in-conference weekend sets against the wild and wacky WAC. One inning at a time they climbed back atop the WAC standings, reaching the top spot just in time for the conference tourney.

They clinched the regular season title on the road at Sacramento State and then traveled 2,000 miles east to Ruston, Louisiana, for the conference tournament. They won four straight to take the tourney, earning an automatic berth to the NCAA Baseball Tournament and an invitation to the Long Beach State regional. They were a number-four seed, the lowest seeding available in a four-team regional, and college baseball's equivalent to earning a number-sixteen seed in the NCAA Basketball Tournament.

In other words, Fresno was expected to do what schools such as Niagara, Iona, and Belmont do each year when March Madness rolls around. Be polite, show up on time, and then be a nice little whipping mule by taking your beating and riding on home.

"What no one knew about these guys is they live for that kind of situation." Mayne placed his hands on the shoulders of his grandson and looked down as Noah looked up and nodded his head in agreement. "The harder it gets, the more injuries they have, the closer they become as a team. Unless you're down here in the dugout or on that bus, there's no way to feel that. You have to have this uniform on to feel it. Right, Noah?"

"Yep."

"It's just another game to these guys."

As the Bulldogs filled the lobby of the hotel, it looked like the field hospital scene from *Gone with the Wind*. First baseman Alan Ahmady was recruited out of high school as a pitcher, but was moved to the corner after tearing a muscle in his right elbow. Across the infield, Tommy Mendonca was playing with a right hand so full of dislocated fingers that it looked like a sack of broken glass. Second baseman Erik Wetzel had a hamate bone removed from one his wrists and right fielder Steve Detwiler was playing with a torn thumb tendon suffered while sliding into the bag at Long Beach State. Fortunately, it had ripped completely through, so it didn't bug him at the plate like a partial tear would have. At least that's how he rationalized the situation. At season's end, doctors were going to fix it with a Tommy John–like surgical procedure, removing a tendon from elsewhere in his body and sewing it into his hand. But for now he was willing to gut out the pain that had become increasingly obvious as he grimaced on every swing and constantly worked his fingers over and over while standing in the outfield.

"If you haven't gotten hurt, the other guys pretty much think you're a wuss," said assistant coach Pat Waer. "If you don't have an injury then the other guys are probably going to pull you aside and give you one just to make sure you're on board."

The only item that team equipment manager Eddie Brewer had ordered more of than bandages was pine tar. These guys put it everywhere. On their hats, their jerseys, even their cleats. After every game Brewer would haul the uniforms to the laundry and scrub them down to get rid of the brown gunk. Before the next game the players had squirted it all over everything again.

What Eddie didn't need to bother ordering was razors.

Fresno led the NCAA in hair, facial and otherwise. After thirty-three straight days on the road, most of the Bulldogs had given up trying to fight the stubble. Then again, maybe they wore the facial hair because they weren't allowed to rub pine tar all over their cheeks. "None of us liked shaving anyway," Tommy Mendonca said with a rub of the cheeks. "This just gave us an excuse to stop."

They were the sons of construction workers, ink salesmen, and accountants (despite what he may have said in the Bulldog media guide, Holden Sprague's father was not an astronaut, though he kept ESPN fooled for at least one game). Most had been passed up by the superpower programs out of high school, evaluated as a step too slow or an inch too short, and every player on the roster hailed from the state of California, most within a short drive of campus.

While Coach Batesole dropped jaws with his impromptu stand-up routine at Friday's coach's press conference, his players walked around The

Blatt as if they owned place. They joked, wrestled, and waved to the small group of fans and family that sported hastily made white T-shirts touting, "From Underdogs to Wonderdogs." During their day off on Saturday several players came and hung out among the shoppers and partiers on Thirteenth Street, closer Brandon Burke grabbing some time relaxing in the shade of the trees on the sidewalk to Zesto.

But when the team came back to the hotel after a workout session that afternoon, Batesole stopped them in the lobby and pointed to the table where an official CWS souvenir vendor sold T-shirts and hats screaming "Fresno State—2008 College World Series."

"Buy what you want to buy today," the coach told his team. "Go see all the stuff you want to see and have all the fun you want to have. But tomorrow, this . . ."—he pointed to the souvenirs and the giant banner welcoming the team to Omaha—". . . this part is over. It's not enough just to be here. Tomorrow we go to work."

It's not enough just to be here.

Just as each year brings its own version of The Pick, it is also kind enough to extend an invitation to The Underdog, one team that manages to crash the annual CWS convention of the juggernauts. When the Buster Poseys come to Rosenblatt, they are expected to do everything short of round the bases atop a golden chariot. The Fresno States arrive with little or no expectations but their own.

The first real Cinderella crashed the ball in 1951, only the second College World Series to be held in Omaha after two years in Kalamazoo and one disastrous stop in Wichita. It was also the second year of the eight-team format, essentially the same bracket structure that exists today. Southern California, already establishing what would become a half-century of dominance, was making its third straight appearance, joined by a pair of one-loss teams in Utah and Tennessee, and an Ohio State squad led by future big-league infielder/manager/mascot Don Zimmer. Their appearances at The Blatt were expected.

"But not us."

Former Oklahoma outfielder Jim Antonio's satisfaction was still audible as he talked about it nearly six decades later, dramatics finely tuned by a fifty-year career as a Broadway and Hollywood actor. (In *Outbreak*, he's the doctor that tells Rene Russo, "The chances of this virus showing up in the U.S. are virtually nil." In the next scene the virus shows up in the United States.)

"Our own people didn't want us to go to Omaha. Bud Wilkinson, the great football coach, was the athletic director and he didn't think we were good enough to go. But thankfully the president of the school made him send us. Still, they gave us barely enough money to get there and back."

The Sooners lacked big names and started the year with a brutal losing streak. But the senior-heavy squad managed to slowly claw its way back, inching over the .500 mark and rallying to win the Big Seven conference championship to earn a postseason invite.

Sound familiar?

Oklahoma swept through the CWS double-elimination bracket without a single loss, bringing their season-ending winning streak to a lucky thirteen. After upsetting Tennessee in the championship game 3–2, they boarded the bus and drove through the night back to Norman. "We would've liked to have stayed and celebrated," Antonio said with his aged Okie drawl. "But we didn't have enough money left to get hotel rooms."

Back home there was little if any attention paid to the victors, a silent treatment likely designed to keep from denting Wilkinson's Oklahoma-sized ego. The team didn't receive championship rings until the fiftieth anniversary of their title in 2001, prompting pitcher Jack Shirley to tell CWS historian W. C. Madden, "They were probably waiting for us to pass away."

After Oklahoma's victory, The Underdogs role became less about trying to win it all and more about heartwarming cameo two-and-'cue appearances. By the time such meteoric teams arrived in Omaha they'd already used up their magic just to get there. Compounding the problem was the rise of the Sun Belt's stranglehold on the sport. The success of programs from Southern Cal to Texas to Miami had resulted in a demoralizing lack of parity. Entering 2008, a total of 106 schools had made at least one trip to the College World Series. But forty-two of the sixty-two championships had been won by only eight teams.

Still, there always seemed to be room for someone to ride in, make some noise, and win over the hopelessly romantic hometown fans. Like Rider University in 1967, Dartmouth in '70, Texas-Pan American and Harvard in '71, or James Madison in '83. Each team unexpectedly blew into town, pulled off at least one win they shouldn't have, and walked off the field at The Blatt to appreciative applause from the underdog-loving Omahans.

In 1986, LSU marched into town having spent most of the season ranked number one in the land. They blew through the Southeastern Conference tournament and steamrolled into Rosenblatt as the prohibitive favorite.

Then they ran into Loyola Marymount. And no, that's not a typo.

"We played in the first game, middle of the day, lot of sunshine," Coach Skip Bertman winced as when he told the story. "Loyola had two men on late in the game with two outs and they hit a high fly ball to Albert Belle. He had it played perfectly. Too perfectly. Had he made a run for the ball, gotten an angle on it, the sun would have never come into play. But where he was standing the sun was directly in his face. The ball just popped out of his glove. They scored twice and we lost, 4–3. It is still the greatest day in the history of the Loyola Marymount program. As far as I was concerned, it was the worst day in LSU history up that point. It wasn't really, but it sure felt like it at the time."

But not even the roar that followed the Loyola Lions off the field could match the series of explosions that Omaha's baseball fans set off four years later. It began when the Georgia Southern Eagles nearly upset number-one Stanford, robbed when an apparent game-winning home run was ruled a double. The Stanford Cardinal went on to beat the Eagles 5–4 in ten innings.

Three days later The Citadel took center stage. The tiny military school from Charleston, South Carolina played their regular season in a ballpark flattened by Hurricane Hugo, but they stunned Miami in the NCAA tourney to earn their trip to Omaha. At the 1990 edition of the pre-CWS coaches' press conference, Citadel skipper Chal Port listened to Marquess, Bertman, and the other coaches talk about their preseason expectations of making it to The Blatt.

"Our aim was a little lower," Port cracked. "When we looked at the calendar last fall, our goal for June 1 was to make sure that the kids had turned in all their equipment."

The Bulldogs were promptly beaten by Skip Bertman's LSU Tigers, but rebounded with one of the most memorable games in Rosenblatt Stadium history. Down 4–1 to Cal State Fullerton after six, Chal Port rallied his troops (they were literally troops) and motioned wildly to the Rosenblatt crowd to come to The Underdog's aid. The Bulldogs took a 6–4 lead in the top of the eighth and Fullerton came back to force extra innings. The Citadel took a one-run lead in the tenth and the Titans tied it up again. Finally, in the top of the twelfth, third baseman Tony Skole stroked a single to score left fielder Anthony Jenkins, whose game-winning slide into home is still one of the most replayed images on The Blatt's big scoreboard screen.

"It's been nearly twenty years since that game," said one souvenir vendor along Thirteenth Street, specializing in classic CWS apparel. "Every year I still get people coming over here looking for Citadel stuff."

The fourteenth and final game of the '90 Series ended with, fittingly, another upset. Unheralded Georgia earned a spot in the finals by shocking Stanford ace Mike Mussina and then held Oklahoma State, who'd averaged twelve runs per game in the CWS, to one run and won the title. On the Bulldog roster was a reserve utility player and local Athens kid named Dave Perno.

"What we did in 1990 was living proof that it pays to get hot at the right time," the UGA head coach said while standing outside his office, looking at the Bulldog trophy case that housed a picture of his much younger self. "You start rolling, the crowd gets behind you, you start believing you can do no wrong . . . and boom, you're the champions. It sounds like stereotypical coach speak bulletin-board B.S., but if a team really believes in itself, really buys into the guys in that locker room, even when no one else does, that's when it becomes something special. It's hard to beat a group like that."

At 10:33 A.M. on Father's Day, Mike Batesole stepped off the elevator into the lobby of Webber Seavey's jailhouse and laid eyes on what he believed was exactly that type of a group, no matter how many bandages it took to hold them together. Dressed in his customary short-sleeve Windbreaker the coach stopped to shake the hand of Fresno State A.D. Thomas Boeh, who'd arrived much earlier to work the room of Bulldog parents and alums (not to mention potential donors), and perhaps the proudest man in the Nebraska Territory, WAC commissioner Karl Benson.

Benson was also a baseball man. He played at Boise State and coached at a junior college in Tacoma, Washington. His conference didn't get many chances to stand nose to nose with the cash-money likes of the SEC, ACC, or Pac-10. Now he wanted to be the first to congratulate Mike Batesole's Bulldogs for giving him that right. The last time the commish made an appearance at a big-time collegiate event was the Sugar Bowl, where his Hawaii Rainbows had their dream season crushed by Georgia, 41–10. Benson's baseball acumen told him that this trip would end differently. His lifelong knowledge of the game meant that he recognized the truth behind Batesole's quiet confidence.

Fresno had talent. Damn good talent. And Mike Batesole, as mysterious as he was, was also a damn good baseball coach.

Rice University's head coach Wayne Graham knew it, too. He had tried to tell the assembled media during Friday's press conference and tried to tell his fellow coaches, but no one took his warnings seriously.

From 1997 to 2005, the Owls had been a member of the Western Athletic Conference, where Graham and Batesole's teams fought for the conference title three straight seasons. Fresno finished second all three times, but did so behind an unstoppable Rice squad that won the College World Series in 2003 with what was essentially a Major League pitching rotation. During Friday's press conference, Batesole had thanked Rice for leaving the WAC so that his team "had a chance" and believed he'd coached against Graham's teams "about fifty times" and didn't think Fresno had ever scored a run against them.

"Yeah, right," Graham said as he stood on the top step of the dugout chatting up his team's civic club host, LeRoy Swedlund. The old coach said he wished he had a media guide to look up the numbers, but he knew without looking that Fresno had scared the hell out of him more often than not. The media guide backed him up, revealing that Graham and Batesole had matched wits eighteen times in the WAC, Rice winning twelve to Fresno's six. But five of those games had been decided by one run and another took ten innings to sort out. "People don't know much about Batesole, especially out on the East Coast and down in the southeast. But he can coach and his teams can play. They don't quit until someone tells them the game is over and threatens to turn off the lights. Anyone not prepared for that hasn't done their homework."

The night before his rematch with Rice, Batesole had done plenty of homework. The first question he asked before any road trip was, "Does my room have a DVD player or do I need to bring one?" He'd watched film all night and figured out how he was going to pitch every player on the Rice Owls roster, his defensive alignment for every potential situation, and had even devised a plan for dealing with All-American closer Cole St. Clair should the situation arise.

But now it was time to get on the bus, the perfect escape hatch to wriggle out of more uncomfortable forced small talk with the administrative suits.

The coach's pause to chat allowed just enough time for the last few players to sneak by and jump onto the red Arrow bus that was parked on Dodge Street. Catcher Jake Johnson hugged his parents. Holden Sprague stopped by his dad's hotel room—the dad that the media now believed was an astronaut—and wished him a happy Father's Day. Alan Ahmady kissed his mother, one hand carrying his gray number 9 road jersey, the other cramming down a Hot Pocket.

By now everyone knew that the coach would be the last one on the bus and they knew he'd show up precisely three-to-five minutes after the announced departure time. They knew where everyone would sit and who would be listening to what songs on their iPod. The routine had been the same in Sacramento, Louisiana, and the first two rounds of NCAAs.

It was the same when they were sent to Long Beach State to face the number-eleven team in the country on their home field, then had to win two of three against number-six San Diego, owners of the nation's top pitching staff.

It was the same during the even more impossible task of visiting number three Arizona State for the Super Regional, where they won back-to-back games against a team that had only lost three home games all season.

Between each must-win was another hotel breakfast buffet, another couple of hours wandering the streets of whatever town they were in, another pay-per-view movie in the room, or another game of *Guitar Hero*. Everywhere they went, the media asked about the distractions of being on the road and the pressures of always being The Underdog.

Coach Batesole, how do you keep doing it?

"We just kept playing."

But what's been the strategy?

"They figured out how to play the game."

But what's the secret?

"They've got a lot of guts."

Okay, uh, thanks . . . just get on the bus, will you?

To a smattering of applause from a half-dozen Bulldog fans, the big motor coach lumbered west on Dodge and turned south toward The Blatt. Directly behind them was the rainstorm, now safely north of the city. "All right," the head coach said as he settled into his front row, right-side seat. "Let's play ball." The ten-minute ride was like an afternoon on a junior-high bus. If a freshman looked nervous, a senior picked on him to loosen him up. Once again, they talked about music, movies, and girls, particularly the cute one behind the front desk at the hotel.

Mike Mayne was right. It was just another bus ride to another ball-game. That was honestly how they felt, even if no one believed them when they said it. The Underdogs knew what Wayne Graham knew . . . what Karl Benson knew . . . what Long Beach State, San Diego, and Arizona State knew. They deserved to be here.

As Fresno rolled toward the ballpark, Graham's Rice squad was already there. The team began unloading their gear into the third-base dugout, everything going into its proper place. The aluminum bats were slid into their notches on the bat rack by the steps to the on-deck circle. The helmets were slid into their green metal cubbyholes. The official NCAA POWERade and Dasani coolers were filled with ice, and the paper cups were stocked.

In the middle of it all, one lone white baseball cap, embroidered with the school's trademark "R," was snapped around a metal power cable to hang over the Owls' bench. The cap was the property of George "Poppie" Thomen, a Houston native and a Rice grad, class of 1941. When Wayne Graham turned the Rice baseball team into a national power, Thomen had jumped on the bandwagon in a big way. He and an old friend named Don attended every home game at Reckling Park, Poppie wearing his white "R" ball cap while Don kept score with a brand-new ceremonial opening day pen, which Thomen presented to his pal at the start of every season.

Soon Thomen's granddaughter Tracey Kuhlman, also a Rice grad, started going to games with the old coots, and the bond she and her grandfather established over Owl baseball brought them closer than they'd ever been. They even planned a trip to the 2008 College World Series, certain that their beloved Owls would be there for the third year in a row.

But as the 2008 season wore on, the eighty-nine-year-old began to visibly slow. He'd quietly held off his cancer for a while now, but had come to the realization that he needed full-time medical care. On May 7, Poppie Thomen sat with Don and watched the Owls defeat Oklahoma State. The next day he checked himself into the hospital. Twenty days later he was dead.

Now, on Father's Day, Thomen's hat hung in the dugout keeping watch over his Owls. Graham had heard about the story and contacted Kuhlman to borrow the cap that her grandfather had given to her shortly before his death. As her hat hung in the dugout at Rosenblatt Stadium, Kuhlman sat eleven rows behind it, honoring her grandfather by making the trip to Omaha without him.

Across the field another grandfather, Mike Mayne, walked to the top step of the first-base dugout, following his grandson as the kid popped up onto the grass. Mayne leaned forward and motioned with his right hand in a big sweeping movement across the field before them.

He explained that during this very same week twenty years earlier Brent Mayne, his son and Noah's father, had been on this very same field playing catcher for Cal State Fullerton in the '88 College World Series. The boy, who'd already phoned his Dad to say happy Father's Day, paused for a moment and smiled at the thought of his old man on this old field. Then the nine-year-old looked up and said, "I love you, Grandpa."

"There you go," Mike Mayne said to a reporter standing next to him, his voice choking up. "Is this place magic or what?"

For The Underdogs, yes it was.

While the Maynes had their moment, Mike Batesole stood directly behind the batting cage, watching his team hit. He barely spoke above a whisper, addressing only the player at the plate, but repeating the same mantra for each hitter. "Show some discipline . . . work the count . . . two-strike hits . . . get the barrel of the bat down . . . hit it down . . . through those holes . . ."

Batesole grabbed his middle infielders, Danny Muno and junior second baseman Erik Wetzel, and walked them to the edge of the infield grass. The former infielder knew that the hard morning rain followed by the sharp midday sunshine would completely change the field from what they'd seen during Friday's infield session. Muno, who looked younger than Noah Mayne and wore a hat that looked three sizes too big for his head, was one step ahead of "Coach Bates."

"It's not wet at all. But it's a lot faster out there today, huh?"

Batesole smiled. Yes, the kid *was* one step ahead of him.

"Exactly. Those balls are going to be coming in low and mean." He motioned with his hand like a stone skipping across the water. "They'll be coming at your ankles in a hurry."

When Game Three started, Batesole's advice instantly looked downright prophetic. More often than not, it always did.

In the first inning with one on and no outs, Rice shortstop Rick Hague hit—you guessed it—a low screaming grounder right at Danny Muno's shoe tops at short. Prepared for it, the nineteen-year-old smothered the ball even as it suddenly hopped up on him just as it had to Florida State's Tony Delmonico. In a flash, Muno whipped the ball to Wetzel at second to start a 6–4–3 double play.

In the top of the second, right fielder Steve Detwiler was up with two on and one out. He slapped an identical hot chopper toward Rice second baseman Jimmy Comerota, who ran in to meet the grounder, snagging it and diving for the feet of the runner from first, catcher Ryan Overland. He missed the tag by inches, then wheeled to throw the ball to first, but the impact of his knees hitting the edge of the infield grass was enough to jar the ball loose.

E-4. Bases loaded.

Two batters later, Danny Muno hit—you guessed it—a low bounding grounder over second base. The next batter, Gavin Hedstrom ripped—yep—another hot low one over the bag at third for a double. *Get the barrel of the bat down . . . let's hit it down and through those holes . . . those balls are going to be coming in low and mean.*

At the end of two innings, the score was Fresno State 4, Rice 0.

Two innings later, the Bulldogs moved the ball off the ground and into the air. Ryan Overland slapped a single to left. Designated hitter Jordan Ribera dumped another single into center. Then Muno shook off any freshman fears by launching a 2–2 grooved fastball into the right-center-field bleachers.

Fresno 7, Rice 0.

Center fielder Hedstrom drew a walk and then scored when Erik Wetzel drove a wind-aided ball against the center field wall. Left fielder Steve Susdorf drew another walk. When Alan Ahmady brought his Hot Pocket-fueled bat to the plate, he quickly went down 0–2 but then drew three straight balls to fill the count.

The sixth pitch from Rice lefty Matt Evers was a good idea, an 88-mph breaker that was supposed to be low and inside. Instead it drifted into the middle of the strike zone belt-high. Ahmady's elbows locked and his eyes grew large.

Tink.

It was the second three-run homer of the fourth inning. Fresno 11, Rice 0. By the end of the game it was 17–5.

Did The Underdog deserve to be here? You bet they did.

As Wayne Graham walked into the Hall of Fame Room for his postgame press conference, he slapped a local Houston writer on the shoulder, saying, "Does anyone want to believe me about Fresno now?"

Danny Muno and Erik Wetzel turned their pregame chat with Batesole into a combined five hits and six RBIs. Muno did commit one error at short, but the blowout meant that it didn't matter. Alan Ahmady's Hot Pocket powered him to a 3-for-4 day. And Justin Wilson, Mr. He-Makes-Me-Go-Through-a-Pack-of-Marlboros, smoked through seven innings of work for the win.

The Underdogs lined up in the infield grass and shook hands with their old WAC rivals, then turned and walked back toward the first-base dugout. "See?" Mike Mayne said as the assistant coach arrived from the bullpen for the celebration. "Just another game."

As the "Red Wave" fans stood and applauded, Wetzel scanned the stands for his father, David. Just two years earlier, the Wetzel family was in mourning. Erik's mother, Cathy, had suffered from cancer all spring, choosing to forgo debilitating medical treatment so that she and David could follow Erik's first season with the Bulldogs. David sold his printing business to buy an RV, which the Wetzels drove over every mile of the bizarrely nationwide WAC schedule. They cheered Erik through a twelve-game hitting streak, they cheered when he was chosen as a Freshman All-American, and they went particularly crazy when Erik hit his first collegiate home run to help the 'Dogs beat San Diego in the first round of the NCAAs.

By the start of Erik's sophomore year, his mother was gone. Now, in his first College World Series appearance, he had honored her memory with one of the best performances of his career. Standing on the field, he honored his father on Father's Day with a point, a smile, and a nod.

Shortly after Fresno moved out of the dugout, LSU moved in for Game Four. Tiger head coach Paul Mainieri unknowingly walked out to the same spot on the grass where Wetzel had waved to his father and did the same, bringing his two boys, twenty-four-year-old Nick and thirteen-year-old Tom, out onto the field to get the attention of their grandfather, sitting a dozen rows up. Paul's love for the game had come from Dr. Demie Mainieri, a legendary coach at Miami Dade Community College who'd tutored the likes of Steve Carlton and Oddibe McDowell. Now here they were, like so many fathers and sons, together in Omaha.

Three hours later the Tigers walked off the field after a heart-wrenching 8–4 loss to North Carolina. They'd never hit their rhythm, kept off balance by the endless number of missile-throwing pitchers the Tarheels seemed to always have in abundant supply.

With Miami on the ropes, Carolina was the overwhelming press-box favorite to win it all, and now LSU knew why.

But Mainieri couldn't stop smiling. He kept looking at his boys and the way they kept looking over at him. Sure, losing the first game of the College World Series was always hard to overcome, but Mainieri was the guy that always preached to his children and his team about "the experience" and "appreciating what's in front of you."

Across town on the banks of the Missouri River, the sting of Florida State's loss on Saturday wasn't hurting quite as bad, either. The Martins, Mike Senior and Junior, and the Delmonicos, Rod and Tony, were elbow-deep in fried steak and hot dogs, pausing only to enjoy a ride on the River City Star riverboat, all compliments of the Omaha Cosmopolitan Club.

Like the Seminoles, Paul Mainieri wasn't feeling the pain of suddenly being one loss away from going home. Instead, he was oddly emotional, truly moved by what he saw in front of him, in the Rosenblatt grandstands above and all around his disappointed team. He saw fathers and their children, and he later admitted that it made him think about those poor Boy Scouts that had been lost, the ones whose funerals would share the local headlines with the Series for the next week. They were all the same age as his son Tom. And tonight he was just that much more thankful to have his sons here with him, win or lose.

Outside the ballpark, Bob Bruns and his two boys were already on the road back to Michigan. It was tempting to stick around for a few more days, but Bob had to be back at work on Monday morning as did Jacob and Sam. They'd be pulling weeds in the morning and had baseball practice that night. And all of that was 900 miles away.

They watched the Rosenblatt lights disappear over the horizon in their rearview mirror, and for the next four hours talked nonstop baseball. They talked about the big leagues, minor leagues, and high school ball, but mostly they talked about what they'd seen over the last two days. At one point Sam declared to his father that he wanted to play college ball and hopefully come back to Omaha in uniform.

As they crossed into Illinois, the boys were talked out and fast asleep. Bob was all alone, replaying the weekend over and over in his mind.

It was . . . yes, it had to be . . . the grandest Father's Day celebration on planet Earth.

FOUR

THE PROGRAM

Monday, June 16
Game Five: Florida State vs. Miami
Game Six: Stanford vs. Georgia

At five o'clock on Sunday afternoon, about the time that the Fresno cele-bration bus was arriving back at the hotel and the generations of Mainieri men were waving to one another, University of Miami head coach Jim Morris strode onto the field at Bellevue East High School, home of the Chieftains. His Hurricanes—the ACC champions, the number-one team in the land, The Program—suddenly found itself laboring in the loser's bracket, potentially twenty-four hours from going home. Morris would deal with that later. Right now there was a much more pressing issue to tend to.

"Where's Miss Marilyn?"

"Who?"

The reply came back from his players, who were laughing and joking like a team that was 1–0, not 0–1, razing relief pitcher Rene Guerra for missing the bus and showing up ten minutes late.

"Miss Marilyn."

"You mean the Gatorade Lady?"

"Yeah, but her name is Miss Marilyn. Where is she?"

"Here she comes."

Easing down the grassy hill toward the first-base dugout, banging along carefully with a giant white cooler in tow, was Marilyn Ralston. She was doing what she always did this time of year, bringing cold drinks to Belle-vue's Don Roddy Field Sports Complex to keep her boys cool on a searing hot summer day. As soon as she was spotted, people began running up the hill to meet her halfway and take the load off her hands.

"Hello, Coach," she said as the aluminum gate swung open by the first-base dugout. "How's my favorite team?" In one fluid motion, she flung open the top of the cooler, wiped her wet hands on the fronts of her legs, and pointed to the green and orange lettering across the front of her white T-shirt.

MIAMI.

The truth was that her favorite team was whichever squad was scheduled to show up that day. But it didn't hurt that the Hurricanes had given her the shirt. As Morris walked over to hug Miss Marilyn's neck, he spoke to a small group of South Florida sportswriters standing by to grab a quick quote about the next day's elimination game with archrival Florida State. "This here is who you need to be interviewing. Teams come and go, but she's always here. Wouldn't feel right without her . . . isn't that right, Marilyn?"

"Thank you, Coach," she said as she received her hug. "But it'll never really feel right again."

"Yes, ma'am, I know."

Here, on a high-school baseball field fifteen minutes south of Rosenblatt Stadium, was the greatest display of how the teams of the College World Series are embraced by the people of Omaha. Here, in the suburb of Bellevue, where the locals came to sit in the sunbaked wooden bleachers of a municipal ballpark to watch the NCAA's number-one-ranked team take batting practice.

Throughout every College World Series that anyone can recall, the eight teams have shown up at local Omaha schools to grab a quick workout and stay loose between game days. In 2008, four locations volunteered their fields—including Creighton University downtown, Millard West High, and Boys Town, a location made famous by the 1938 film starring Spencer Tracy and seventeen-year-old Mickey Rooney. (During their 1927 Omaha visit, Ruth and Gehrig made a trip out to see Father Flanagan's kids. Ruth was deeply moved, reminded of his days at St. Mary's Industrial School for Boys in Baltimore.)

The fourth, and the most popular, practice venue was here at Bellevue East.

During every practice the blue wooden grandstand was typically pretty empty. The crowds could be found lined along behind the outfield wall, where dozens of kids wait, glove in hand, for long balls to come sailing over the chain-link fence. When a right-handed batter came to the plate, the designated spotter peered through a corner gate and shouted, "Righty!" sending the herd sprinting along the wall to stand behind the left-field fence. When six-foot-two, 215-pound Yonder Alonso stepped into the cage, the kids scrambled to the right to haul in balls hit by an only slightly older kid who was a few weeks away from receiving a two-million-dollar signing bonus from the Cincinnati Reds.

But one boy named Alex stayed dug in behind left center. "I heard the coaches talking to him earlier," he said with a wink. "He's gonna work on his opposite-field hitting. Those guys are in the wrong place. He'll be hitting them over here." Four pitches later, Alex caught a big fly on the fly, stuck the ball in his pocket, jumped on his bike, and rode off for home, making sure to cruise past his buddies and shout, "I told you so!"

In the third-base dugout Roddy Field groundskeeper Steve Jarrett watched the Canes blast away, happy to grab a few minutes out of the hot sun. As his crew educated the Miami equipment managers on the best places for "real Omaha steaks," Jarrett nodded without even knowing he was doing it. Every year he tried to time out the grass so that it was in perfect condition for the year's most important visitors. This year's cycle process started back in mid-March. In the weeks since, the field had somehow successfully survived more than seventy Bellevue East varsity, JV, and reserve games, not to mention city leagues and a CWS-affiliated American Legion tournament. Between that and the horrible weather, it was a miracle there was any grass at all. Instead, it was the by-God nicest high-school field one could ever hope to play on.

"Awesome job, guys," Miami assistant head coach Gino Dimare said with a point as he walked by the resting crew. "It's always an awesome job."

Across the diamond, Miss Marilyn offered a drink to anyone who happened by, from the team to the sportswriters to a handful of church friends who'd shown up just to check on her.

"I've been doing this for, I guess, twenty years now," she explained between pleads to not have "a big deal" made of her. "My husband and I always tried to take care of anyone who came down here to our ball field."

When she said everyone, she truly meant everyone. From the high school to club teams to the biggest names in college baseball, Gene and Marilyn Ralston always greeted every team with a car trunk full of cold drinks and anything else they thought a ballplayer might need.

In 1989, local college Bellevue University decided to start a baseball program, headed by Omaha native Mike Evans. The coach had once built Omaha's Creighton Prep into a national high school baseball machine that produced, among others, local pitching hero Kyle Peterson. Evans was lured to college baseball by Gary Ward, the hitting savant of Oklahoma State, and served as an assistant with the Cowboys. He later moved back to Nebraska as an assistant with the Cornhuskers. As a young boy, Evans attended CWS games at Rosenblatt and dreamed of returning to sit in the dugout as a coach. He came within one out of making that happen, but the Huskers lost to Stanford at Stanford in 1985.

"We had a massive collision at home for what would have been the final out. But the ball popped free. Now there's a rule in college baseball against those kinds of big hits at home. If it had been in place in '85, I would have made that dream come true."

When he returned to Omaha to work at Bellevue U., it presented an opportunity to return to his small-school roots, a chance to teach and coach at the small private college with a little more than 5,000 undergraduates. But it was a school without a baseball team.

When Evans announced his desire to start a baseball program, Gene and Marilyn Ralston were among the first people to show up at his office to pledge their support. Soon the Ralstons were pounding the pavement to help raise money. They showed up at practices and games, popping open that trunk so Gene could hand out soft drinks and Marilyn could distribute still-warm homemade cookies. They had players over for dinner. They helped them find apartments. During games the Ralstons sold tickets, ran the concession stand, kept score, did whatever the Bellevue Bruins needed done.

Coach Evans eventually built the program into a Miami-like small-college version of The Program, reaching the National Association of

Intercollegiate Athletics (NAIA) World Series for the first time in 1995. Like its NCAA counterpart, the NAIA tournament is a one-week, double-elimination bracket, though it invites ten teams instead of eight. Like the College World Series, it has been held in the same location nearly since its inception, in their case Lewiston, Idaho. And like Miami, the Bellevue Bruins are in their division's World Series much more often than not.

And just to be safe, Evans began each season working with catchers on holding on to the ball during big collisions at home.

"We won the national championship in that first visit in '95," Coach Evans said proudly. "Our twelfth trip in fourteen years was in 2008. Without the Ralstons I don't know if we'd ever gotten the program going, let alone had the kind of success we've enjoyed. The big NCAA Division I schools have multimillion-dollar budgets and people who take of things for them. For small schools like us, people like Gene and Marilyn are what keep us going."

Like the Bellevue Bruins, the Hurricanes, Seminoles, Tigers, and Longhorns quickly realized that the Ralstons weren't just great people, they were good baseball karma. Head coaches started seeking out Gene and Marilyn whenever they earned a visit to Omaha, anxious to catch up, sip a cold beverage from the Ralstons' big white cooler, and soak up some luck.

But in 2000, every team that rolled into Bellevue noticed that something was missing. As always, the field looked great, the fans showed up, and Miss Marilyn came down the hill with her cooler. But there was no Gene. The previous December his health had taken a sharp downward turn. He collapsed in the door of his doctor's office, victimized head to toe by ailments ranging from cataracts to kidney stones. Throughout the holidays poor Marilyn sat by her husband's bedside, heartbroken over her beloved's sudden suffering. By spring Gene had recovered enough to sit in the car in a handicap parking spot by the stadium to watch Bruin baseball games. Now, instead of waiting on the Ralstons to come down the hill, the team would run up to meet them, win or lose.

By the time the College World Series came back around, Gene was stuck at home, too ill to make the one-mile trip from his house to the high school to greet the teams. When Florida State came in for its first practice, Gene made Marilyn go on without him. "We don't want any-body out there thirsting to death, do we?"

A couple of hours later, she returned home and reported to her husband that practice was fine, everyone sent their well wishes . . . but, wait . . . was that the doorbell? She went to answer it, making sure Gene was looking, and flung open the door.

Sitting in Gene Ralston's driveway was the Florida State team bus.

Into his living room walked the Seminoles, still in uniform. In walked All-Americans John-Ford Griffin, Matt Lynch, Marshall McDougal, and Daniel Hodges. They lined up behind head coach Mike Martin and each shook Ralston's hand, wished him good health, and told him that practice at Bellevue East wasn't the same without him.

It still wasn't, years after his passing. But when Florida State arrived for their first 2008 practice, Marilyn and her entire family were there waiting on Martin, anxious to introduce him to her new grandson. "You want to know what Omaha is all about?" Martin choked up as he recalled both moments. "Winning games is great. But it's people like Gene and Marilyn that make you want to come back every year, that make it just hurt your heart when you don't make it back. And there are too many people like them in that town to count."

The Gatorade Lady and her late husband were walking saints on Earth. On that fact, Mike Martin and Jim Morris are in total and complete agreement.

Past that, they agreed on nothing else.

The two head coaches of the two most successful southeastern collegiate baseball programs of the last quarter century (at least outside of Baton Rouge) didn't merely disagree or dislike each other. They despised one another.

On Monday morning, June 16, a few hours before the start of Game Five, each coach spent his obligatory half hour visiting with that day's ESPN broadcast team, in this case play-by-play man Karl Ravech and color commentator Robin Ventura. Each coach was asked to describe his relationship with the other. One replied, "Icy," the other, "Next question."

On paper, Martin and Morris should have been baseball soul mates. They both grew up in Charlotte, North Carolina, played baseball at rival high schools, and both attended small Carolina colleges—Martin at Wingate Junior College, and Morris at Elon College, just up the road in Burlington.

In 1980, it was Martin who gave Morris his big coaching break, hiring him away from a highly successful run at Atlanta's DeKalb Community College to become an assistant at Florida State. In their first year together they made it to Omaha, though they went two-and-'cue. Two years later, thanks to Martin's recommendations, Morris landed the head job at Georgia Tech, where he spent the next twelve years building the Rambling Wreck into a national power and, after Florida State joined the ACC, a conference rival of the Seminoles. Then, in 1994, Morris took the head job with the Hurricanes and soon his relationship with Martin was ripped apart by one of the most treacherous, destructive rivalries in collegiate athletics.

Florida State versus Miami.

"People think about football first when they think Florida State-Miami," FSU outfielder Jack Rye said as his team started stretching down the first-base line before Game Five, one eye on the direction of team trainer Jack Pfeil, the other on the Hurricanes, who were already taking batting practice. "But there is a lot of straight-up hatred when it comes to baseball. Hatred between teams, between players, even coaches. You hate to use the word hate, but that's what it is. There's always a lot of tension. Can't you feel it already this morning?"

For decades the two programs had battled for wins, recruits, booster money, and home-state loyalty. Such battlefields are common among big in-state athletic departments across the nation and across all sports. What separated this matchup, as is the case with the football rivalry, was that their showdowns routinely transcended local or even regional interest, when battling for a conference championship was merely a stepping stone to a larger fight on a much larger stage—Rosenblatt Stadium.

Like the gridiron grudge, the baseball rivalry between "State" and "The U" had been very much about what one team had and what the other did not. For so many years, Miami's flashy, braggy football coaches Howard Schnellenberger, Jimmie Johnson, and Dennis Erickson won national championships and a national following at the expense of aw-shucks

FSU coach Bobby Bowden, whose teams always seemed to come up one yard short, typically one yard wide right and always against the Hurricanes. The programs and the schools have long been as different as the city of Miami has always been from the rest of its own state.

The 2008 season marked Florida State's twenty-ninth consecutive trip to the NCAA baseball postseason. This trip to Omaha was its thirteenth. But back in Tallahassee there was not a single national championship trophy to show for their efforts.

Zero-for-flippin'-28.

Miami had made the NCAA field for the thirty-sixth straight season and was playing at Rosenblatt for the twenty-second time. Back in Coral Gables there were four national championship trophies on display, fourth most all-time. They were 4–2 in national title games. Florida State was 0–3, including a 1999 loss to (swallow hard) Miami.

Dick Howser and Mike Martin's approach to building the Seminole program was much like Bowden's blueprint across the hallway. Be stern when you have to, but for the most part play nice, and the people and players will love you for it. Martin and Bowden's tendency to draw the spotlight from their student-athletes had never been as much of their own doing as it was a by-product of years and years of building relationships and success. Both likely could have drawn much more attention to themselves had they gone out and sought it, but in the end they received the attention anyway for their affable ways, even in the face of perennial disappointment, most of which had been handed to them by the Hurricanes.

Before Jim Morris, the man who made life so hard for Martin was Miami Hurricane head coach Ron Fraser, the owner of a personality so strong that it always somehow managed to keep his employer from remembering that he was a Florida State alum. He was so likeable that his alma mater never completely disowned him, despite his lifetime of success at their expense.

And any attention Fraser received was never coincidental. He'd gone out and gotten it.

Ronald "Ron" George Fraser came to the University of Miami in 1962, when the private school was very much an athletic afterthought and baseball was, well, it was nothing, really. The program had started in 1946 and enjoyed moderate success at best. The baseball field was little more than a stopover for former Hurricane athletes and something for the football coaches to do to earn extra cash over winter. Baseball Hall of Famer Jimmie Foxx even sat on the bench for two seasons, the man known as Double XX compiling an equally symmetrical record of 20–20.

On a summer night in 1962, Miami president Henry King Stanford settled into his recliner to catch the wildly popular television show *What's My Line?* He proceeded to watch a magnetic leprechaunlike smile of a man stump the panel of journalist Dorothy Kilgallen, Random House cofounder Bennett Cerf, and actress Arlene Francis. Ron Fraser's job title was the night's chosen mystery, and the twenty-six-year-old jokester had the audience guffawing as Kilgallen came close, but was ultimately stumped.

Fraser finally revealed that he was the head coach of the Dutch National Baseball Team, recent winners of the European Championships and a squad led by Hannie Urbanus, aka the Babe Ruth of the Netherlands. *That,* President Stanford thought to himself, *is Miami's next baseball coach.*

Miami offered Fraser a part-time job at the university for $2,200 a year, along with a day job to help pay the bills as director of the Coral Gables Youth Center. He took the gig, despite the fact that there was no equipment, no scholarships, no uniforms, and a baseball field filled with more rocks than blades of grass.

"Don't ask me why I took the job," he recalled years later, pointing out that his salary stayed at $2,200 for nearly a decade. "I didn't have a good answer for that then and I don't have a good answer for it now. I just remember parking my old beat-up Volkswagen outside the fence and walking from the outfield all the way to home plate. Then I turned around and looked over that terrible field and said, oh man, I've got to get to work."

Fraser had served in the U.S. Army before accepting a job offer from the prime minister of the Netherlands, so he talked the Army into sending him some secondhand uniforms. When his first team took the field, the "A" and "Y" were still visible on either side of "Miami," so he convinced a tailor friend to design gaudy orange and green jerseys. He soaked used baseballs in milk to make them look white. They looked great, but smelled like hell.

Despite his best efforts to make something out of less than nothing, he was soon informed that the school was considering scrapping the baseball program. So he dug into his Nutley, New Jersey, roots and started calling on the South Florida–obsessed athletes of the Big Apple to come to his aid. Fraser brought in player-turned-broadcaster Joe Garagiola to come down and speak on behalf of the program . . . then Stan Musial showed up . . . and Joe DiMaggio . . . and Ted Williams. In 1971, he convinced Miami supporter George Light to underwrite the construction of a state-of-the-art baseball field. Two years later, he filled Mark Light Field (named for George's son) with a little help from another Fraser first, the Sugar Canes, a team of female coed "ambassador" batgirls.

"Say what you want about the Sugar Canes," he said with a laugh. "But a lot more guys started showing up to the games after that."

That same year, after a decade of begging, Fraser finally talked the school into a few scholarships for baseball so he could go out and prevent some of all those great Miami high-school players from leaving town to play elsewhere. In 1974, only their second season with scholarship players, the Hurricanes earned their first invitation to Omaha.

When the team arrived in Nebraska, it did so as a total outsider. Almost since its inception, college baseball was a West Coast game. More specifically, it was a California-Arizona game. Beginning with Jackie Jensen and his '47 Cal Bears, fifteen of the previous twenty-seven editions of the College World Series had been won by teams from California and Arizona. The last seven had been split between just two programs—Arizona State and Southern Cal. In 1972 and '73, those two went head-to-head in the Series finals with USC taking both crowns.

The Southern Cal Trojans were in the midst of a sports dynasty that in terms of championships won was in the same league with the New York Yankees, the Boston Celtics, and UCLA basketball. As of 2008, USC's twelve CWS championships were double that of the next closest school, Texas, and the Trojans were 12–2 in championship games at Rosenblatt Stadium.

Like Fraser, USC head coach Rod Dedeaux won games and supporters through force of personality. He was Tommy Lasorda before there was Tommy Lasorda, embracing his team's place in the midst of the Hollywood universe and routinely inviting the biggest stars of stage and screen to come out and see his Trojans play ball. He served as a technical adviser for baseball-themed movies, the actors absolutely mesmerized by his New Orleans drawl as well as his ability to draw up incredible stories from the diamond.

After so many visits and so many victories, Dedeaux became Rosenblatt royalty; Omaha became what he called "our second home-field advantage behind Bovard Field." In '74, Dedeaux's team was going for its fifth straight title when it ran into a Miami team with a head coach that reminded Coach Rod of . . . Coach Rod.

Said Fraser, "When we got to Rosenblatt in '74 it was like a drug, like an instant love affair. We won three games, including a win against Southern Cal with a big comeback in the eighth inning. That game was the turning point for our program. My kids had heard about USC and Coach Dedeaux, but we'd never seen them before. All of the sudden, there they were, the Trojan army in flesh and blood. They had us down 3–1 in the eighth and we came back and beat them. Those people in Omaha went crazy over us. We were a brand-new team, an underdog, which they've always loved. Our uniforms looked crazy. We beat Goliath at his home away from home. Even when they came back and beat us in the championship game, we were the talk of the town. Once we got a taste of that atmosphere, how good it could be, once the university got a taste of it, that's what drove us all, just to get back."

That taste of how good college baseball could be convinced U of M administrators to cut loose Fraser, giving him free rein to do whatever it took to accelerate The Program. Coach Ron hired the best assistants, including Ron Polk, who went on to take three different schools to Rosenblatt, and Skip Bertman, a former Cane catcher whom Fraser hired away from nearby Miami Beach High.

By the 1980s, Fraser was referred to as "The Wizard of College Baseball," and his promotional mind was perhaps second only to that of former Major League team owner Bill Veeck. In 1977, he paid off the remaining debt on Light Field by hosting "An Evening with Ron Fraser," where patrons paid $5,000 a plate to dine in formal wear on the Light Field infield, sitting among ice sculptures and violinists while eating Iranian caviar prepared by internationally renown chefs. ("We flew in truffles from the Black Forest. I had no idea where the Black Forest was.") He started luring fans to Light Field with giveaways, from used cars ("They looked great at night") to vacations ("We called it 'Trip to Somewhere' and told fans to come to the ballpark packed. They had no idea where they were going.") to open heart surgeries ("The coupon had to be used within a year"), and promotions such as Income Tax Night, when accountants were stationed throughout the stadium to help fill out fans' 1040s.

"One night we did a ten-thousand-dollar money scramble. We wadded up all of these one-dollar bills and scattered them across the field. We chose two fans to see how many bills they could pick up in thirty seconds. We got lucky. One of the contestants was an older woman with bad hands and she didn't go to her left very well."

Much of the modern Major League ballpark experience has its roots in Fraser's antics at Light Field, from the Miami Maniac mascot to wearing green on St. Patrick's Day to inviting local kids to stand with players on the field during pregame ceremonies to asking local corporate suits to come and throw out the first pitch (but only if they opened their wallet first).

"He made college baseball cool," says Alex Rodriguez. Before he was A-Rod, he was just a kid growing up on Miami's south side, as big of a Canes fan as everyone else in the city. "You always knew that even if you couldn't get to a game in person you were going to be able to watch them on TV every summer from Omaha."

Those games were carried on ESPN, yet another fruit of Fraser's labor.

In advance of a big regular season series against USC in 1981, Fraser hopped on a plane to Connecticut and set up shop in Bristol, across the street from the cable network's then-tiny headquarters. He set up meetings with every executive, producer, and secretary who would agree to see him, pounding on doors for nearly two weeks until the cable channel agreed to televise the three-game set in Coral Gables. Initially they agreed to carry only one game on tape delay, but Fraser convinced them to broadcast all three games live, a first for college baseball. Miami won all three, including a thrilling thirteen-inning 10–9 victory in the weekend finale.

When Fraser's team finally won the title one year later, they became the first school east of the Mississippi to win a College World Series since

1966. What's more, his as-labeled "nonrevenue" sport began to turn a profit for The U. Before long, every large school in the southeast was moving into Miami's slipstream, increasing their emphasis on the lone spring sport with true return on investment potential, though still an admitted distant third behind football and basketball.

Fraser's efforts had a sweeping impact on the game he loved far beyond Mark Light Field. Nowhere was that change in the wind more apparent than in his second home of Omaha.

NBC televised its first CWS game in 1981. ESPN, eyeing a cheap yet entertaining property to fill their summertime programming lull, was televising every game of the Series by 1984. Four years later, CBS signed on to televise the championship game. Rosenblatt's attendance numbers began growing by leaps each year, topping the 100,000 mark in '81 with more than 12,000 people per game. And the little baseball tournament that had been once been so happy to break even financially managed to cross the one-million-dollar mark in revenues for the first time. Seizing the momentum, the NCAA Baseball Tournament was expanded from thirty-two teams to forty-eight in '87.

"The West Coast guys don't like to admit this," said Fraser disciple Ron Polk, "but Ron Fraser is the guy who woke this sport up and turned it and the College World Series into what they are now. The '82 Series alone put college baseball on the map."

Call it Rosenblatt's perfect storm. The year 1982 was the first time the NCAA altered their tournament to ensure that the top teams were seeded in a manner that would get them to Omaha. The move resulted with a field of superpowers, including Cliff Gustafson's number-one-ranked Texas Longhorns, Augie Garrido's number-two Cal State Fullerton Titans, along with Oklahoma State, Wichita State, Stanford, South Carolina, and the prerequisite annual version of The Underdog, this year in the uniform of the Maine Bears.

Fraser's '82 Canes blew into Nebraska with brutally ugly Houston Astro–style horizontally striped polyester pullover jerseys, shown in glorious orange and green on ESPN, who was televising all fourteen CWS games for the very first time.

In Game One, the Canes beat Maine 6–1. In any other town that would have been a ho-hum score. Not in Omaha. Third baseman Phil Lane was born in Council Bluffs and had lived in Omaha until he was nine. He learned baseball in Omaha youth baseball leagues, and he went to countless games at Rosenblatt to watch the O Royals and study how the infielders set up for certain situations and how the hitters attacked at the plate.

In the second inning, Lane dug in at that same plate to face future big-league ace Billy Swift. Sitting in the stands were Lane's grandparents, aunts, uncles, and cousins. He rewarded them, and the very partisan hometown crowd, with a 360-foot three-run shot that iced the game nearly before it had begun.

The Hurricanes had won over The Blatt during their first CWS appearance nine years earlier, but had frustrated their new fans by coming back nearly every summer only to fall short. Phil Lane won them back with one swing. Fraser won them over forever with one play two days later.

During a quiet off-day practice at Boys Town, Fraser huddled with his assistant coaches, Skip Bertman and Dave Scott, to try and figure out how they would counter the Wichita State Shockers and coach Gene Stephenson's legendarily aggressive running game.

The assistants had an idea. While scouting at a junior-college tournament earlier that winter, Scott had watched West Palm Beach Junior College run a complicated-looking yet actually very simple hidden-ball trick. He walked Fraser through it and Fraser immediately began to choreograph a version right there on Father Flanagan's old ball field. The Canes ran the play a few times on the high school diamond, each repetition bringing in another member of the team to amplify the sales job. The players soon had it down pat, and immediately wanted to know when they would get a chance to try it in a game.

The answer was simple—during the biggest game of their lives . . . live . . . on ESPN.

With the score tied 6–6 in the bottom of the sixth, Wichita's Phil Stephenson, younger brother of Gene, reached first on a walk. The first baseman was nothing less than the greatest base-stealer in college baseball history, with a single season record of eighty-six stolen bags in ninety-one attempts. When Miami pitcher Mike Kasprzak stepped off the rubber to check the runner, Stephenson dove back into the bag.

Kasprzak and first baseman Steve Lusby immediately looked to the dugout. They didn't say or signal anything. They didn't have to. Their faces said it all.

C'mon, Coach . . . this is the perfect time!

The assistant coaches looked at Fraser, who nodded back with a look of "Oh, what the hell?" Skip Bertman looked back at his pitcher and signaled by sticking his finger in his ear.

The Grand Illusion was officially in play.

"The conditions had to be perfect and they were," Bertman recalled in the Rosenblatt press box twenty-six years later. "It was dusk, so the light was kind of tough. Stephenson was all riled up and ready to run, which we learned when he dove back into the bag when all we did was take a step off the rubber. And they had a player coaching first, not a coach. As soon as I signaled for it, the entire team stood up, even down in the bullpen. Everyone was in on it."

Once again pitcher Mike Kasprzak stepped off the rubber, this time making a hard throwing motion toward first base. Once again Stephenson dove back and Steve Lusby dove over the runner, letting loose a curse word and taking off running for the right-field bullpen. Clearly, Kasprzak had overthrown the ball, right?

The relievers sitting in the bullpen jumped up in reaction to the ball supposedly heading their way. Second baseman Mitch Sloane and right fielder Mickey Williams took off running to join the pursuit. Miami fans seated behind the home dugout stood and pointed, trying to help their fielders locate the ball, but no one could spot it. Shortstop Bill Wrona, visibly angered by the turn of events, did his duty and moved over to cover second base.

Phil Stephenson might as well have had a fish hook in his cheek.

Reacting to the chaos around him, the speedster jumped up and rocketed toward second. As he looked back to the commotion over his right shoulder, he failed to see the pitcher calmly tossing the ball to the shortstop, who applied the tag as the runner arrived, very confused, at second base.

The Hurricanes tried not to laugh, but they couldn't help it.

Derailed and deflated from the play, the Shockers never recovered and lost the game 4-3. When the two teams met five days later for the championship game, Wichita was still complaining about what had happened and Miami won its long-sought first CWS title in a come-from-behind victory that was anchored by another three-run homer from Omahan Phil Lane.

That summer, for the first time in its thirty-six-year history, the College World Series led every sportscast in the nation, every talking head anxious to give his or her take on the Grand Illusion. The play placed The Blatt prominently on *SportsCenter*, *This Week In Baseball*, and Fraser's big-stage gamble immediately became a staple of every baseball coaching clinic from coast to coast.

Coach Ron led the Canes for another decade, adding a second CWS title in '85 and making a dozen trips to Omaha. The little dumpy ballpark in Coral Gables was now the crown jewel of collegiate baseball. His department, once nearly dumped because it was a consistent money loser, now made a profit when no other program did, and his 1,271 wins ranked second only to Dedeaux. Prior to his arrival, Miami players had been drafted three times in two decades. During his tenure, they were chosen more than 150 times with twenty-seven making it to the Majors.

"The guys I'm most proud of are the ones you've forgotten about," the coach said while fidgeting through retirement. "The doctors and the lawyers and the teachers and the coaches. People always think that a successful college coach is full of it when he says things like that. But it's the truth."

After Fraser's final game at Light Field, he was driven around the bases in a Rolls-Royce as his number-one jersey was retired, during which he thought about the Volkswagen he'd arrived in. A few weeks later he coached his forty-seventh and final College World Series game, a semifinal loss to Cal State Fullerton, after which he received a standing ovation from the rain-drenched Rosenblatt Stadium crowd.

In '93, longtime assistant and head coach heir Brad Kelly went two-and-'cue in the NCAA Tournament with losses to (gulp) South Alabama and Western Carolina. Kelly was quickly shown the door and Fraser was asked to find a more suitable replacement.

He called Jim Morris at Georgia Tech.

———

Morris had built the Yellow Jackets into a winning machine, thanks to current studs and future Red Sox teammates Nomar Garciaparra and Jason Varitek. But when Fraser called, he was on the first plane to Florida, saying, "I'm leaving the best team in the country for the best program in the country." All Morris needed to know about The Program became crystal clear during his initial tour of the facilities with athletic director Paul Dee during the interview process. Propping open the door to one of the clubhouse bathrooms was a trophy engraved 1974 NCAA MEN'S COLLEGE WORLD SERIES RUNNER-UP.

Tough place to coach.

His first day on the job, the team made him participate in the Cane rookie ritual of standing on a chair in public and singing as loud as possible. Morris crooned "Old McDonald." Like Fraser, he earned his players' respect by teaching more than preaching, and by asking as many questions about their lives off the field as on it. He earned the respect of fans in Miami—and Omaha—by taking Miami back to The Blatt in each of his first six seasons. In '99 he won his first CWS championship. Two years later he equaled Fraser's total with title number two.

Morris, though admittedly quieter than Fraser (who isn't?), won over local business leaders with his Carolina drawl and his ability to carry on a conversation on practically any topic, a mind honed while earning a master's degree at Appalachian State and coming to within one finished dissertation of earning a PhD at Georgia. ("Too lazy," he likes to say with a wink.)

He squeezed millions out of those who were once only interested in Cane football to start an overhaul of Light Field. Anchoring that effort was Alex Rodriguez, who played high-school baseball for coach Mike Lusby, the first baseman from the Grand Illusion, and had signed a letter of intent to play for Morris before the Seattle Mariners came up with a one-million-dollar signing bonus.

Out of loyalty to Morris, maybe even out of guilt, A-Rod committed $3.9 million toward the ballpark, now known as Mark Light Field at Alex Rodriguez Park.

Morris kept The Program running and winning. Even while the friendship with his mentor ground to a halt.

When Morris took the Miami job, Mike Martin was among the first to call and congratulate him, and among the first to warn him about the dangers of following a legend. At first the calls were regular and came from both ends of the state. Then they began to slow and eventually, like a garden hose being slowly stood upon, the flow between the two coaches was crushed under the boot of the FSU-Miami rivalry.

They faced off six times in '94, splitting the series 3–3 and ending each game with a handshake. They continued to shake hands for a while. Then it stopped. No one wants to say exactly when it stopped or precisely why, but the standoff's roots have long been the topic of conversation among college baseball coaches, a group that enjoys their gossip as much as a bunch of old ladies sitting around a game of bunko.

In 2004, Martin filed a complaint with the ACC claiming that Miami was using a television camera in center field to intercept pitch signals and then relaying those signals via walkie-talkie to the Hurricane dugout, transmissions that were accidentally intercepted by Seminole equipment manager Bob Holland.

Five years earlier, longtime Fraser and Morris assistant coach and master recruiter Henry "Turtle" Thomas left Miami for a similar job at LSU. Some with Morris's staff accused Thomas of handing over secrets to the enemy when the Hurricanes' signs were found on a crib sheet accidentally dropped onto the field by a Seminole coach. Later that same year, it was Florida State and Martin that Morris's team beat 6–5 to win the CWS title.

"It's Florida State versus Miami," Nole outfielder Jack Rye repeated during his Game Five warm-up tosses. "What else do I need to say?"

Their meeting here in the CWS would be their fourth of the 2008 season, the first three played two months earlier at Mike Martin Field in Tallahassee, where the Canes were ranked number one in the nation by *Baseball America* and the Noles were ranked number one by *Collegiate Baseball*, one of those rare boxinglike moments where an undisputed champ would have to emerge.

They, of course, split the first two games. In the rubber match, Miami jumped out to an 8–1 lead, powered by a three-run shot by Yonder Alonso.

But FSU came back, trailing 11–5 in the bottom of the sixth inning (everyone knew the game would only last seven so that Miami could make their flight home), when Buster Posey answered Alonso with a three-run homer off his own. With two outs in the bottom of the last inning and the tying run at third, Miami closer Carlos Gutierrez struck out leadoff man Tyler Holt to end the game.

That's when a great game took an FSU-Miami turn for the worse.

The Hurricanes walked out to midfield for the customary lineup of handshakes . . . and no one came out to reciprocate. As soon as they recognized the diss, a handful of Miami players started gesturing to the home dugout.

This time someone came out to see them.

The two teams advanced toward each other as the coaches and support staffs ran out and made sure they never made it all the way. After a lot of noise and a lot of threats, the two teams left the field. But the 6,700 Florida State fans made sure their opponents' walk to the bus was as miserable as possible.

The next time Morris and Martin were on the field at the same time came fifty-seven days later, at 1:00 P.M. at Rosenblatt Stadium for Game Five, a go-or-go-home showdown in the College World Series. They approached home plate from their respective sides of the diamond and handed their lineup cards to umpire Jack Cox. They never made eye contact as Cox went over the ground rules of the old ballpark they both knew so well. When the discussion was over they shook hands with every member of the four-man umpire crew, never even as much as hinted at the possibility of shaking hands with each other, then turned heel and scuffled back to their respective dugouts.

Icy.

Next question.

Florida State started the game by banging and running like they'd been expected to do in Game One. They smashed four hits in their first seven at-bats, the seventh ricocheting off the throwing shoulder of Miami pitcher David Gutierrez, little brother of closer Carlos, and knocking him out of the game.

But even with all those hits, FSU's Game One problem was resurfacing in Game Five: they were stranding runners again. With Posey up in the first, second baseman Jason Stidham tried to steal second, but was thrown out. Posey's slapped a run-less hit on the next pitch.

Over the first three innings, FSU scored one run and left seven runners on base. It got worse.

Miami went up 4–1 in the third inning, 6–2 in the seventh, and 7–2 in the eighth with a suborbital blast from center fielder Blake Tekotte, who went into an unmistakable we're-The-Program-and-you're-not home-run trot.

Entering the top of the ninth, Florida State had scored two runs and left a staggering fourteen runners on the bases. Even worse, the bottom half of the order was up. Posey had redeemed himself from Game One with a 4-for-5 day, scoring one of his team's runs and driving in the other, but Miami had successfully kept the hitters around The Pick from reaching base, minimizing the damage he could do to the scoreboard.

Buster would have to be a spectator now as his teammates faced closer Carlos Gutierrez in the final inning. Sure, Gutierrez had blown Game Two against Georgia, but there was no way he was going to do that again. Was there?

First baseman Dennis Guinn led off the inning by working the count and singled on a 3–2 pitch. Shortstop Tony Delmonico, who had thankfully recorded no errors this day, singled to center. Then a sacrifice groundout by designated hitter Tommy Oravetz moved them around to second and third, and another sacrifice scored Guinn. A single scored Delmonico. And then another single drove in a third run.

The inning had started with Miami up 7–2. Now that deficit had been cut to 7–5 with two outs. Run number six was standing on third, the tying run was on second, and the winning run . . . the potential winning run was walking to the plate and Rosenblatt Stadium was suddenly booming as the crowd came to its feet, everyone arriving at the same conclusion at the same time.

Holy crap . . . it's Buster!

As The Pick—and his .463 batting average, 25 homers, and 93 RBIs—walked out of the on-deck circle, Nole head coach Mike Martin came to the top step of the dugout and drew a breath like he was going to dole out some advice for the at-bat. But, perhaps hearing the chants of "Bus-ter Pose-eeee" behind him, he stepped back to let the Player of the Year do his All-American, too-good-to-be true best.

First pitch—*big* slider and a miss, strike one.

Second pitch—low, ball one.

Third pitch—high, ball two.

Fourth pitch—is it the curve again? No, it's a changeup, looking, strike two.

Fifth pitch—there's that second curve, in the dirt, full count.

One pitch to shut up Miami. One pitch to send their asses home. One pitch to back up Coach and let him go get that handshake on his own terms.

In the dirt and outside . . . ball four.

That's okay, The Pick thought to himself as he trotted down the line to first. *Jack is up next with the bases loaded. It's his turn.*

Back in the Miami dugout, Jim Morris kept his customary position at the end of the bench with his notebooks. Martin stayed posed at the top step of the Noles dugout. Neither coach visibly reacted, but both admitted later to thinking the same thing at the same time.

Damn classy move, kid.

Outfielder Jack Rye, himself a .374 hitter, was up next and fired a screaming shot toward second . . . but it was scooped up nicely by Jemile Weeks, who snared the ball and tossed it to second for the final out . . . Buster Posey. The Pick slapped his hands together in disappointment and then quickly got into line with his other teammates as they formed up to shake hands with their "hated" rivals. Suddenly, all the venom between the players seemed to vanish. The Noles were disappointed, but they wished the Canes well, one even proclaiming, "Go win one for the ACC." Alonso and Posey paused as they shook hands, adding slaps to the opposite shoulders as if to say, "I'll see you later on a bigger stage."

Jim Morris waited on his team to welcome them back to the dugout as Mike Martin did the same. Morris headed to the Hall of Fame Room to answer questions about his team's survival and to bid a fond farewell to Buster Posey, for whom he admitted he had so much respect but was glad to see him go.

Mike Martin had to face the music about another trip to The Blatt without a trophy to bring home, and the pain of coming up empty while tying a CWS record with seventeen runners left on base. In their two-and-'cue games they'd left twenty-seven runners stranded.

One day the two head coaches might get past the past. One day they might have a beverage and swap stories about that first trip to Omaha they made together nearly thirty years ago. One day they may even shake hands.

That day was not this day.

Exhausted from the daytime blood match, the people of The Blatt had little energy remaining to truly appreciate what they witnessed in the night-cap. Good ol' dependable Stanford, just like good ol' dependable Miami, was being chased down, caught, and put away by . . . Georgia?

On Friday, Bulldog head coach Dave Perno had picked up a bracket and pointed out to anyone who cared to listen that his side of the tournament was packed with "traditional programs"—Florida State, Miami, Stanford, and his overachieving Dawgs. Those three had been to Omaha an average of nineteen times apiece. Georgia was making only its fifth trip, and all five had taken place with Perno on the bus.

He was a player on The Underdog of 1990, an assistant under Ron Polk in 2001, and the head coach in 2004, 2006, and this year. The University of Georgia had already posted one of the greatest all-around athletic years in school history, a long line of national accomplishments that only underlined where Perno's squad stood on the totem pole of Dawg athletics, despite so much recent success.

Football (2008 Sugar Bowl champions), women's gymnastics (2008 national champs), men's tennis (2008 national champs), and equestrian (2007–08 national champs) . . . then baseball.

"Yeah," Perno said with a knowing chuckle, trying not to reveal his frustration of living in the shadow of others. "They set the bar kind of high, don't they?"

In Game Two, the Bulldogs had trailed Miami three different times before exploding in the top of the ninth to put away The Program. On Monday night, they took the same gut-wrenching route against Stanford.

Starting pitcher Nick Montgomery produced an outing that had become all too familiar to Perno and pitching coach Brady Wiederhold. He looked solid in the first two innings, then faded in the third, victimized by Stanford's version of The Pick, catcher Jason Castro, who hammered a two-run homer in the third to put the Cardinal up 3–0.

That's when Perno unleashed the team strength that had allowed the Bulldogs to survive its starting troubles—the best bullpen in the southeast. Righty Stephen Dodson, a tenth-round pick of the Colorado Rockies, entered the game in the fourth inning with two one and no one out.

From his first pitch, the momentum of the evening shifted.

He smoked a fastball into the waiting bunt stance of right fielder Toby Gerhart, who popped up weakly to first. Two pitches later third baseman Zach Jones grounded out to short. The fifth pitch to shortstop Jake Schlander was popped up to third. Inning over. Two runners stranded.

In the Stanford dugout, head coach Mark Marquess felt as helpless as a man with a three-run lead could feel. Game Six was on the verge of spiraling out of control and directly into his favor. But Dodson had slowed down everything. He'd hushed the Stanford crowd and jarred the Dawg Pound back awake. For four innings, the right-hander held Stanford in check, allowing only one hit. He handed the ball to lefty Alex McRee, who entered the game in the seventh inning and chopped down all four batters he faced.

While the Cardinal scoring stalled, the Bulldogs chipped away at their lead. The foreman of the excavation was center fielder Matt Cerione, pronounced Sir-rone-ee. Thus his nickname, Rice. As in Rice-Cerione . . . Rice-A-Roni . . . get it?

In the fourth inning, Rice sliced a 77-mph outside curveball into the left-field corner, a two-out double that drove in Georgia's first run of the night. In the sixth, the normally impatient Cerione drew an eight-pitch walk from tiring starter Jeffrey Inman to load the bases and set up another one-run inning.

But the center fielder, who sported a dark leather tan and a face straight out of a Clint Eastwood spaghetti western, saved his best work for the bottom of the seventh. Trailing 3–2, the left-handed hitter stood at the plate with the bases loaded and two outs.

The previous batter, catcher Bryce Massanari, appeared to have hit a three-run homer down the right-field line, but in what was easily the finest call by an umpire in the 2008 Series, first-base umpire Mitch Mele called a ball foul off the top of the yellow-painted padding beneath the foul pole. The mixture of the vertical yellow stripe on the wall, the horizontal yellow strip of padding, and the giant yellow pole was described by *Omaha World-Herald* writer Rob White as a "Bermuda Triangle of yellow lines."

A play that took ESPN multiple high-definition replays to determine had been called correctly by Mele as he ran down the baseline, watching from 240 feet away. Not until the *Herald* printed a once-and-for-all full-page photo in Tuesday morning's paper was the Georgia bench fully convinced that the call had been the right one.

Turns out, none of it mattered.

Stanford reliever Austin Yount's next pitch thunked Massanari in the back to load the bases, which brought Cerione to the plate.

The center fielder watched the first pitch strike, a very nice curve ball that looked to be high but dropped off a shelf and over the plate. *That worked,* Yount and pitching coach Jeff Austin simultaneously thought. *Let's try it again.*

This time Rice was waiting on the curve. He let his knees break just a touch, and brought his left hip around to dip with the pitch, making solid tinking contact and lofting the ball into center.

Gordon Beckham strolled in from third and big first baseman Rich Poythress shifted into whatever high gear his linebacker frame would muster, breaking for home from his starting spot at second. The throw from center fielder Sean Ratliff looked to be right on target to nail the lumbering Poythress, but the first hop came off the pitching mound to negate the excellent strike.

"The righty and the lefty out of their bullpen shut us down," Stanford coach Mark Marquess said afterward. "Then the big guy nailed the door shut in the ninth."

The "big guy" was Josh Fields, who usually meant the outcome was a foregone conclusion. Not tonight.

He threw five pitches to Sean Ratliff before forcing a grounder to second for out one and then popped right fielder Toby Gerhart in the ear hole with a 96-mph fastball. Then he committed the ultimate sin by walking the pitcher, Austin Yount (perhaps he realized that this particular pitcher was the nephew of Hall of Famer Robin Yount, so there had to be some hitting DNA in there somewhere). With one out in the bottom of the ninth, Stanford had the winning run standing on first.

Entering Game Six, Georgia was 34–0 when leading after eight innings. David Perno wanted to hear none of it. "That's great," he sarcastically told ESPN dugout reporter Erin Andrews. "Miami was 45–0 after eight before we beat them two nights ago."

Fields received a visit from pitching coach Brady Wiederhold, who reminded his closer to calm down. Everyone in the UGA dugout knew that Fields looked calm on the outside, but inside his nerves were typically knotted up like a box full of Christmas tree lights. Whenever Georgia was in the field, he always became so wound up he had to go back and sit in the clubhouse, unable to watch. When the Dawgs came back to the plate, a teammate would come and grab him and bring him back out to the bench.

He fell behind early to freshman pinch hitter Colin Walsh, the Stanford staff hoping that the infielder wouldn't be intimidated by the NCAA Closer of the Year because he was too young to know better. The rookie worked the count full, then made solid contact with a 96-mph fastball on the outside corner, but the ball rocketed to shortstop Gordon Beckham, who cranked it into a 6–4–3 game-ending double play.

Georgia 4, Stanford 3.

Three days into the College World Series, Georgia had blown through the more impossible side of an impossible eight-team bracket, sitting 2–0 and only one win away from playing for the national championship. How big of an advantage was their position? Sixteen of the eighteen previous CWS champs had started out 2–0.

Georgia's championship-berth clincher would have to come against one of the two teams they had already beaten, Stanford or Miami, who would meet in an elimination game, Game Nine, two nights later.

To prepare for that do-or-die matchup, the Cardinal would spend Tuesday hitting in the cages and on the artificial turf at Creighton University.

Not Miami. Jim Morris was taking his team back to Bellevue.

Back to run drills on that perfect grass.

Back to see Miss Marilyn.

FIVE

THE NEIGHBORHOOD

Tuesday, June 17
Game Seven: Rice vs. LSU
Game Eight: North Carolina vs. Fresno State

In the dark dawn hours of Saturday, June 9, 2000, Jeff Hyde and Stan Evans had no idea where they were going or what they were doing. They just knew they wanted to go to Rosenblatt Stadium.

Five days earlier their beloved Louisiana-Lafayette Ragin' Cajuns were inexplicably one game away from earning their first invitation to the College World Series, pitted against the hard-hitting South Carolina Gamecocks in Columbia, South Carolina. They had a freshman pitcher on the mound and on the road against the number-one team in the nation. Evans made Hyde promise that if the Cajuns won, they would drive from Lafayette to Nebraska to root them on.

"Sure," the oil-field worker said as he agreed to the proposal, "but it'll never happen."

The Cajuns beat the Cocks 3–2.

Thursday night after work Evans was sitting in Hyde's driveway leaning on the horn of his wife's Toyota Camry, packed with little more than some maps, a duffel bag, and one small cooler. Without tickets, a hotel room, or a single friend west of Texas, they hit the road, arriving at The Blatt on game morning to watch 2000's version of The Underdog. The Cajuns bleached their hair in an act of unity and upset Clemson to reach the semifinals, coming to within one game of facing in-state nemesis LSU for the championship.

"It didn't matter that they lost," Hyde remembered while standing over a boiling pot of some sort of alien-looking, yet delicious-smelling crustaceans. "We were hooked."

Hooked by the games, sure. But what really won their hearts was The Neighborhood.

Two years later they were back, this time with a friend, a pickup truck, a barbecue pit, and enough meat on ice to eat for a week. They circled the stadium looking for a parking spot, finally spotting an empty space along Bob Gibson Boulevard, located at the bottom of the hill behind the Rosenblatt outfield.

Randy Workman and Larry Berray, Nebraska natives and drywall subcontractors, were already preparing a stack of Omaha steaks when Hyde jumped out and asked if the empty space was reserved. "They noticed our license plate and said, 'You guys from Louisiana?' When we said yes, they were like, 'Well then, you boys come right on in.'"

Soon Evans and Hyde were serving up boudin, gumbo, and chicken sausage to what quickly became a growing number of Omaha locals. Before their friend Doug Guidry left Lafayette to come up on day four, they called and told him to load up on as much food as the airline would let him pack because they had already run out.

That week the two camps hit the golf course together for a little two-man scramble, one player from Louisiana matched up with one player from Nebraska. They dubbed it the Boudreaux Thibodeaux Classic. In 2008, they played the Classic for the seventh consecutive year. Only now Evans and Hyde made the trip up with a couple of trucks and a tandem axle trailer packed with eleven 100-quart coolers and enough tents and cookers to feed anyone and everyone who came along, from their friends to the police department, from the firefighters to the bomb squad to the employees of the zoo. People don't just hope that the Cajuns are cooking their dinner. They're counting on it.

"At first we'd throw some Cajun food down and everyone would say 'What the heck *is* that?' Now they don't even ask. They just eat it."

Decade-long friendships forged over 1,000 miles, thanks to baseball, strange foods, and a thin strip of grass, all leading to laughter and lies beneath a mixture of Husker, Ragin' Cajun, and LSU Tiger flags that looks like the outside of the United Nations.

From the north end of The Neighborhood, they sent up a smoke signal. On the south side, they were more than happy to reply.

Mark Samstad was born and raised in Omaha, but eventually landed in Fort Lauderdale. For thirty years he'd returned home for the College World Series. For the last twenty-five he'd occupied the same parking spot, at the bend in the road where College World Series Boulevard becomes South Tenth Street.

Like Evans and Hyde, Samstad was serious about his tailgating. Very serious. Hanging from the trees as traffic crawled by was a giant white banner, decorated with a stylish green alligator, a bright red baseball, and the unavoidable lettering that read, CWS TAILGATERS. As Samstad cooked up bacon and eggs for a couple dozen friends and a few nameless strangers drawn to the scent, he sipped a 10:00 A.M. Newcastle, and handed over a business card with the 'Gater logo (which is trademarked) and the address of his soon-to-be-launched Web site: www.cwsprofessionaltailgater.com.

Told you he was serious.

Samstad's followers gathered 'round their giant bearded leader, each wearing a different Tailgater T-shirt, which connected the dots of their years together. This year's edition read: BASEBALL AND BEER BOTH BEGIN WITH "B." COINCIDENCE? I DON'T THINK SO! They sipped suds from custom-made Tailgater cozies.

The décor of alligators was outshone only by the endless number of pink flamingos. They hung from trees. A FLAMINGO CROSSING sign dangled from a street post. One woman wore a hat fashioned after a flamingo's head. And lined along the road were eight plastic flamingos, each bearing the logo of a CWS team. One of the birds sat a few feet away from the other seven, separated from the flock with a black cloth bag tied over its head and a handful of dead flowers at its feet.

"That's Florida State," Samstad said, pointing to the tiny black-and-white Seminole insignia taped to its back. "They're gone, so that bird is dead."

Thirty minutes after a team was eliminated, the CWS Tailgaters gathered around the birds for the "Hooding Ceremony," when Samstad would say a few words about the deceased, place the flowers on the ground, pour a beer over the bird's head, and tie on the hood. "It's surprisingly emotional," explained Bill Nash, a Chicago resident with a Rollie Fingers mustache who, along with wife Diana, had parked alongside Samstad for nine years. "Then again, after a dozen beers about anything will make you cry, won't it?"

If only the Hooding Ceremony was the strangest tradition along CWS Blvd.

A few hundred feet to Samstad's right, the Dale family sat in lawn chairs, lining the curb side by side and identified by a custom black flag—THE DALES—flying over their perch. Out in the street laid the smashed remnants of at least two dozen frankfurters, victimized by the family's favorite game, Beat the Meat. The premise was simple: toss a hot dog into the road, throw a dollar in the hat, and pass it down. Whoever was holding the hat when, ahem, the meat got beat, took the cash.

"We started when my mother was here in her wheelchair," Mike Dale said, grinning and shaking his head to acknowledge the ridiculousness of what he was trying to describe. "Instead of cars running over hot dogs, Mom did it. We've been here twenty-five years and we've been playing Beat the Meat for at least fifteen. You do something that long it qualifies it as a tradition, right?"

Between the Dales, the Tailgaters, and The Blatt were rows upon rows of cars, vans, tents, and flags. Baseball wrapped in a football atmosphere.

For decades CWS-ticket holders simply showed up for game time, walked in, walked out when the game was over, and went home. Then the Texas Longhorns towed in a group calling themselves the "Wild Bunch." The Bunch set up camp in the cinder-and-dirt parking lot and stayed there until the Horns went home, drinking beverages, burning meat, and playing horseshoes. They even came to Omaha on those rare occasions when their ballclub did not. Like Samstad's bacon-craving masses, the locals were drawn to the Wild Bunch's big-as-Texas pregame rituals. Soon Husker Nation caught wind of a place to party somewhere other than Memorial Stadium.

That migration begat the Tailgaters, the Dales, JLC's Crew, Dingerville, and the Row J Party, where a group of city planners, politicians, and journalists have made more municipal decisions over Bud Light and brats than they would ever be willing to admit. By the 1980s, LSU was arriving with regularity and their fans turned The Blatt parking lot into a northern cul-de-sac of Bourbon Street. And when Nebraska finally made its first Series appearance in 2001, the entire experience officially graduated to off the hook.

Take, for instance, "Little Big Cheese," a retired yellow short bus up-fitted with mirrored ceilings, a smoke machine, and a rooftop inflatable swimming pool. A well-toasted individual half-dressed in Big Red Nebraska gear to match his big reddening shoulders tossed a football back and forth from his pool position to some friends below. "We started coming up when the Huskers came, but we weren't this well equipped then. Today we're even considering going in to see a game. Yesterday we just sat here and guessed what was happening by the crowd noise."

When the parking lots became solid concrete in the 1980s, horseshoes were out. The game that fans improvised became a CWS staple all its own, constructing homemade wooden platforms wrapped in plastic turf to play a horseshoes-ish game called Washers, where players toss metal washer rings into holes in the boards. The sounds of classic rock and sports-talk radio have long been punctuated by the sounds of Washers—either wooden thunks followed by cheers or metallic clinks followed by choruses of "awwwww!"

Kids played catch. Parents fixed lunch. Grandparents took photos of it all. Everyone shared whatever they brought with whoever needed it, from ice to sunscreen to bacon and eggs. Every American neighborhood should be as happy as The Neighborhood.

CWS season ticket holder Jody Rusnak ended up sharing more than he'd planned to. The Omaha native purchased a decommissioned ambulance and converted it into perhaps the ultimate tailgating apparatus. He tricked it out with a brain-melting stereo system, a forty-two-inch plasma television, a satellite dish, and custom-built benches that doubled as coolers. His future plans for the party wagon included changing the words on the side from "Mobile Intensive Care Unit" to "Mobile Intensive *Tailgating* Unit," but he hadn't had time to complete the paint job before the 2008 Series, so the old title was still visible. That explains why the weak and wounded kept stumbling toward him in search of medical assistance.

"We've had three people come by so far. A cut leg, a migraine, and a diabetic guy whose sugar was getting too low. We had some Band-Aids,

Tylenol, and a Coke, so we got them fixed up. But I probably need to get that name change finished, don't I?"

One hundred sixteen years before Stan Evans and Jeff Hyde first arrived on the banks of the Missouri from Louisiana, Meriwether Lewis and William Clark were in the midst of their own journey into the unknown. A mission spurred by, fittingly, the Louisiana Purchase.

On the morning of July 27, 1804, their team left "White Catfish Camp" near present-day Bellevue and floated upriver with a gentle northern breeze at their backs. In his journal, Clark made note of a wooded island, a sandbar, and a "thick and troublesome" cloud of mosquitoes. There is no way of knowing if the explorers looked to their port side to see the sharp rising hillside upon which The Blatt now sits, but it was certainly looking down on them. Perhaps the spirit of Johnny Rosenblatt was already present as they drifted by, because later in the trip they did attempt to teach the Nez Perce Native American tribe how to play "the ball of base."

Fifty years later the Council Bluffs picnickers declared their desire to create Omaha City. Soon afterward the pioneers tumbled in off the prairie, followed by the railroad, and cows. A lot of cows.

In 1883, a Wyoming cattleman by the bound-to-know-how-to-make-money name of Alexander Hamilton Swan stopped over in Omaha on his way home from a sales trip to the massive Chicago Stockyards. Maybe it was the dusty streets or the smell that convinced Swan the city was a good place to herd cattle. Or perhaps it was because the commute from Wyoming to Illinois had worn out his ass. Whatever the reason, Swan immediately set out to convince local businessmen, including telegraph pioneers John and Edward Creighton (as in Creighton University) that Omaha should build its own stockyards to pull business west from New York and Chicago.

Over the next seventy years, Omaha's Union Stockyards grew into one of those only-in-America images that today would have to be recreated by Hollywood CGI artists, a horizon-covering labyrinth of fences and roads, with a city's worth of brick processing buildings and smokestacks rising from its center. By 1910, more than 20,000 animals were passing through the Stockyards daily, brought in from all four corners of the nation to be examined, sold, and slaughtered. At one point 80 percent of Omaha was employed by Stockyard-related businesses, all taking place within smelling distance of where Johnny Rosenblatt would eventually build his ballpark.

South Omaha became known as "Packingtown," and the city's population base shifted from downtown to the hilly side streets that surrounded the Stockyards and the four giant packing plants it supported. Packingtown residents came from all over the world. Germans arrived and opened local breweries with which to soak the workers and visitors heading south from Union Station to the Stockyards. There were Lithuanians, Estonians, Italians, and Mexicans. The Czechs, Poles, and Irish all took jobs in the packing plants, while the Sicilians maintained the railroads. Closer to the Stockyards, the neighborhoods were subdivided by nationality. But The Neighborhood was an unusual blend of all of the above. A century later, it still was.

Packingtown's residents went to Riverview Park, just a few hundred yards from where Samstad's hooded flamingos stood in 2008, and at what would become the Henry Doorly Zoo they gawked at dozens of animals, including a pair of bison donated by Buffalo Bill Cody.

They also played baseball. Man, did they play baseball. They played at city parks and on empty sandlots. They held company picnics on the weekends, which were little more than an excuse to play ball until the sun went down. The packing plants, the rail companies, and the Stockyards sponsored teams. The Union Pacific Enginemen played Eatmore Candy as the Northwestern Bells took on the W. Electrics. In 1939, when the Stockyards were approaching 50,000 cattle, pigs, and sheep run-through per day, the Omaha McDevitts electrified the city by winning the American Legion national championship.

The packers and railroad workers built their South Omaha homes in neat rows that covered the surrounding hillsides like graph paper, lining Thirteenth Street and fanning out toward the west. They were modest wood-frame houses that reflected the varied heritages of the people who built them. The residents sat on the front porch, hoping to catch a cool breeze off the river while watching their neighbors head south toward the Stockyards for work.

In 2008, a new group of locals sat on those same porches, watching the endless stream of out-of-towners coming to and from The Blatt.

For two weeks every summer, they serve as the hosts of college baseball's grand bazaar, beginning at the bottom of the hill near the Boudreaux Thibodeaux lovefest and rising a half-dozen blocks southward toward Bellevue and the old Stockyards site, which has been stuck in a slow decay since the packing business splintered in the 1960s. During CWS weeks, the residents willingly rent out their lives, handing over yards to vendor tents, from mom-and-pop T-shirt makers to the corporate likes of Lids, New Era, and Borsheim's Jewelry (hey guys, it's never the wrong time to buy your baseball fan that diamond she's always wanted!).

Some homes become the unofficial headquarters of visiting teams, from the wooden bungalow known as the Titan House, rented out by Cal State Fullerton loyalists and adorned with a giant orange "F" on its roof, to Cal-Irvine's rowdy HQ for 2007's Anteater Nation.

One house was completely outfitted with a full commercial kitchen and indoor-outdoor dining, becoming a two-week full-scale Famous Dave's barbecue joint. Another received a Ty Pennington–style extreme makeover to become the Nike Fieldhouse, complete with an Astroturf floor, an outdoor batting cage, and an upstairs lounge where college and high school coaches sat in air-conditioning and watched games in high-definition . . . but only if they were willing to hear a pitch from the team sales rep.

The highest concentration of commerce was found on the front lawn of the old Rosewater School, built in 1910 to educate the children of Packingtown. In 1985, the school was converted into apartments and every June it was transformed into The Neighborhood's version of a shopping mall, home of giant white tents and overpriced officially licensed merchandise. While the youngsters ogled at flat-billed high-rise caps, the older set sifted through bins filled with the gotta-have-it items of College World Series past, one man thrilled to plunk down five bucks for a 2006 OREGON STATE CWS CHAMPIONS golf shirt.

Set up on the sidewalk between the tents sat high school student Cade Hassel and an older gentleman identified only as Grandpa Dolven. To their right and left, vendors sold $30 hats and $25 T-shirts. Cade and Grandpa sold pop at $1.50 a pop. In 2007, they moved 3,000 units. The vendors around them paid thousands of dollars for their spot of Rosenblatt-friendly real estate. Hassel's modern-day lemonade stand landed its location for free.

It helps when your family owns the building.

"Dad's in the back parking cars," the high school junior said as he wiped sweat from his brow and handed over two bottles of water for three bucks. "The money we make goes into my college fund. I'm thinking UCLA. Have you ever been there?"

Half a block north of the Rosewater School sat the red, white, and blue spiritual center of The Neighborhood. The building, which looked like it might slide backward into the ditch off the back door, was finished in 1898, doubling as the neighborhood grocery store and the home of the family that ran it. For more than a century the old wooden floors had withstood the bloody boots of meatpackers, the clogs of school kids, and since 1992, the sneakers and flip-flops of College World Series visitors, on the prowl for memorabilia, air-conditioning, and, oh yeah . . .

"Wanna beer?"

Greg Pivovar greeted every visitor to Stadium View Sportscards the exact same way every single time. By his estimation, the pre-2008 count of brews given away had topped 30,000. (If you wanted to buy a T-shirt stating that fact, he could hook you up.) There was also free food at meal times, free TV coverage of the games going on across the street, and free B.S. for as long one could stand to stomach one of Piv's trademark gaudy Hawaiian shirts.

For years the wood and glass shop door featured his locally famous motto "Management reserves the right to bend the bill of your cap if you come in looking like a dork." (If you wanted to buy a T-shirt stating that fact, he could hook you up with one of those as well.) In 2008, he amended that warning with another: "Management reserves the right to pull up your damn pants."

"I don't know how these kids keep their damn pants from falling down," he said as he wrapped a can of Busch Light in a paper towel, looking down to a customer's waistline before handing it over and smiling beneath his shrub of a mustache. "You're okay. We don't need you to pull up your damn pants."

On display in the cases throughout the old store were vintage CWS ticket stubs, programs, posters, and autographs. The left-hand side of the store was covered in old Series apparel and autographed bats. The back storage room belonged to what he proudly proclaimed, "Has to be the best collection of old sports magazines and books this side of the Mississippi." There was an old Willie McCovey glove, an aluminum bat signed by the entire 1996 U.S. Olympic Baseball Team (coached by Skip Bertman), and plenty of Nebraska football stuff. Stacks of baseball-card boxes covered shelves from the floor nearly all the way to the twelve-foot tin-covered ceiling.

"There used to be some offices in here," he said with a point to remnants of wall moldings. "We wanted to do a lot more work in here to really bring out the character of the place, but there's no real point in doing that now."

No point because after 2008, Stadium View had only two years left on its colorful life as the unofficial anchor of the CWS experience. Pivovar didn't need to keep the store open for the money. He made a good living as an attorney, known for taking cases as colorful as his shirts, including a golfer who attacked another with a long iron because he was playing too slow, and a carnival worker accused of killing a fellow thrill-ride operator. Truth was, the place was really open only to the public during Series weeks. The remainder of the year he might come down and piddle around for a few hours a week, but he made enough moving product on eBay to pay the bills on the building.

Since '92, he'd been welcoming first-timers along with a constantly growing number of regulars. This year they'd all asked if he was planning to move downtown alongside the new stadium in 2011. Like so many of the houses along Thirteenth, Stadium View once sported SAVE ROSENBLATT posters in its windows. When the questions about the future arose, Pivovar was always ready to blast the NCAA and Omaha officials for "selling out" and warned fans about the impending "clean zone," which will ensure that businesses like Stadium View would be kept at arm's length, six blocks away. He always talked tough, like a good attorney should. But deep down, the thought of moving cut much sharper than mere municipal politics.

When the excellent Omaha World-Herald columnist Tom Shatel (coworker of Greg's brother Steve, keeper of the greatest Series tales), posed that question for a column, Pivovar started describing his defiant plans to have every fan sign their name on the walls of his beloved old store in 2010. As he talked, he became so emotional he had to leave the room to regain his composure.

"People come here for this. Not my store, but the whole atmosphere. Everybody wants to know if I'm moving downtown. Where? The younger generation, they're used to antiseptic, corporate events," to which he pointed out the door and across the street to the NCAA Fan Zone. "It's going to be weird downtown. We'll get used to it. But it'll never be the same."

With that, he snapped out of his speech and swept his hands across the room to display his domain. "But let's enjoy this now, right? People can't figure out how I stay in business with all the beer we give away. But I don't lose money on the deal. They either buy something out of guilt, buy something because they like a guy that hands out free beer, or they at least contribute to the Harper Lee College Fund."

As he said it, he pointed to a lineup of jars adorned with the colors of the eight participating schools, then to his seven-year-old daughter—yes, Harper Lee—perched on a bar stool by a stack of dusty Topps year sets. "Whichever jar ends up with the most money is where she'll end up going, right, baby?"

"Sure, Dad."

"Hey, Piv," a visitor shouted from across the room. "You forgot the other reason that you don't lose money on the deal." With a smile he picked up an abandoned Busch Light can from atop a box of ball caps, still three-quarters full, proven by a taunting shake only slightly sloshier than his smile. "You give out crappy beer."

When the laughter died down, someone asked Pivovar who had donated the most money to the Harper Lee Fund. The answer comes back before the question was even finished. "LSU. Always LSU. Whether the team is here or not, the LSU fans come in here and buy stuff. You walk the streets of Omaha and ask what team they love the best and they'll always answer LSU. Why? Because when they leave, their money stays behind."

It's true.

The Neighborhood loves 'em some Louisiana State.

Unlike Southern Cal, Texas, or Miami, the Bayou Bengals are relative latecomers to the CWS inner sanctum of superpowers. Their first appearance didn't come until 1986, the fortieth edition of the Series and the thirty-seventh at The Blatt. But they partied hard, talked funny, and ended all their words with an "x." They also fed everybody within ladle distance and tossed them strands of beads without even asking them to first pull up their shirts.

When Bertman left Coral Gables for Baton Rouge in 1983, the program he inherited wasn't as bad off as the one his mentor, Ron Fraser, had taken over at Miami. But it wasn't in great shape, either. Between 1893 and Bertman's arrival ninety years later, the Tigers had qualified for the postseason once and been ranked in the top twenty-five only twice. Alex Box Stadium—"The Box"—was named for an LSU alum and decorated World War II tank commander. It was adequately sized but always empty.

With guidance from Fraser, Bertman had the program turned around in one season, making the NCAA Tournament in '85 and riding Ben McDonald to the school's first CWS appearance in '86. During his eighteen seasons at the wheel, Bertman's teams managed to eclipse every other program in the nation, including his former employer. He won 870 games, put twenty-seven players in the big leagues, and won six Southeastern Conference (SEC) championships. He also transformed Alex Box Stadium into a rowdy, perpetually packed college showcase, routinely bringing in 200,000 fans a year when other schools were lucky to draw a third of that. The magic of The Box eventually convinced administrators and alumni to kick off a Miami-style fund-raising program that would replace the old park with a new multimillion-dollar ballpark in 2009.

But as much as he loved The Box, Bertman saved his best work for The Blatt, making eleven CWS appearances and winning five NCAA titles with a perfect 5–0 record in championship games.

"You watch these people walking by out here," Pivovar said while standing on the front stoop of his store. "LSU apparel outnumbers everyone else. You think everyone wearing it is from Louisiana? Nope. Most of them are locals who have been fans of LSU since they were little kids because they grew up watching them win."

Bertman fans also included coaches, who flocked to the Gulf of Mexico to study his teaching techniques and legendary ability to motivate. He published a book and produced a how-to coaching video, which high-school and college coaches gobbled up. He kept motivational speeches and sayings meticulously filed by subject, situation, and opponent. Big game this Friday night against an out-of-conference foe in front of a hostile crowd with a wicked left-hander on the mound while in the throes of a three-game losing streak? Chances are Coach Skip had a speech ready to pull out of a file folder and to fire off.

At the end of the 2001 season, Bertman hung up his cleats, choosing to focus on his duties as LSU's athletic director. He chose longtime assistant Smoke Laval to take over the team, an experiment that lasted four seasons. Miami's decision to stick with a loyal assistant had resulted in a one-year slide toward mediocrity. The decline under Laval was slower, but just as unsettling to Tiger fans. Laval got the team to Rosenblatt twice, but went two-and-'cue in both visits. The 2006 season ended with LSU's first absence from the NCAA Tournament in twenty-two years. As painful as the decision was, Bertman had to let go of his longtime lieutenant.

Enter Paul Mainieri, a chatty Miami-raised Italian with a smile permanently stuck on his face and a cell phone permanently stuck in his ear. "Who do you want to talk to?" he said while holding up the phone as if it were made of gold. "I've got everybody in here. Tommy Lasorda, Roger Clemens, you name it. One of my players told me the other day that his favorite movie was *Rudy*. I said, I've got Rudy on speed dial, you want to call him?"

Mainieri's specialty, other than talking, was turning around dormant baseball programs. At the age of twenty-four he took over at Florida's tiny St. Thomas University, a school that had never posted a winning season, and transformed them into a top twenty-five program in NCAA's Division II for smaller schools. Then he became the first civilian baseball coach at the Air Force Academy, where he guided the Falcons to their first winning season in more than a decade.

Mainieri even woke up the echoes at old Notre Dame, going against conventional college baseball wisdom that a cold-weather school can't compete nationally, and in 2000, earned the Fighting Irish their first

CWS berth in forty-five years. Soon that cell phone was ringing with a 225 area code flashing on the caller ID. It was Skip Bertman.

Mainieri and Bertman had more in common than anyone in Baton Rouge realized. In 1967, when ten-year-old Paul wanted some help with his hitting, Demie Mainieri took him to Miami Beach High for pointers from slugging professor Bertman. One year later, when Bertman decided that he wanted to make the jump from high school coaching to college, it was Demie whom he sought out for advice. When Paul was coaching at St. Thomas, he scheduled games against Miami so he could visit with and learn from Bertman and Fraser.

Mainieri had even played one year in the LSU outfield, long before Bertman arrived, meeting wife Karen on campus before realizing he couldn't pass up the chance to play for his father at Miami-Dade, and finished up at the University of New Orleans.

So when Coach Bertman phoned the perfectly happy Catholic boy in South Bend, Indiana, Mainieri told him to first call everyone else and then call back if he was still the guy. Ten days later he called back. Yes, he was the guy. After the interview in Baton Rouge, Karen and Paul sat up in their hotel bed, wrestling with their happiness at Notre Dame and the specter of following the greatest coach of the last twenty years.

"The idea was so intimidating," Mainieri recalled as his cell vibrated . . . again. "You don't follow Bear Bryant or Dean Smith. But maybe because I'd known Skip for so long, it wasn't as intimidating as it would have been for someone else." Then he smiled. "At least that's what I tell myself."

His first year on the bayou quickly exposed the shaky foundation Laval had left behind. As the 2007 season began, the new head coach quickly realized that getting to Omaha, hell, even making it to the SEC tournament, wasn't the goal. Finishing above .500 was the mark, which the team barely achieved after dropping six of the season's final eight games.

The 2008 season started no better. They padded their record early with a soft nonconference schedule but they were punched in their collective mouths once SEC play began. The low point came at the hands of Perno and Georgia, who came to Alex Box Stadium and scored twenty-five runs in three games. The 2008 Tigers were looking a lot like the 2007 squad, stuck on a highly generic record of 23–16–1, sitting eleventh in the twelve-team SEC. Fans were growing restless. With each loss, Mainieri's trademark smile became less charming and more disingenuous in the eyes of the Tiger faithful. This was how they were going to tear down and replace The Box for 2009? By sucking?

Then came a breezy Tuesday evening just down the road at Tulane's Turchin Stadium.

On April 22, the Tigers were threatening to settle into yet another spiritless loss to an inferior ballclub. The Green Wave led 4–3 in the eighth and yet another Tiger opportunity was falling flat. With two on and no outs, the next LSU hitters promptly grounded out weakly to the mound and went down on strikes.

"You could feel it," recalled designated hitter Blake Dean, stuck on third. "We weren't going to get the big hit . . . again."

That's when shortstop D. J. LeMahieu stepped into the batter's box. Despite the Louisiana name, he was a California native raised outside of Detroit with stops in Las Vegas and Wisconsin, and seemingly unaffected by the pressure of playing in the LSU fishbowl, hitting .322 in his freshman season. The nineteen-year-old calmly took the first pitch. He smoked the next one. LSU 5, Tulane 4.

"It was like D. J. turned the light on," LSU sports information director and broadcaster Bill Franques recalled weeks later, standing outside the batting cage at Creighton University. "Someone finally got the clutch hit. From then on, everyone expected to get the clutch hit. Mike Hollander, Matt Clark, everyone. Blake Dean had enough clutch hits down the stretch for one team, let alone one player."

They swept South Carolina and Mississippi State at home. They swept Kentucky and Auburn on the road. They swept through the SEC Tournament and their NCAA regional at The Box. After dropping the Super Regional opener to the Cal-Irvine Anteaters, they came from behind to win the second game and then posted a football score of 21–7 to close the old ballpark, to soak up the cheers of the crowd, and to accept LSU's fourteenth invitation to Omaha.

Beginning with LeMahieu's hit they won a mind-bending 25 of 26 games, including 23 in a row to close out the regular season. And in the middle of it all, Skip Bertman had survived a heart attack.

"I told Paul I wasn't going to blame my little heart condition on the wild season," the seventy-year-old said with a wink. "But a few people that obviously know my penchant for speeches did tell me I could have at least milked a 'Win one for the Gipper' moment out of it."

As Game Seven began against Rice, Mainieri said a little prayer to the baseball gods, hoping they would grant his team a little more back-against-the-wall magic. It wasn't impossible for a team to lose its first game of the CWS and come back to win the title. Oregon State had done it in 2006. And it was surely easier to do since the NCAA had started a clean-slate best-of-three series for the championship. But still, it was surely a lot more difficult than taking the Georgia '08 route of winning early and often and waiting on everyone else to catch up.

The greatest thrill of the day for the fifty-year-old coach, win or lose, was the pregame handshake with Wayne Graham. During Friday's coaches press conference Mainieri sat and grinned at Graham as if the Rice skipper had just handed him the deed to Graceland. When the old coach made his comment about surviving a vampire bite, Mainieri proclaimed to the media, "Don't you just love Wayne Graham?"

He loved Graham because his heroes had always been baseball coaches. In Graham he saw the same characteristics that he loved so much about Bertman, Fraser, and his father. He loved that Graham quoted poetry during practices and got his players motivated with phrases such as, "It would behoove your ass to get in gear." He loved that Graham took half a day to walk out to the mound and talk to his pitchers and he loved that the coach had toiled for two decades as a high school and junior-college coach before landing, and winning, at Rice. At *Rice!* Hell, President John Kennedy had once invoked the preposterous idea of winning at Rice to illustrate the difficulty of getting to the moon.

And Mainieri loved Graham's stories, especially the ones about his brief Major League playing career, getting called up for ten games with Gene Mauch's Philadelphia Phillies and twenty more with Casey Stengel's New York Mets.

Stuck in the downward spiral of their legendarily bad 1964 season, Stengel chatted with a group of beat writers on the Mets team plane. Well within earshot of his twenty-seven-year-old journeyman infielder who was hitting around .125 at the time, the crusty manager shouted, "How do they expect me to win when they keep sending me mediocre players like this Graham?"

The player took the hint and went into coaching.

But as Game Seven wore on, the romanticism of facing Graham had quickly faded for Mainieri. Almost immediately, the master took the apprentice to school. Senior starting pitcher Chris Kelley put on a typically sleepy Rice CWS pitching clinic, following the blueprints drawn up by his predecessors such as Jeff Niemann, Wade Townsend, Phil Humber, and David Aardsma, the backbone of the school's dominating CWS championship in 2003 and all MLB first-round draft picks.

Kelley cruised through five and two-thirds innings, allowing no runs on only four hits and three walks. He left the mound with a five-run lead, handing the ball off to All-World lefty Cole St. Clair for a long relief appearance. St. Clair was the recipient of the Senior CLASS Award, given annually to the nation's top senior player. He had pitched the final inning of Sunday's beatdown by Fresno State, but looked plenty fresh as he struck out the first batter he faced, none other than Matt Clark, the nation's home run leader, and motored through the seventh and eighth.

Entering the bottom of the ninth, Rice led 5–2 and St. Clair was in total control. LSU's last likely threat had died when catcher Micah Gibbs was thrown out at home to end the previous inning, an out that sucked away whatever oxygen had been left in the Tiger dugout.

"All right," a newspaper writer said as he stood up in the press box and headed for the exit. "I'm outta here. This is a classic Rice game right here. It's over. I'm going to Zesto for a milkshake."

As left fielder Nicholas Pontiff grounded out to first to start the bottom of the ninth, the Tigers stood on the top step of the dugout, their hats turned backward in full-on Rally Cap mode. But no one cheered. Coach Paul Mainieri's smile was officially in absentia as he lurked in the back of the dugout and thought about the fact that the mighty purple and gold was about to be handed its sixth consecutive CWS loss. Back-to-back-to-back two-and-'cues. Yikes. And where the hell was he going to take Karen out for dinner on this, what might end up being her worst birthday ever?

Fifteen hundred miles away, in the visitor's clubhouse at St. Petersburg's Tropicana Field, the mood was just as glum. The Chicago Cubs had just arrived for a three-game interleague set with the suddenly hot Tampa Rays. As soon as the Cubbies got into town, they made sure the television was tuned to ESPN and the Series.

The man who had signed or dealt for them all, general manager Jim Hendry, had known Mainieri since he was a college kid, having served as an assistant coach with Demie in the Cape Cod League. Two of their best players were Paul and his college roommate Randy Bush, who was now Hendry's assistant GM. What's more, former LSU infielders Mike Fontenot and Ryan Theriot, members of LSU's 2000 CWS championship team, were on the Cubs roster. "We turned it on," Theriot said later. "And immediately it was like, oh man, this isn't good."

Then the Cubs watched as Derek Helenhi, LSU's number-eight hitter, smacked a bounding single past the outstretched glove of second baseman Jimmy Comerota. Mainieri sent freshman catcher Sean Ochinko to the plate to pinch hit, and he was promptly plunked in the back and sent to first.

Two on, one out.

Suddenly The Blatt crowd woke up.

Senior third baseman Michael Hollander singled up the middle, one run scored. Rice 5, LSU 3.

Still two on, one out.

"Wait!" Cubs pitcher Kerry Wood jumped onto a chair and started waving a rally towel in the direction of his LSU teammates. "Here we go, Tigers! L-S-U! L-S-U!"

At The Blatt, the crowd started to echo Wood's cheer. The game started with 19,103 fans, but had significantly thinned out as the outcome grew apparent. Still, they were plenty loud. The Thirteenth Street bead-wearing bandwagon was fired up.

"L-S-U! L-S-U!"

Tiger left fielder Jared Mitchell fouled off what should have been a gift from Cole St. Clair, running the count to 2-2. Still angry at himself, he hacked at ball three, sending an easy double-play ball to shortstop Rick Hague. Hague had nineteen errors on the season coming into Game

Seven and had already been drilled in the Adam's apple by a Helenhi bounder in the seventh inning.

Now he had twenty errors. Bases loaded, one out.

Designated hitter Blake Dean, the lethal number-three hitter, wisely laid off an 88-mph fastball. This was bad and in the Rice dugout Wayne Graham knew it. High pitches meant his pitcher was tired and overreaching. But St. Clair was his guy and he was staying on the mound.

The next pitch also registered at 88 . . . coming and going.

Dean's opposite field drive thwapped off the left-field wall just inches shy of going out. Three runs scored. Game over. LSU 6, Rice 5.

Almost instantly, Coach Mainieri's cell phone started ringing in the clubhouse. The call came from the other Tiger clubhouse, the one in St. Petersburg where the Cubs were leaping around like they'd finally won a World Series game themselves. The coach never heard it ring. He couldn't for the ringing from The Blatt's big grandstand. The crowd raised their arms, hugged whoever was within hugging distance, and stomped on the metal floors.

Upstairs in the press box, Skip Bertman was the recipient of more hugs than he could count. "I'm going to have to talk to Paul," he joked. "My cardiologist isn't going to let me sit through any more games like that." Then the old coach leaned out of the window and looked down at the crowd, listening to the chant that he had taught them all so many years ago.

L-S-U! L-S-U!

It's true.

The Neighborhood loves 'em some Louisiana State.

The nightcap of Game Eight featured two candidates ready to win the hearts of Omaha had LSU stumbled and gone home, and they couldn't have been more different.

North Carolina was in Omaha for the third consecutive year. Their first trip started as something of a novelty and ended within one pitch of winning the 2006 CWS title, falling to Oregon State. One year later they lost to the Beavers again. Head coach Mike Fox won over the local residents with his soft Carolina Piedmont lilt and stories of shooting his own home movies to distribute post-Omaha DVDs to his players and staff.

When the Tarheels returned in 2008, there was nothing feel-good or folksy about it. This time they were The Favorite. Fox's team started the year ranked fifth in the nation and never dipped lower, spending one week at number one. They blew through the first two rounds of the NCAA Tournament, averaging ten runs over five games and hitting a cool .337 as a team. Seven of their starting nine players came in with at least five starts in CWS games. Their Game Eight starter was Adam Warren, who carried a college career record of twenty-two wins to one loss—22 and 1! The Heels looked buttoned up in their blue and white uniforms, a group of "yes sir, yes ma'am" clean-shaven veterans not the least bit bowled over by the Rosenblatt experience.

Then there was Fresno.

The Bulldogs had slogged their way through the postseason by winning three elimination games. No one on their roster had even as much as attended a CWS game until their win over Rice. Starter Justin Wilson was a junior-college transfer from Bakersfield sporting a workmanlike if not unspectacular 7–5 record in sixteen starts. What's more, first baseman Alan Ahmady added another injury to the Fresno medical report when he woke up the morning of Game Seven with a chipped tooth. At least that was his story.

All you needed to know about one program versus the other was to take a look at their CWS media guides. Carolina's, like Miami, Florida State, and the other superpowers, distributed books of stats that had merely been updated from years before and professionally bound. Fresno State's was a stack of papers stapled in the top left corner.

Perfect.

In the early innings those contrasting styles were illustrated perfectly. Warren threw impressive heat, giving up some hard contact, but the only real damage came when catcher Ryan Overland hit a solo homer in the second inning. Almost immediately the Heels' classic playing style punished Fresno's aggressiveness, picking off two runners and catching another off base on a bang-bang double play at first. In the fourth, Carolina nearly hit for the cycle, posting three runs to chase Miller off the mound and taking a 3–1 lead. Bulldog leader Steve Susdorf looked like he'd been slapped with a shovel, his jersey covered with grass stains after diving for a double to left off the bat of UNC second baseman Kyle Seager.

The Underdog was getting a lesson in how to play Omaha baseball from The Favorite.

"You looked at those guys and thought, there's a College World Series team," Susdorf said later. "They looked the part. They walked like you're supposed to walk. They didn't make mistakes. But then you also thought, so they've been here before, but we're both here now. Like it or not, we're on equal ground. We just had to show that to them."

On the fourth pitch he saw, Steve Susdorf reset the tone for his team. Adam Warren hung a breaking ball out over the plate and with a cut eerily reminiscent of former Mississippi State Bulldog Will Clark, Susdorf flicked the ball over the right-field wall. The supposedly light-hitting Fresno State team had now hit six home runs in a game and a half, produced by six different hitters.

Almost immediately, the Bulldogs came off the bench and to the top step of the dugout. Susdorf carried the momentum of his homer directly into the dugout, vocally reminding his teammates that The Favorite could fall. Alan Ahmady, chipped tooth and all, nearly hit one out in the next at-bat.

When the infielders gathered for their customary glove-slapping dance in the third-base coach's box, Susdorf was already thinking about his team's next trip to the plate. "He's dropping off," the Academic All-American said to Tommy Mendonca, Gavin Hedstrom, Danny Muno, Erik Wetzel, and Ahmady, leaning in to ensure the ESPN camera didn't broadcast his lesson into the UNC clubhouse. "A lot. He was throwing a lot harder the first time around. We need to jump on that."

Susdorf was right. Adam Warren had started the game with a fastball in the 92–93 mph range, but by the third inning it was down in the mid-80s, and in the last half of the fourth he was tossing off-speed breaking balls almost exclusively. When he came out overthrowing in the fifth, Fresno was ready, thanks to Susdorf's ten-second seminar. Muno singled, Hedstrom singled, and Wetzel laid down a perfect bunt on a 79-mph breaker.

With the bases loaded and no outs, Carolina coach Mike Fox pulled Warren for another fireballer, lefty Brian Moran. Two batters later, Ahmady stroked a two-run single. Fresno 4, UNC 3.

We need to jump on that.

"That's when we maybe got a little tight," Fox admitted weeks later. "For whatever reason, we didn't play well when we were behind. We swung at a lot of bad balls. In that game in particular, the strike zone was very small but we still kept swinging away. That's a sign of a worried bunch."

Looking back, it was a warning sign. The Tarheels, the team that was supposed to know how to handle Omaha, was suddenly feeling the pressure of being the team to beat and, for one night at least, wilted.

Final score: The Underdog 5, The Favorite 3.

Fresno State, like Georgia, was now strapped into the driver's seat of its bracket. For two days they could sit and watch UNC and LSU beat the hell out of each other while they sat in the hotel and waited to see who they would end up playing for a slot in the championship series.

As the Bulldogs packed their gear, a group of friends and fans gathered behind the dugout chanting, "Let's go, Bull-dogs!" Clap clap clap-clap-clap. As closer Brandon Burke walked off the field, a group of boys asked him to throw them a spare baseball.

"Sorry," he said, dripping with sweat. "After the championship game."

As if it was a foregone conclusion.

Back out on College World Series Boulevard, Mark Samstad was packed up for the night. For security reasons, every reveler, even the Professional Tailgaters, were required to tear down and take everything home . . . though veterans like Samstad typically had deals worked out with buddies on the police squad to leave their tents, as long as they were chained to a tree to keep from blowing away.

To his left stood the eight flamingos, but one had been moved since breakfast. Sitting alongside the Florida State fowl was now a second hooded bird, its back still damp with beer.

"That's not a flamingo," Samstad said with a hops-laden laugh. "That's an owl. A Rice University Owl. Now they're dead, too. Two down, five to go."

SIX

THE MASTERMIND

Wednesday, June 18
Game Nine: Miami vs. Stanford

While The Blatt was rocking on Tuesday afternoon, the Stanford Cardinal (whatever you do, don't call them Cardinals with an "s") took batting practice at Creighton University, preparing for their Game Nine matchup with Miami. Unlike Bellevue, the scene wasn't heartwarming, it was just warm. The day had become very hot and the artificial turf at the Sports Complex made it feel even hotter. In fact the whole scene felt a little too sterilized.

There was no Miss Marilyn, no grass, and no charm.

Then the preschoolers came waddling in. On the metal bleachers high above the sunken field, a dozen day-care toddlers wobbled down the stairs and down one row of seats, each with one hand clutched to the kid in front while the other flailed around like a detached sail.

"All right, kids," their teacher said with a singsongy tone. "Here we go. The baseball men are around here somewhere. I can hear their bats . . . Excuse me, sir, is Stanford here? The College World Series Web site said they would be."

"Yes, ma'am," Matthew Ritson answered back, not realizing that he was shouting over his radio earphones. The forty-something assistant equipment keeper was in his twenty-something year of working with the Stanford baseball team and at this moment he was sorting through a stack of equipment bags as he listened to Game Seven between Rice and LSU.

No one had more fun in Omaha than Ritson, whom the players referred to as Matty, Ritter, or Doc, a nickname earned after he convinced a woman at an airport that he was the team doctor, despite his obvious mental challenges. The unofficial team mascot had watched his beloved Cardinal knock off second-seeded Florida State and then celebrated by making a much-desired visit to the Bluffs Run Dog Track across the river.

When the team paid a visit to their assigned civic club, he had a different kind of canine experience. Over at Offutt Air Force Base, the team's ambassadors asked for a volunteer to participate in a demonstration of the USAF's finest pack of military working dogs. Ritson jumped at the chance and pulled on a black padded "bite suit" that resembled the outfit minor-league teams use for between-inning sumo wrestling. The resulting scene of Ritter being yanked to the ground by an angry German shepherd became an instant viral video sensation back in the Bay Area.

"Hey, kids!" Matty shouted at the two-year-olds with a wave and a point to the Kitty Gaughan Pavilion, a tall stone building to his left. "The team is inside taking batting practice and they will be here soon! By the way, LSU is coming back!"

On the wall where he pointed were five larger-than-life pictures of Creighton's larger-than-life baseball heroes, including Major Leaguers Scott Stahoviak, Alan Benes, and Scott Servais. They were fashioned after baseball cards and the one closest to the door from where the *tink-tink* of BP could be heard was of Jim Hendry. Yes, the same Jim Hendry of the Chicago Cubs who was halfway across the country cheering on Mainieri and the Tigers, the one who was now bolting to the airport to come to Omaha and support his pal in person.

In 1991, Hendry was Creighton's head coach, leading the school to its first and, as of 2008, only CWS appearance. For six days the Bluejays ruled the roost in their own town, embracing the role of The Underdog and electrifying a city that typically forced them to play second chair to the big red school down in Lincoln.

Fresno State (in their last CWS appearance before 2008) upset number-one-ranked Florida State and Creighton quickly matched the effort by doing away with number-two Clemson. In the semifinals, Benes took the mound against Midwestern rival Wichita State and another future big leaguer, Tyler Green. The game went twelve innings in front of a then-record crowd of more than 18,000. With two outs in the bottom of the thirteenth, Creighton pinch runner Steve Burns, the tying run, barreled home, but was thrown out by Shocker center fielder Jim Audley, who'd scored the go-ahead run in the top of the inning.

"To me, it was Omaha's finest moment," Skip Bertman recalled. His Tigers beat Wichita for the title the following day. "I was scouting the two teams and I had the best seat for the best play in the best game. Even in the loss, Creighton did so much for the Series. They were so disappointed, but when Jim Hendry and his team walked off the field, they received the greatest round of applause I've ever heard at Rosenblatt. From that moment on, anyone in the town who hadn't been sold on the magic of the College World Series started standing in line for tickets. It turned a football town into a baseball town."

Seventeen years later, as Hendry celebrated LSU's comeback against Rice, the Stanford players filed past his picture and onto the Creighton field, where Ritter was waiting with the news. "LSU won! LSU won! You guys said they were finished, but they came back and won!"

Stanford head coach Mark Marquess blew out of the batting cage and into the dugout, that rare diminutive figure who can fill a room just by walking into it. He stomped into the dugout where his players lounged and told his team to grab their stuff and get on the bus. He shook the hands of some alums who had stopped by to see their team practice, and headed for the gate.

Then he stopped and turned to Matty for the delayed reaction.

"Did you say LSU won that game?"

"Yes sir, Coach. Scored four runs in the bottom of the ninth."

"Welcome to Omaha," the coach said with a chuckle as he snapped closed his black briefcase and headed up the stairs. "Why not, right?"

As the bus pulled away and the toddlers teetered off, a father and son walked out of the building, where they'd watched Stanford hit and scored Jason Castro's autograph. When they came to the portraits on the wall, the dad stopped and tapped his finger on the one in the middle, the card that featured one very scary looking right-hander in a St. Louis Cardinals uniform about to unleash one very scary-looking pitch.

"That's Bob Gibson," he said to his son. "He might be the greatest right-handed pitcher that ever lived. I had no idea he went to Creighton."

Pack Robert Gibson was born on November 9, 1935, in the worst neighborhood in North Omaha, the youngest of seven children and the only one of those children to never meet his father, Pack, who died of tuberculosis shortly before Bob's birth. That left poor Victoria, a worker at Omaha Lace Laundry, to literally fight for her family's survival, especially baby Bob, who suffered from a heart problem, asthma, rickets, and pneumonia, all while living in conditions so poor that he was once awoken in the night by a rat nibbling at his ears.

He eventually outgrew his poor health, only to face the racism of a rough-hewn heartland city. At the age of nine, he was already destined to become a meatpacker, a janitor, or a dead man. Enter Josh Gibson. Bob's older brother's first name was Leroy, but his friends called him Josh because of his love of baseball, a nod to the great Hall of Fame Negro Leaguer Josh Gibson. (Gibson actually played ball in Omaha as a member of Satchel Paige's All-Stars in 1936. Immediately following the game, League Park, the city's only pro-worthy ballpark, burned down, opening the door for The Blatt.)

Josh was smart and persuasive, not long and lean like his brother, but big and bulky like a catcher, like the other Josh Gibson. He graduated high school when most of his peers did not, then took it one step further and earned a degree from Creighton. When he returned to Omaha after three years with the Army in World War II, he had hoped to land a job as a teacher, but Omaha Public Schools wouldn't hire him because of his skin color. So he turned his attention to Bob and the other kids in the Logan Fontenelle projects, becoming program director at the North Side YMCA, immediately going to work to get children off the streets through sports, especially baseball and particularly Bob. He built a rudimentary mound at nearby Kellom Elementary and started teaching Robert (he never called him Bob) how to pitch. That instruction continued as Josh coached YMCA-sponsored youth teams and hauled them all over Nebraska, Iowa, and Missouri to play whomever would agree to schedule them.

While Josh converted his racism-created anger into fuel for his work, he taught Bob to transfer it into his pitching. The Y Monarchs rode Bob's arm to the Nebraska state title, a first for an African-American team. At Tech High School, Johnny Rosenblatt's alma mater, Bob ran headlong into racism again, denied a spot on the baseball team and told that blacks could only run track. He became a three-sport star, finally allowed to play baseball when a new coach came in for his senior year, and earned a basketball scholarship from Creighton. He wanted to go to Indiana University, but the Hoosiers sent him a letter to say, "We have already filled our quota of Negroes," so he became a Bluejay legend in both sports. Out of school he signed a minor-league contract with the Cardinals and even played hoops with the Harlem Globetrotters for one year.

Bob Gibson threw his first professional pitch in 1957, and he threw it from the mound at Municipal Stadium as a member of the Class AA Omaha Cardinals, the team Rosenblatt had lured with his new facility. Friends and family, including Josh, came to the ballpark and braved the segregated grandstand to see baby Bob's debut. Seven years later that ballpark became Rosenblatt Stadium, and decades later one of the roads that the Gibson family took to see their boy pitch was renamed Bob Gibson Boulevard.

For Josh, going to see his little brother play wasn't just the fulfillment of a dream, it was a business trip. He used the example of Bob time and time again, leveraging the image of a North Omaha kid getting paid to play baseball as a motivator to get his kids at the YMCA to want a better life. When he could score tickets he'd bring his kids to the College World Series to see African-American players such as Hubie Brooks and Ken Landreaux, though there never seemed to be more than one or two black faces on the field at one time.

Bob made the big club in 1959 and won 251 games and two World Series titles during the 1960s, all the while fighting to fully integrate the Major Leagues, going so far as to demand that the Cardinals purchase a hotel in St. Petersburg, Florida, so their black and white players could all stay together during spring training.

During that same time, Josh helped counsel his children through the brutal process of school desegregation. He brought Bob back to keep his young troops inspired, the brothers hammering on them with "If you don't want to try hard, then don't waste our time." In 1981, Bob was elected to the National Baseball Hall of Fame and spent nearly half of his induction speech talking about his big brother. Josh died of a heart attack one year later.

NFL Hall of Famer Gale Sayers, Denver Broncos quarterback Marlin Briscoe, Heisman Trophy winner Johnny Rodgers, and pro basketball players Bob Boozer and Ron Boone all grew up in the same North Omaha projects and all learned sports and life from Josh Gibson at the North Side YMCA.

"Everyone knows about Bob Gibson, but even he will tell you that Josh is the hall of famer in the Gibson family," sixty-year-old Jerry Bartee said it from the office of the Omaha Public Schools, noticeably emotional at the mere mention of Josh Gibson's name. He was once one of Josh's kids at the North Side Y, and 2008 was his seventh year as assistant superintendant of the very place that once refused to give his mentor a teaching job. "We are all proud of Bob, but without Josh I am not here. I don't survive. Neither does Bob nor any of the other thousands of kids that Josh took the time to coach. No one loved baseball more than Josh Gibson and no one teaches it anymore like he used to. He used a proper batting stance to teach you how to stand up to life. He was truly a mastermind."

At 10:00 a.m. on Wednesday morning, eight hours before Stanford's elimination game against Miami, another mastermind, Cardinal head coach Mark Marquess marched into Room 4034 of the Omaha Hilton.

He shook hands with the ESPN on-air team of play-by-play man Mike Patrick, color analyst Orel Hershiser, and sideline/dugout reporter (or as *Monday Night Football*'s Mike Tirico calls her, "ESPN's It Girl") Erin Andrews. Producer Scott Matthews, a three-year CWS veteran, offered the coach some coffee before their pregame production meeting, but Marquess held up the gigantic Starbucks cup in his hand. "Thanks, but I'm already on number three."

The coach had no idea what time these people had gotten out of bed, but he knew that it was well after he did. It'd been that way his entire sixty-one years. Early to bed . . . you know the rest. Growing up in

Stockton, California, Marquess was never big enough or strong enough to athletically overpower his way to wins, so he decided at a young age that he would simply outwork his competition. *If you don't want to work hard, don't waste my time.* Measuring five-foot-ten (maybe) he played baseball and football at Stagg High School and would have been more serious about basketball, but his dedication to the other two sports wouldn't allow it.

At Stagg, his life was forever altered by the influence of football coach Bill Gott. Coach Gott was demanding and his regimen was structured, but like Josh Gibson, he ultimately cared more about the kind of men he was creating than the number of points they scored.

"It's sad that when you say something like that, today's cynical world reacts like, 'yeah, okay, rah rah,' but it's the truth," Marquess said as he polished off the last drop of that third cup, sounding more than a little like Josh Gibson disciple Jerry Bartee. "If Coach Gott hadn't demonstrated that approach to me when I was fifteen, sixteen years old, then we aren't here today talking in Omaha, Nebraska. That's a fact."

The man known around Stanford as simply "9" excelled at both football and baseball on the campus they call The Farm. He was awarded a football scholarship by head coach John Ralston, who promised the kid that he could play baseball in the spring. His gridiron career began as a knockout safety, then he moved to quarterback before wisely relinquishing that job to future Heisman Trophy winner Jim Plunkett, who tossed passes to his newly assigned split end, Mark Marquess. There he was introduced to another major influence, fellow diminutive coach and eventual Super Bowl winner Dick Vermeil.

As great as Marquess's gridiron exploits were, his baseball career was even better. He started at first base for three seasons, earning All-American honors in both his junior and senior years. He hit .404 in 1967 (a number the assistant coaches like to dangle over the players when they think their head coach doesn't know what he's talking about), leading the Cardinal to their second ever College World Series appearance and making the All-Tournament team. Their next trip to Omaha would come in 1982, his sixth as head coach.

"You think about all the people that have come through there and

Coach Marquess is the one constant." As John Elway said it, he did a quick rundown of all the great Cardinal coaches and players, from Bill Walsh and Tara VanDerveer to Tiger Woods and Tom Watson. In 1981, Elway helped Stanford return to the NCAA postseason for the first time in more than a decade. He was also a pretty good football player. But the two-time Super Bowl champ is quick to point out that Marquess did the two-sport double long before he did. "There's not one of those athletes or coaches that didn't want to at least go down and talk to him. Even if they were a little intimidated. Okay, a lot intimidated."

Marquess is a Stanford man to his core, the strongest, most durable pillar of what has long been held up as the gold standard for everything that is right about college sports. The year 2008 marked his thirty-second at the end of the Cardinal bench, his thirty-seventh including his five seasons as an assistant. Dean Stotz, his associate head coach, had been at his side ever since he took over as head coach, the perfect buffer between his hyperintense boss and their hypersensitive young players. Assistant coach Dave Nakama was with the team for his ninth campaign while pitching coach Jeff Austin was back on The Farm after winning the 1998 National Player of the Year Award and three years in and out of the big leagues.

The Mastermind and his staff were rare bedrocks of stability in the quicksand world of college sports, stability that has resulted in two CWS titles, a dozen Pac-10 championships, and nearly seventy big-league players. Monday's game against Georgia was Marquess's 2,000th as Stanford head coach. He'd won 1,325. College baseball had moved from hit-and-run to Gorilla Ball to somewhere in between. It had grown from being totally invisible to being nationally televised. Through it all, Marquess had managed to keep winning by constantly adapting to the playing style of the times, even if his buttonless polyester pullover jerseys had not.

"I get asked all the time when am I going to get rid of the 1970s uniforms. We'll get rid of the '70s uniforms when we get rid of the '70s coach."

With the old school unis came an old-school approach. Everything, *everything*, happened according to plan. Midweek practices were scheduled to the minute and pregame warm-ups were an unparalleled, well-scripted baseball ballet. Seeing his 2008 team go through batting and infield practice was no different than watching his '98 team, '88 team, or '78 team.

In the hour before Game Nine that approach was on display for the world to see. As it was all season every season, pregame was a lesson in system and symmetry. Marquess himself threw BP, a rubber-armed spectacle of nothing but strikes cranked out in perfect 1-2-3-4 rhythm. When he had to grab a new ball out of the bucket, that dance became a seven-step maneuver. Players split into groups of six, and took four turns each in the batting cage, three rounds of six pitches and one bam-bam round of two pitches.

Each hitter banged the lead donut off his bat, took his whacks at six pitches, then slipped the round weight back on and waited for his next turn. Donut off, six swings, donut on, donut off, two swings, you're done.

The assistants slapped balls off their wooden fungo bats to each side of the infield, Coach Stotz to the right, Coach Nakama to the left, and each assistant was assigned an off-day pitcher to retrieve incoming balls.

To the hitters, 9 shouted two-word commands over the blaring sound system, nodding his approval when they got it right, shaking his head when they got it wrong, and never, ever smiling.

"Go right."

"Back to me."

"Hands up."

"There you go."

"We played down at Texas earlier this year," Stanford pitcher Erik Davis telling the story as he soft-tossed with a teammate. "They made this big deal out of the coach down there and all his wins and how he had been there ten years. I was sitting on the bench and I said to the guys, 'Do you realize Coach has been here thirty-two years?' We all just started laughing. It's unbelievable to think about. And I don't think he's slowing down any time soon."

For decades, coaches from around the nation have migrated to Omaha even when their team hasn't qualified, merely hoping for a chance to rub elbows and perhaps absorb a little baseball knowledge from the living legends. The American Baseball Coaches Association holds its official annual meeting each January, an anthill of activity and ass kissing. But it is Series Week in Omaha where the most shameless résumé swapping takes place, as staffs are already shuffling and reshuffling before the summer recruiting season officially begins on July 1. What's more, a pair of very large national youth tournaments is usually occupying every diamond on both sides of the Missouri River for the two weeks, every team led by ambitious young coaches eager to become the next Mastermind.

Before and during every Series game the yellow seats behind The Blatt's home plate are constantly filled with coaches from big universities and tiny colleges you've never heard of, ID'ed by the logos embroidered on their shirts and hats. They stay locked in on the demigods of the diamond, anxious to mimic everything from pregame practice drills to a coach's trot as he runs out to argue an umpire's call. As Mark Marquess threw batting practice, the yellow seats were standing room only. "God almighty," one young coach said to another, his eyes never breaking contact with the mound. "I've sat here and counted 602 pitches and Marquess has thrown 600 strikes."

Every sport has its pantheon of legendary coaches and college baseball is no different, though its biggest names tend to be big only among the most hard-core college baseball fans and, of course, other coaches. The "coach down there" at Texas that Erik Davis had referred to was Augie Garrido, former head coach at Cal State Fullerton and a longtime friendly rival to Marquess and Stanford.

Garrido topped most greatest-ever lists, having won four CWS titles across four decades at Fullerton (1979, '84, '95) and Texas ('05). As of 2008, he was also the all-time leader in wins with 1,668. LSU's Skip Bertman is also in everyone's top ten, as is Fraser, Gene Stephenson, who won the '89 College World Series with Wichita State, Jerry Kindall of Arizona, Bobby Winkles and Jim Brock of Arizona State, and the Texas two-step of Bibb Falk and Cliff Gustafson, who built the Texas Longhorn program that Garrido inherited.

Each legendary coach has his own family tree of former assistants, players, and devotees. Down south there are the Fraser Fanatics, which produced Bertman and Ron Polk, who begat, among others, LSU's Paul Mainieri and

Georgia's Dave Perno. In the southwest is the Church of Stephenson. Out west, there are the Apostles of Augie and the Disciples of Dedeaux.

Rod Dedeaux was an assistant on the 1948 Trojan team that denied George H. W. Bush and Yale a chance to avenge their loss to Cal in '47. In forty-four seasons as a head coach he produced ten CWS titles and more than 250 professional players, from Tom Seaver to Randy Johnson to Mark McGwire. From his retirement in 1987 until his death in 2006 at the age of ninety-two, he returned to Rosenblatt Stadium every summer, moving through the crowd like the Pope while leaning on a cane fashioned from a baseball bat, autographed by dozens of former players. In 2001, he and Bertman sat together for the opening game, their greeting handshake sounding like two trains colliding as all their championship rings clacked together.

"Here at North Carolina they love to connect the generations of basketball coaches," UNC coach Mike Fox illustrated through comparison, pointing to his Chapel Hill coworker Roy Williams, who served as assistant under Dean Smith, who played for Kansas coach Phog Allen, who played for Dr. James Naismith, the man who invented basketball. "College baseball is the same. Everyone is connected to everyone else. You played or coached with a guy who played or coached with another guy. Two coaches will sit and talk for an hour just to figure out how they're connected."

But as stakes have risen, friendly interaction has faded. A head coach is so busy running the business of a team on the road that the days of grabbing dinner with an old buddy in Omaha are all but extinct.

As in basketball, their fiercest competition is away from games. They attend the same high school camps to scout the same potential recruits. During more genteel times, they tipped one another off on hot prospects and undiscovered gems. But camaraderie has eroded in the name of finding an edge, even if it means throwing a friend or a mentor under the bus.

Southern coaches try to lure California hitters by saying that West Coast hit-and-run baseball will take the bat out of their hands. West Coast coaches try to coax southwestern pitchers to the Pacific by pointing to the inflated offensive numbers of the Gulf Coast.

They tell impressionable high school kids that young coaches like Mike Batesole and Dave Perno are too inexperienced and guys like Mark Marquess and Mike Martin are too old and out of touch. They tell tales of other head coaches screwing over loyal assistants (*You don't want your son to play for a guy like that, do you?*) and of former coworkers who just don't know what the hell they are doing (*Trust me, I coached with so-and-so at State U. and all the pro scouts hate him, so they'll never come to see you play*).

"It's sad," one coach said while telling a tale of a former assistant who had spread false rumors about his failing health. "But that's just how it is now."

Every program begins recruiting season with a national grid of a wish list, but in the end most schools are forced to focus solely on their regions due to budget constraints (a big football program will spend more than a million dollars annually on recruiting; the biggest baseball programs are lucky to get a tenth of that), lack of manpower, and time-sapping administrative duties.

"I don't think people realize how difficult it is to put together a college baseball team," Coach Perno explained while sitting in his "War Room" above the University of Georgia's basketball arena in Athens. His football friends down the road have a row of offices dedicated solely to recruiting, with a full staff and a massive budget that allows them to comb every corner of the continent for the strongest and fastest athletes to fill their eighty-five scholarships.

Perno, like every other NCAA Division I baseball coach, goes shopping with 11.7 full rides—not 11, not 12, but 11.7. He puts together his shopping list in a conference space smaller than a cheap motel room, with two assistant coaches and some marker boards. There are file cabinets, Post-its, and maps all over the place. On one table are two loosely arranged stacks of papers—one containing hundreds of e-mails from high-school coaches, overeager fathers, and pro scouts, the other all the signing bonuses paid out by pro teams during the last five MLB drafts.

"We essentially recruit the same kid three times. We compete with professional baseball for kids during their junior and senior year in high school. Officially, the pros can't touch them in their junior year, so that's when we have to go after them. They commit to come to Georgia, but then they get drafted the summer after their senior year and I don't know if they are coming to school or signing with a big-league team, and the deadline to make that decision is the first week of school. Once they go to class, I have them. But until then, they can go pro at any minute. Then, at the end of their junior year, we do it all over again. Is my number-one pitcher leaving because the Yankees drafted him in the tenth round and are offering him $200,000? Or is he coming back to Athens because he wants to win the national championship and hopefully get drafted just as high at the end of his senior year?

"People think my main recruiting competitors are Georgia Tech, LSU, Florida State, people like that. But I'm also racing against the Boston Red Sox and the Atlanta Braves."

The biggest weapon college baseball has against the bottomless pockets of the big leagues is education. The promise is simple: Come play ball, you'll probably be drafted anyway, and you can work toward your college degree in the meantime. (MLB teams counter with college money to use after a player's tenure is over, but those offers often come with short expiration dates and a player's outdated high-school transcript keeps him from getting into the school he once passed up.)

When it comes to education, no one is carrying a bigger stick into the recruiting street fight than Mark Marquess. Stanford will always be Stanford, and for every Tiger and Elway, there is a Sandra Day O'Connor and a John Steinbeck.

It's a helluva sales pitch.

"Everybody's going to the Major Leagues, right?" As the Cardinal skipper said it, he sat up straight to emphasize his point. "How many players have I coached in thirty-two years? I've got maybe five guys who have made a living playing professional baseball. I'm talking about they went to the big leagues and when they were done they'll never have to work again. Five guys! Nearly everyone I coach will get drafted or will sign as a free agent, but only one or two will make a living at it. All these nineteen-year-olds, when I give that speech, they all look around like, 'Well, I feel sorry for these other guys because I'll be one of the five,' but you have to have that degree to survive after baseball. And if you're going to have a college diploma, Stanford's a pretty good one to have."

Drew Storen was a fireball-throwing All-American high-school pitcher at Brownsburg High School in Indiana. His lifelong love of the game came via his gene pool, compliments of his father Mark Patrick, longtime Indi-anapolis sportscaster and host of *Baseball This Morning*, the anchor program of XM Satellite Radio's Major League Baseball channel. His junior year he was 10–1 with 114 strikeouts in seventy-one innings pitched, popping up as a high school All-American in *Collegiate Baseball*, a publication consumed by the logoed residents of The Blatt's yellow seats as if it were water.

The race to sign Storen was on.

Letters flooded in from around the nation and during summer camps his family was constantly surrounded by pro scouts and college assistants. Patrick and Storen visited more than a dozen schools, making a southeast-ern swing through Clemson, Auburn, and Kentucky, among others. Out west, Southern Cal viewed Storen as a key to finally recapturing the glory of Rod Dedeaux's days of winning ten CWS championships.

Then Stanford called.

When Drew and Mark finally made it out for their official visit, they got off the plane expecting the usual drill. They'd drive to campus, get a facilities tour from one of the assistants, and then be ushered in to meet the head coach as if he were a priest waiting to hear their confession. One SEC head coach hadn't even bothered to take his feet down off the desk, flipping channels with his TV remote while Storen asked questions. On The Farm they expected more of the same.

What they hadn't expected was the tornado known as 9.

Coach Marquess called and said he was on the way to pick them up at the airport. No need, Coach, we have a rental car. "Okay," he said, "I'll pick you up at the hotel in the morning." When they arrived on campus, the coach rarely, if ever, talked about himself, despite a résumé built for bragging. Instead, he asked Drew about Drew. They spent the entire day together, including a visit with the head of the mechanical engineering department, where Marquess asked more questions of the professor than anyone else. At one point he turned to Storen and said, "Gee whiz, Drew, this is amazing stuff, isn't it?"

Unbeknownst to Storen and Patrick, visiting with the academics was a regular part of 9's routine. Marquess had long operated his program with the assumption that his players would be around only three years and then be drafted as a junior. So he and the academic office devised a "one extra class per quarter" strategy that ensures student-athletes will be only a few credits shy of graduation when they leave, making it more tempting to come back and finish up. Year after year, former Cardinal players do just that. More often than not, they do it because they don't want to let 9 down.

"There's just something about him," Stanford-turned-Yankees ace Mike Mussina explained. "He might drive you crazy with all his rules, but when you leave you realize how much you want to do well for him. My last year of college was almost twenty years ago and I still talk to Coach when I can."

When's the last time you talked to him?

"An hour ago."

Moose isn't the only one. Those who know describe the long-lasting relationships as college baseball's version of North Carolina basketball or Notre Dame football. Players graduate, but never leave. Former players constantly call, drop by, and schedule their years around the fall alumni game. No matter how old they get they know that the ballpark known as Sunken Diamond will still be there. And Coach Marquess and Coach Stotz will still be in the dugout.

One year after their first meeting, Marquess made his NCAA-allowed visit to Storen's home in Indiana. Everyone knew he'd be drafted out of high school and he was. The Yankees threw a six-figure signing bonus in his lap and assured him that he'd be fast-tracked through the minors to his waiting locker at Yankee Stadium.

"If we need to I can always use my secret weapon on Pam," Marquess told Patrick, referring to Drew's mother, who had gone upstairs and left the coach alone with her husband. "I ask the mom, would you rather your son meet his future wife on the Stanford campus or in some minor-league ballpark somewhere?"

In the end, the secret weapon stayed in the holster. Storen was headed to The Farm. Less than one year later, he was headed to Omaha.

At noon, four hours before the first pitch of Stanford's Game Nine matchup with Miami, Mark Marquess sat restlessly in yet another room of the Omaha Hilton, huddled around yet another table. This time his conversation was with his assistant coaches as they mapped out the game plan for Miami.

As soon as the head coach had woken up that morning, he began bugging sports information director Aaron Juarez for "his stats," any and every numerical computation concerning his team as well as the Hurricanes. In return, Juarez bugged Marquess for his starting lineup, particularly the starting pitcher. Marquess knew it was going to be freshman righty Danny Sandbrink—he'd already told ESPN, the team, and Sandbrink himself. But until he handed the lineup to Juarez to be turned in to the NCAA, it wasn't official. Which meant Jim Morris was sitting in a conference room in his hotel wondering if Stanford might make a last-second change to Erik Davis or even ace Jeremy Bleich to survive the elimination game.

"During the regular season Coach Marquess has the pitching rotation set up for the entire year," Juarez said while staring at his cell phone, waiting to see a coach's number chime in. "Once the postseason starts the rotation becomes a total mystery. Just a little friendly Omaha gamesmanship."

The coaches mapped out their defensive alignment for every batter in every situation. During the Pac-10 season, the assistants typically did advanced scouting of their familiar West Coast foes. Today, they based their strategies on what they'd seen on a DVD of ESPN's Game Five broadcast. "Nobody knows Miami better than Florida State," Coach Stotz explained with a wink. "Instead of charting that game we let their coach, Mike Martin, do it for us."

As controlling as they may have seemed, the staff of admitted control freaks always took a conscious step back when they came to Omaha. They'd been playing ball since February 22. Today's game would be their sixty-sixth of the year. The time for big movements was long gone. They worried less about the opponent, more about themselves, and most important, they let their players play.

"Early in the year I might grab a player before an at-bat and go over some very specific things with him," Marquess explained. "But by now he knows what he's doing. The last thing I want to do is scream 'lay off the high fastball!' as he's leaving on the on-deck circle. Now he's going to go up there and swing at it. That's the perfect way to ruin a nineteen-year-old mind."

They agreed on four keys to beating Miami:

1. Get four innings from Sandbrink, four from Davis, one from Storen.
2. Take advantage of Sandbrink's great move to first and Castro's even better move to second to shut down Miami's lightning-fast first two hitters, Blake Tekotte and Jemile Weeks.
3. Don't let Yonder Alonso beat them at the plate.
4. Score early and often, and commit no errors.

Marquess was still visibly irritated about the Game Six loss to Georgia, when his hitters stranded six runners, walked five, and blew a 3–0 lead. Heck, he was still irritated about the 2001 CWS championship game, when outfielder Carlos Quentin lost a can of corn in the high Omaha sun, the ball bouncing off the ground and opening up a four-run third inning. Miami won the title, 12–1. One year earlier, Stanford blew a three-run lead in the title game, handing LSU its fifth CWS championship.

"No one likes to lose," said assistant coach Dean Stotz. "But Coach *really* doesn't like to lose."

In 1993, Marquess took his team to Cal State Fullerton to face Augie Garrido's Titans in a huge early-season three-game series. They won the first but dropped the last two with some sloppy early-season play. When the team boarded the bus for home, Marquess merely took his seat at the front of the bus and let the heat waves come off the top of his head. Too pissed to eat, he instructed the bus driver not to stop until he needed gas. Four hours later they stopped and Coach stood.

"You have ten minutes."

Thirty miles past the stop, the players realized someone was missing. "Oh hell," they whispered, "Jimmy Noriega missed the bus." Someone, probably a freshman, was sent up front to tell 9. They turned around to pick Noriega up, but the glare that was unleashed on the rows of that bus was radioactive.

"It was rare that Coach Marquess ever actually exploded," recalled

ESPN's Kyle Peterson, who joined the team as a starting pitcher two years later. "He never really yelled or screamed and I've never heard him use a swear word. But the fear of what it would be like when he finally did explode kept us in line."

As it was in Peterson's day, as it has been since 1977, all Stanford players are clean-shaven, wear ties on the road, and take their hats off indoors. Curfew is always exactly two hours after the team returns to the hotel and bed check is always performed by 9.

"Mark is just right of Attila the Hun," Skip Bertman said, his laugh booming through The Blatt's concrete concourse as he scribbled out a couple of autographs. "But there's two ways to run a ship as tight as Stanford's. You can either do it in a manner that makes your kids love you for making them better men, or you can go bark and yell and carry on, and make everyone hate you. No one hates Mark."

In other words, had Bobby Knight made a conscious decision not to be an asshole then he could have been Mark Marquess.

As Bertman walked away, he stopped and added one more comment. "I have seen the Bus Glare, by the way. Ask him about the Japanese meat incident."

In 1987 and '88, the same years as Stanford's back-to-back CWS titles, Marquess served as head coach of the U.S. Olympic Baseball team. He wisely chose Bertman as an assistant coach. Strapped for cash, they barnstormed nineteen countries in three months, sharing cargo planes with cattle and sheep.

The last stop before Seoul was Japan, where the team found itself stuck in downtown Tokyo traffic, sleep deprived, and forced to survive on boxed lunches containing what former Stanford slugger Ed Sprague described as "some sort of meat covered in some sort of sauce, we think it might have been a pork chop." Hot, tired, and a hemisphere from home, the Olympians were disgusted by the mystery meat. That's when a police car pulled them over and an officer began chattering at Marquess through an interpreter.

Something about . . . a window . . . a car beside the bus . . . a lady . . . and ketchup . . . ?

The Stanford Man, the All-American, the owner of a master's degree in political science, The Mastermind, stepped back onto the bus, digging out the Bus Glare to speak the following words:

"All right, who threw their meat out the window?"

Silence.

"Who . . . threw their meat . . . out *the window* . . . and onto this *woman's dress?!*"

More silence.

"This bus is not moving until I have *an answer!*"

Future big-league stars Ben McDonald of LSU, Robin Ventura of Oklahoma State, and Jim Abbott of Michigan all pleaded ignorance. Even his own Stanford players, Sprague and Doug Robbins, held their ground until the swarming traffic forced the bus to move on.

"*Fine.*"

Three weeks later, Team USA defeated Japan on the arm of one-handed pitcher Abbott to win the gold. Their medals around their necks, the squad sat in exhausted silence as they rode back to the Olympic Village. Then Ventura jumped up and pointed to a University of New Orleans outfielder sitting across the aisle.

"Ted Wood did it! Ted Wood threw the meat!"

Up front, the Bus Glare was gone, replaced with the laughter of Mark Marquess.

One hour before game time, Marquess took a seat at the far end of the dugout and flicked open his briefcase. The black hard-shell bag looked as if it had been dragged up and down Tenth Street behind the team bus, but to The Mastermind it was more important than even the bats and balls. For a man who doesn't do e-mail, it is an external hard drive for his brain.

Of all of Coach Mark's rules, perhaps the most important was the one that dared not be spoken. "Do not," Dean Stotz said, the longtime assistant clearing his throat for emphasis, "I repeat, *do not* touch the briefcase."

Earlier in the year, Marquess told Aaron Juarez to grab the lineup from his briefcase. As the baseball newbie reached out to grab the card from one of the pockets, Stotz, a dead ringer for Hollywood go-to mafia actor Paul Sorvino, leapt across the dugout to stop him. Even with permission it just didn't feel right.

The Mastermind rummaged through the carefully selected contents: pens, a box of pencils, sunglasses, ChapStick, stopwatch, calculator, two clipboards, a white towel ("I hold it when I am shifting my outfielders. It makes it easier for them to see me"), and the most important item of them all, a roll of white athletic tape. The entire team, it seemed, was obsessed with white tape. They'd fashioned an impromptu lucky charm out of cups and white tape, and during the first round of the NCAAs they created the Voodoo Bat, which they plastered to the dugout wall with, of course, white tape.

From the pockets of his briefcase, Marquess carefully removed his precious charts, the ones that the coaches had prepared earlier in the day. He looked them over one more time . . . then another . . . and another. Using the white tape, he affixed the charts to the dugout wall, the pattern always the same. Team stats stacked two high on the left side, the opposing team's roster and lineup across the top, defensive charts across the bottom.

If these charts worked and Stanford won, they would be placed back into the briefcase just as carefully as they'd been removed. If they led to a loss, like the ones he'd used in Game Six, then he'd rip them off the wall, shred them into tiny pieces, and carry them back to the hotel to throw away.

"The handwritten notes were always everywhere." Catcher A. J. Hinch was a three-time first team All-American catcher from 1994–96. "They could be about anything. He's an information maniac. But he won't touch a computer. Go figure."

For the last twenty-one years, he hadn't needed a computer. He had Kathy Wolff.

Wolff's official title was administrative associate. In reality, she was the team mom. Every time the Cardinal hit the road for a game, she was the literal image of the mother standing at the door, making sure everyone's jackets were zipped and they had their lunch money.

In the Stanford directory, her phone number and her e-mail address were the same as Marquess's. That was no accident. He didn't know how to send an e-mail or check his voice mail. He didn't want to know. And as long as Wolff was stationed outside his office he didn't need to know. She booked travel, kept the schedule, and knew how to translate his manic note-scribbling and schedule-making into a digestible form for the outside world.

When 9 summoned a player to his office then that was bad news for the player. But the last person they saw before they went into The Mastermind's lair and the first person they saw when they came out was Kathy Wolff, who quickly restored their ashen faces with an assuring smile.

"When you call back to Stanford, you don't talk to Coach Marquess," Mussina said. "You talked to Kathy. And she knew everything that was going on with you. My kids' names, their birthdays, what grade they're in. She knew if I had won a game the night before or if I'd lost. And if you asked about any player, even a walk-on from twenty years ago who never pitched an inning, she could tell you where they were and what they were doing."

On Tuesday evening, June 10, Kathy Wolff finally had taken care of all of the travel arrangements to Omaha. It had been a wild forty-eight hours since Stanford had clinched their seventeenth CWS trip by winning at Fullerton. She celebrated with the crowd at "her ballpark" and then walked back to the office to get to work. She synced up with the folks in Nebraska, got the rooms at the Hilton, and manned the phones as alums and boosters started calling for tickets.

We have no idea what Kathy Wolff did before she went to bed that night. Perhaps she thought about her boys, about Jason Castro's bases-clearing double that put the Titans away. Maybe she thought about Drew Storen, the fresh-faced wannabe product designer who locked up the win. Then again, she was probably preparing herself to reign in 9 the next morning. She knew he wasn't going to be happy with the flight. He liked to get into town as early as possible, but the best she could do was get them in during the evening. Oh well, she could handle him. She always did.

We have no idea what Kathy Wolff did before she went to bed on the eve of her eleventh trip to Rosenblatt Stadium. What we do know is that she never woke up.

Panic set in around the athletic department offices by midmorning. People were calling with questions that only Kathy could answer. But she never came to work. When someone finally went to her home, they found her peacefully gone.

Tom and Gloria Davis were driving across the Utah Salt Flats en route to Omaha when their son Erik called. He was sobbing as he broke the news to his parents and soon they were crying with him. Two years earlier, Erik was hit in the face by a line drive while pitching in the Cape Cod League. His face was smashed and doctors were initially concerned that he might lose use of one eye. Through the two surgeries it was Kathy who had been in constant contact, asking what the school could do, but more to the point, what she could do. It was Kathy who first greeted Erik back to campus with a hug and it was Kathy who stood and cheered at Sunken Diamond when he hit the field for fall practice.

The bad news outraced the team to Omaha, where equipment manager Gary Hazelitt scrambled to have "KW" patches made, which he and Matty Ritson sewed onto those classic pullover jerseys.

Game Nine was played on a Wednesday, exactly one week after Kathy's death. When asked about it that morning in the hotel lobby, 9 looked at the floor and shifted his jaw to one side as if he'd been slapped. "You know, it doesn't seem real. When I get back to the office and she's not there, it will become real. Until then, I just . . . I don't know. I don't know how I'm going to do this without her. I don't know how any of us are. Right now we are standing in a hotel and riding on a bus and eating meals that she took care of. I honestly just can't think about it."

Finally, at 6:00 P.M., Game Nine had arrived.

Right on cue, Marquess took off running in what had become the symbol of his new, easier-going approach. A seemingly simple little drill that bowled over former players as if he'd hit them with a pillow. Kyle Peterson didn't believe the stories until he saw it himself. "Have you seen him do this new thing where he runs the length of the field and jumps into the arms of the team? He would have never, never, ever done that when I was playing there ten years ago." Then he added sarcastically, "I hope he's not getting soft."

The only running 9 ever did with his previous teams was during punishment laps. Embarrassing road loss? Hit the field, we're running. Blew off a Western Civ midterm? Let's go, we're running. Playing poker in your hotel room instead of studying during a preseason exhibition tour? We're running. In Taiwan. In the rain. He always ran with them, just to show that he could.

Game Nine had started with a running leap into the waiting arms of outfielder Jeff Whitlow. Once the first pitch was thrown, Coach was running again. Up and down the length of the dugout.

"You get used to the pacing after a while," explained "Black" Jack Mc-Dowell, ace of the '87 CWS-winning staff and the 1993 Cy Young Award winner for the Chicago White Sox. "At first you're like, what the hell is he doing? It never stops. One end to the other, checking his charts, talking to players as he goes by, then checking his charts again."

During the Game Six loss to Georgia, the Mark Marquess Show was in plain view of the Rosenblatt press box as he went up and down in front of the first-base bench, fifteen steps up and fifteen back. It was four steps from the railing at the top step of the dugout back to his charts on the wall. In the bottom of the sixth, Bulldog left fielder Lyle Allen locked horns with Cardinal pitcher Austin Yount for an epic thirteen-pitch at-bat, lasting seven minutes, during which Marquess was unofficially scored with eight chart checks, twelve up-and-back walks of the entire length of the dugout, ten half-dugout walks, twelve leans on the railing, and he put his pen in and out of his mouth five times. The only time he came to a complete stop was when Yount struck Allen out with a shoulder-high heater.

His total number of steps walked during the at-bat: 540.

"Believe it or not, he's actually slowed down." Ed Sprague, now the head coach at Pacific University, first noticed it when his Tigers visited Sunken Diamond earlier in the 2008 season. "He actually sits down on the bucket every couple of innings. It might not last but a few seconds, but it's more than he ever did before."

Across the field, Miami head coach Jim Morris was in his usual anti-Marquess routine of sitting on the bench with his notebooks in hand. Never one for pacing, he certainly didn't feel like it on this night, suddenly stricken by some sort of stomach bug.

In the first inning, The Program manufactured a West Coast–style run, validating The Mastermind's fears about their running game. Center fielder

Blake Tekotte—speed threat number one—singled and stole second. Then Jemile Weeks—speed threat number two—reached first on a bunt base hit and also stole second. One sacrifice fly later, the score was Miami 1, Stanford 0.

Weeks put a charge into the crowd and, thanks to a little work by his father, that energy traveled all the way home to Altamonte Spring, Florida. That's where his seventy-three-year-old grandfather had the game tuned in on ESPN, but couldn't see it. As a young man, Victor Weeks roamed the outfield and dug into the batters boxes of the Negro Leagues as a member of the Newark Eagles during the 1940s. Thirty years later, the eyes that had looked in fly balls and tracked fastballs began to darken. Eventually, the glaucoma left him so blinded he could only make out the darkest shadows and brightest lights. But thanks to his son Richard, Jemile's father and a former college outfielder at Rutgers and Stetson, Victor never missed a pitch of Jemile's career, delivered via cell phone by his very own personal play-by-play commentary.

"I don't know how we're going to do it when Jemile makes it to Oakland," Dad said as he sat with Victor on the other line, referring to his son's recent drafting by the A's. "Bob Uecker tells us what (older son and Brewer outfielder) Rickie is doing in Milwaukee. I don't know who does play-by-play for Oakland, but he's going to have a very important job to do."

By the third inning, the four-step plan to beating Miami was threatening to burn holes in the soles of 9's cleats. Starter Danny Sandbrink struck out slugger Yonder Alonso with two men on, but hadn't been able to slow the running game as the Stanford coaches had hoped. What's more, the Cardinal batters were hitting Miami pitcher Enrique Garcia hard, but had nothing to show for it, having already left five runners on base.

When Blake Tekotte walked on five pitches to start the third, Marquess signaled for pitcher Erik Davis to get up in the pen. The good news was that Sandbrink had thrown Jemile Weeks out by inches on another bunt attempt. The bad news was that Alonso was back up with Tekotte on second . . . wait . . . make that third after a wild pitch. Wait again . . . Sandbrink struck out Alonso and Mark Sobolewski to end the inning.

Whew.

Pace, worry, clap, shout, pace some more. Mark Marquess was exhausting just to watch.

As the team ran back to the dugout, The Mastermind was waiting for them. He had looked over at the Miami dugout and seen the drooped shoulders. He saw Alonso throw his helmet after the strikeout, his second K of the day. The big guy had driven in only one run in three CWS games and the pressure to perform had become visible. Steps 1 through 3 of the How to Beat Miami plan were coming together. Now was the time to fix step 4.

"Guys," 9 shouted in the corner of the dugout. "We're hitting this guy. Now it's time to actually turn those drives into hits. They're worried. You can feel it. The top of the order is up. Be aggressive and we can get them on the run."

Be aggressive.

Leadoff man and second baseman Cord Phelps started the third inning by smacking the third pitch he saw into the gap for a double.

Be aggressive.

Left fielder Joey August smacked the first pitch from Garcia to center for a single.

Be aggressive.

Catcher Jason Castro singled in Phelps and moved August to second. When designated hitter Randy Molina drove a fast-moving fly ball into deep left, Marquess jumped to the top step of the dugout and shouted "Go!" matching Dean Stotz and his identical scream from the third-base coach's box. August hit the dirt face-first, reaching around the tag from catcher Tommy Grandal to score. Cardinal 2, Canes 1.

From there, the How to Beat Miami plan went into full effect.

Danny Sandbrink went four innings, followed by Davis for four and Drew Storen for one. Check. Tekotte and Weeks each stole a base, but scored just one run between them. Check. The team scored at least one run in four different innings, Cord Phelps had nearly hit for the cycle, and Stanford finished with zero errors. Check. Yonder Alonso went 2-for-5 at the plate, but struck out three times in crucial situations and drove in no runs. Check.

Your Game Nine final score: Stanford 8, Miami 3.

And that, ladies and gentlemen, is how you beat The Program, just like

The Mastermind and his inner circle planned it. As their team headed into the clubhouse, Coach Marquess chatted up Coach Stotz, carefully pulling his charts off the green wall and placing them back into the briefcase. These weren't going to be torn up. They'd worked just fine, thank you. Now it was time to start writing up some new charts on Georgia.

"Aaron! Do you have my stats?"

During Miami's half of the postgame press conference in the Hall of Fame Room, Yonder Alonso said next to nothing. Through red eyes he stared at the microphone six inches from his face, unsuccessfully fighting off tears.

As the media asked their questions, his mind was a thousand miles away, thinking about his father Luis. About how Luis Alonso had risked his life, had sacrificed his career, so that his children could come to America. Yonder's father was once a national hero, a player and a coach for the Havana Industriales, Cuba's New York Yankees. Now he was cleaning offices in South Florida, a job that had forced him back home after the weekend, and now Luis had missed his son's last game as a Hurricane.

"Not a day goes by that I don't think about what he gave up so that I could have a better life," Yonder said as he walked to the team bus for the final time, amid spontaneous applause from the tailgating citizens of Omaha. "I really wanted to take that trophy back home to him."

Luis Alonso had missed Game Nine and so had Bob Gibson. There'd been talk that he was going to be in attendance, but it turned out to be just a rumor. Gibby didn't come to The Blatt much anymore. Hell, he didn't come to anything much anymore. After retiring from baseball he moved back to Omaha, buying a house in Bellevue just a few blocks away from Roddy Field.

He invested in some local business, a radio station, a restaurant, and even helped start a local bank with some assistance from Warren Buffett. Gibby divorced, remarried, and for a while hosted a highly successful charity golf tournament, but shut it down in 2004. After that he could be found in the old wooden grandstand at Bellevue East, where son Chris was a Chieftain before signing a minor-league deal with—who else?—the St. Louis Cardinals in 2008.

Gibson made an appearance at the 2000 College World Series, per the request of CWS of Omaha, Inc. Other than that, if he'd been back to The Blatt no one remembered it, though he was still listed as an emeritus board member in the 2008 Series media guide.

"Nope," the same answer came back from at least a dozen different people. "I haven't seen him in a while. I think he's had his fill of the public life."

That same question was posed the night after Game Nine, to a bartender at a community cornerstone restaurant known as M's Pub, home of the most diverse wine list in Omaha. *When's the last time you saw Bob Gibson?* He leaned forward, his hands busily swabbing out a goblet, and motioned for the inquisitor to lean in for a secret.

"That's him at the end of the bar. The guy sipping on champagne. But don't bother him. He doesn't like to be bothered."

Two months later, he still didn't. On August 9, Josh Gibson was inducted into the Nebraska Black Sports Hall of Fame, but his little brother declined the invitation to attend the ceremony in North Omaha. When the emcee realized that there were no members of the family present to accept the award, Jerry Bartee stood and suggested that anyone in the room whose life had been influenced by Josh should come up and do the accepting.

"Forty people walked up on that stage," Bartee said proudly. "They wanted Josh's family to accept the award on his behalf and you know what? His family did."

SEVEN

THE END OF THE ROAD

Thursday and Friday, June 19–20
Game Ten: North Carolina vs. LSU

If the meatpackers could have seen The Neighborhood today.

After nearly a solid week of baseball, the streets that were once pounded under the hooves of livestock were still packed with slow-moving cars. Among the most repetitive classic complaints about The Blatt had always been the lack of parking. In truth, it was only a problem two weeks out of the year. The Omaha Royals, who averaged only about 4,000 fans per game, had all the parking they needed.

It's when 20,000 people showed up that it became a problem, transforming every curb, yard, and empty six-foot space into an impromptu parking lot and entrepreneurial opportunity. Every gap along Thirteenth Street was filled with homemade signs:

PARKING—$20.
CWS PARKING—$10 PER GAME.
$25—WILL NOT BLOCK IN.

Just below the crest of the hill overlooking The Blatt was the corner of Garfield and Kavan Streets, sitting within earshot of the tinks of the Nike Fieldhouse batting cage and the thumping classic rock of Starsky's Beer Garden. Below the hubbub above sat a weathered storage shed, down off the road, and at the far end of a muddy two-tiered slope of a lot. A plastic

Budweiser banner was stretched over its roof, mere garnish for the tan Port-A-John below, reading WELCOME TO VICKY'S VALLEY.

As a white Cadillac Escalade drove gingerly across the mud, Vicky herself guided it in, using two Tootsie Pops to signal as if they were airplane-marshaling beacons. "Be careful! We don't want you sliding down the hill!" Once the vehicle came to a stop, she walked to the window to collect her ten bucks and to hand the driver a wad of lollipops.

"You have to do whatever you can to get someone to park in your yard instead of someone else's," explained Vicky's daughter Nika, sitting beneath a tent on the curb and pointing to her neighbors to the north, who were coaxing customers by offering up a cool-down splash in their small inflatable pool. "Candy, cookies, public toilet, whatever it takes."

"This is the best parking bargain in The Neighborhood," Vicky added as she trudged back up the hill to join her daughter. "But it turns into a freaking mud bog when it rains like it did late last night. Want a Tootsie Pop?"

A spot directly off Thirteenth Street cost $25. Each street over represented a five-bill discount, the price dropping as the hillside rose up through Fourteenth, Fifteenth, Sixteenth, and so on until one hit the free lot five blocks away and alongside the roar of Interstate 80. The math was pretty much straight up—the farther the walk, the smaller the charge.

The residents wheeled and dealed. They sent their kids into the madness of Thirteenth Street to intercept cars before they paid twice as much as they needed to. Some even tried renting golf carts to shuttle their customers to and from Rosenblatt, but the police nixed that practice in 2006. If you were willing to be blocked in, you'd pay a little less. If you insisted on being right on the road, then you'd pay a little more. No matter what they charged, every homeowner knew precisely how many cars would fit on their lot, thanks to years of practice and carefully crafted plans of execution. One yard took a dozen, another twenty-one, and one way-too-tiny space on Fourteenth Street somehow shoehorned in forty-five vehicles on the busiest days. At the north end of Fourteenth, George Cardenas guided cars down his long side driveway while his wife gently rocked on the front-porch swing reading a book. It was all just another part of the annual routine. New Year's . . . Easter . . . Memorial Day . . . park cars.

At 3477 Fourteenth Street, cars were greeted with a homemade flag, its red, white, and blue letters proclaiming COLLEGE WORLD SERIES PARKING $15 as a machine cranked out bubbles into the street. Beneath the fence on which the machine sat was a small blue sign reading KYLE SHELTON'S MOMMY AND DADDY PARK HERE. GO HEELS.

"It's true," Linda Willis said as she stepped off the front porch with a nod to the sign. Left fielder Shelton, along with the rest of the Tarheels, was in Omaha for the third year in a row. "His dad has been parking here for years. They're regulars. It's funny how you get to be friends with the people who park in your yard. I've had a group of guys coming here every year forever. They tell me that when the games move to the new ballpark they might still drive out here just to park and have me drive them downtown. That's not a bad idea. Maybe I'll start that business. I know I'm going to miss the money."

When Terry and Linda Shelton pulled into the Willis yard for Game Ten, they knew it could be to watch their son's final game in a college uniform.

Yonder Alonso's 665th and final collegiate at-bat was a good one.

In the bottom of the ninth of Game Nine he'd crushed a big slow breaking ball to slap a double off the wall in right, missing a two-run homer by only a few feet. But his college career ended stranded on second base, helplessly watching as Storen relieved Davis and put his teammates away 1–2–3 in nine pitches.

Alonso's sadness was eventually eased by the fact that his playing career was just beginning. He could finally start thinking about that Cuban-style celebration in Cincinnati. The one that Coach Morris had asked him to put on the back burner.

But, as The Mastermind is so fond of pointing out, players like Alonso are the exception, not the rule. With every final out of every elimination game of the College World Series, playing careers end. Every year a handful of seniors sit in their Omaha hotel rooms until morning, refusing to take off their uniform. Since they were children they have always had a game to go play in somewhere. Tee ball. T-shirt League. Little League. Junior Varsity. Varsity. American Legion. Fall ball. College ball.

Then, with one cruel pitch, it ends. And the pain of that finality is a sensation that can make a player forget all the good times in an instant.

In 1978, senior second baseman Mike Fox led his beloved Tarheels to Omaha with a steady yet unspectacular .277 batting average. He doesn't remember much about the trip nor did he remember a lot about The Blatt. What he remembered was the sense of urgency that he felt while playing for his playing life. In an elimination game against St. John's, his seventh-inning three-run homer extended his baseball career one more day. (More than a decade later he received a call from an Omaha resident who'd been standing outside the stadium that day. "Coach Fox, I have your home run ball; would you like to have it?") One day later he earned another stay of execution by defeating Michigan, and earning the honor of facing Dedeaux and Southern Cal in the semifinals.

"We lost to them on a passed ball," Fox recalled two decades later. "I still remember it. We led 2–0 late and were in control. Then suddenly the game was over and we'd lost 3–2. The next day they won the national championship. I don't remember a lot about the experience of that trip. But I vividly remember the reality of taking my uniform off. The depression of it."

Fox played half a summer of independent minor league ball in Birmingham, but his career had essentially ended, like Alonso, standing out at Rosenblatt's second base. One year later another second baseman, Paul Mainieri, experienced that same sudden feeling of extinction in Starkville, Mississippi, when his University of New Orleans team was eliminated by Mississippi State in the NCAA's South Regional.

"I played two years of minor-league ball," the LSU head coach said as his team ate lunch prior to Game Ten. "But it wasn't the same. It was so, so sad when we lost that game in Starkville. At first I was like, oh man, our season is over. Then the reality set in of, wait, they're taking my uniform away."

The eight schools of the 2008 College World Series brought a total of thirty-five seniors to Omaha. About half of them were drafted. The other half would play the final out of their careers at The Blatt. For every Alonso and Posey there were always twice as many Foxes and Mainieris.

Included on the ridiculously long list of a college baseball coach's duties is psychiatrist. They help their kids deal with trouble in class, nagging girlfriends, and, when time allows, how to hit, catch, and throw. During a crucial late-season conference game one small college coach ran out to the mound when his pitcher began to look visibly stressed in the final inning. The game-winning run was on base and there was only one out.

"Are you okay?" the coach asked his trembling ace.

"Coach, I don't think I'm going to be able to graduate on time."

"Don't worry, son, we'll figure it out. But can we get these two outs first?"

Added Stanford skipper Mark Marquess: "My mother is eighty-one; she's here in Omaha. And when I get frustrated she always tells me, 'Remember, they're kids.' And that means you have to deal with the emotional swings of a kid. One of the most difficult times to deal with that is after a season-ending, or worse, a career-ending loss. Especially for those kids who grew up dreaming of wearing the uniform of their university."

Michael Hollander was one of those kids.

He was born on October 30, 1985, on the outskirts of New Orleans. Ninety miles up the road in Baton Rouge, Skip Bertman was wrapping up his third fall practice at LSU with what would become his first CWS squad. The following spring, the Tigers played to packed houses at Alex Box Stadium, a crowd that included LSU alums Mike and Shelia Hollander and little baby Michael.

Michael grew up in section L2, just down the third-base line. Seemingly every summer he sat and cheered as yet another Tiger team won its regional and headed off to Omaha. When he was eight, he went to his first LSU baseball camp and sat in Bertman's lap beneath the menacing outfield billboard listing all of the Tiger's championships. They call it The Intimidator and Hollander and Bertman posed in front of it as if the coach was Santa Claus.

One year later, Michael turned to his father in the midst of a typical rowdy night at The Box and proclaimed he would be playing on that field one day. Other kids dreamed of becoming Roger Clemens or Ken Griffey Jr. Hollander's heroes were dressed in purple and gold. Guys like Todd Walker, Andy Sheets, Lyle Mouton, and Wally Pontiff, the baseball gods of Baton Rouge.

Michael Hollander loved Wally Pontiff most of all. The Hollanders had been friends with the Pontiffs for years, and Michael and Nicholas Pontiff had been playing ball together since they were ten years old. The boys followed Wally during his career at Jesuit High School in New Orleans as he slugged his way to All-State honors and earned a scholarship to LSU. Hollander sat in L2 and watched Wally lead the team to the 2000 CWS title. Soon, Michael was making the drive across Lake Pontchartrain every day because he wanted to experience the tradition that Wally had helped build at Jesuit, and in 2002, he closed out his sophomore season with a 5A state championship.

On July 24, 2002, Wally passed away unexpectedly at his parents' home in Metairie, victim of what doctors called "heart abnormalities." His death served as a rallying cry for his team, a symbol of the hard times that were suddenly settling in atop the LSU baseball program, and as a motivator for Hollander and Nicholas. They played together in the middle infield at Jesuit and eventually both landed in Baton Rouge . . . just in time for the lean years of the Smoke Laval–to–Paul Mainieri coaching transition.

When Mainieri took over the program, among the first people he sought out was Michael Hollander. He'd tried to recruit the kid to Notre Dame, but was told politely, "Thank you, sir, but I'm going to LSU." Two years later, Mainieri was calling again, this time to tell his shortstop that he was going to be the key figure in turning around his beloved team.

"I look back on those lean years now and I was so frustrated," Hollander explained. "You feel a responsibility to the guys who came before you not to lose. But at the same time, even when we were losing I was so excited every time I went out on that field. I started at shortstop and eventually moved to third, and all I could think about was who had been out there right where I was, the guys I had watched and stood in line to get their autographs. Aaron Hill, Ryan Theriot, Mike Fontenot, Todd Walker, and Wally."

One night during a game at The Box, an old friend of Mike Hollander Senior started talking about the good old days of the Skip Bertman Era. "Hey, Mike," he asked innocently, "whatever happened to your little boy that used to be here at the games with you all the time?" Hollander merely pointed out to third base, where his son was in his defensive stance, kicking the dirt in the shadow of Section L2. His friend began to cry in disbelief.

At the end of Michael's junior year, Mainieri sat down with his leader for another talk. He wanted to discuss Hollander's plans for the draft. Said the coach, "He looked directly at me and said, 'Don't worry about me. I'm not going anywhere. I'll tell every pro scout not to even bother talking to me until all of my eligibility is used up.' He'd waited his whole life to be on this field wearing this jersey. Why cut it short?"

When LSU began its 25-and-1 run purple streak to Omaha, Hollander was the engine that kept it running. During the streak he smacked eight doubles, scored thirty-three runs, and drove in twenty-three more. He also won team honors for the best all-around student-athlete, thanks to a .297 batting average and a 3.3. grade point average—the Wally Pontiff Jr. Award.

In Hollander's final at-bat at Alex Box Stadium, every section in the ballpark, including L2, rose to give him a standing ovation.

His team also credited him with the move that started the win streak, when he discovered a box of Skip Bertman's old motivational videotapes and used them to conjure up the spirits of Bayou Bengals past. He summoned the heroes, his childhood heroes, through the magic of some grainy old VHS tapes.

"Before every game we watched two videos, the highlights of the back-to-back '96 and '97 College World Series championship teams. Those weren't even the best teams to come through LSU, but those were the 'Hold the Rope' teams. Coach Bertman said it was like climbing a mountain or a tug-of-war. If everyone holds the rope then we do it as a team. If someone lets go, then we all fall."

No player on the LSU roster had ever driven to Rosenblatt Stadium in person. They'd only seen it on those tapes. When the Tiger bus pulled up to the ballpark for that first Friday batting-practice session, Hollander felt an eerie sense of déjà vu. On those tapes, the cameraman rode with the title teams as they pulled up to The Blatt for each Series. Now, as if he was in a movie of his own life, Michael Hollander was doing it, too. When the team returned for Game Four, Hollander was the first batter of the game. The fourth pitch of his first CWS at-bat he saw he deposited over the wall for a solo home run.

"That didn't seem real. To spend your whole life wanting to play in Omaha for LSU and hit a home run? But the feeling was even better during the comeback against Rice. I was the tying run and when I crossed the plate in the bottom of the ninth and turned to watch Chris McGhee come flying in behind me, it was like . . . all right, this is how I always pictured it. This is the dream."

As the LSU Déjà Vu Special pulled into Lot A for Game Ten, it was joined by the motor coach assigned to North Carolina. Just as they did for every ride in from their way-out-west suburban hotel, the Tarheels rocked out to the beat of a bizarre little ditty known as "Mike Copeland's Carolina Baseball Rap."

For Coach Mike Fox, seeing his team loosen up was a good thing. On this third trip to Omaha he'd seen more long faces and serious looks than he would have liked. Their practices at Boys Town all week had been eerily quiet and businesslike, the loudest sounds coming from the head coach and his fungo bat, ineffectively trying to get his guys to loosen up and have some fun. But the fun stopped even for Fox when his bat broke.

"Now that's not a good omen," he said as ran his fingers over the cracked handle. "This bat had lasted all season long."

A fractured fungo was far from the worst trip that a Tarheel team had ever made to Boys Town. During Carolina's first CWS trip in 1960, head coach Walter Rabb, the man who recruited Fox as a player, decided to push his team through their wind sprints by pulling a Mark Marquess and becoming a participant. While sprinting into the lead, Rabb felt himself inspiring his team to work harder. Then he felt a hamstring snap like a rubber band and crashed to the turf, breaking his wrist. The following day, he was brought to The Blatt in an ambulance and coached his team from a stretcher, at one point jumping up and cracking his head on a bat rack. To very literally add insult to injuries, the Heels lost to eventual champion Minnesota 8–3.

Forty-eight years later and right on cue, Carolina's bus hit its parking spot outside Rosenblatt just when the "Carolina Baseball Rap" ended. And right on cue, there was Omaha resident Scott Walters, dressed in blue and ready to greet each and every Tarheel by name as they stepped off the bus. For three years he'd been there, waiting for his team. Thirteenth Street may have belonged to LSU, but this curb belonged to North Carolina. From this spot Walters had watched a group of no-name sophomores— outfielders Kyle Shelton and Seth Williams, pitchers Mike Facchinei, Tyler Trice, Rob Wooten, and third baseman Chad Flack—return year after year to become unofficial residents of his hometown, turning a basketball school into a baseball school . . . well, okay, for a few weeks a year anyway.

Flack, like his LSU hot-corner counterpart Michael Hollander, was the cornerstone of his team, the quiet leader of that magical class of North Carolina natives. This would be his unbelievable sixteenth College World Series start.

Like Hollander, Flack grew up in a house of home-state diehards. He was raised in the foothills town of Forest City, the center dot of a baseball-mad Carolina corridor. There was Shelby, home of UNC associate head coach and master recruiter Chad Holbrook, and Cherryville, hometown of teammate Tyler Trice and one of the southeast's great American Legion baseball towns. Grandfather Ray Guy, a local hero and former minor leaguer, tossed catch and talked baseball with Chad the kid's whole life.

Flack's parents Tripp and Angela both attended UNC, as did his older sister, but unlike Hollander, Flack was willing to allow his love for The Blatt to trump his love for the Heels, which is why he leaned toward signing with nearby Clemson out of high school. The Tigers had been to Omaha a dozen times. Carolina had made just four visits and only two since 1966. Fox threw down the only card he had to play, the same one he'd used to win over Flack's future teammates all over the Old North State.

"Clemson? They've got a great program. But they've been there and done that." Then the coach reminded the kid of his light-blue blood, the blood that made him despise Clemson orange his entire life. "Don't you want to be one of the guys who turned North Carolina into the next Clemson?"

Where do I sign?

Unlike Hollander, Flack's team won immediately. They won 41 of 61 games before losing two heartbreakers in the 2005 NCAA tourney, one to Florida and the other to Paul Mainieri's last Notre Dame squad. His sophomore year, they made it past the first round to earn a tough trip to Tuscaloosa, Alabama, for a best-of-three Omaha-or-bust weekend set with the Crimson Tide. When they split the first two games, Flack's Omaha dream came down to one game and one at-bat.

In the eighth, he'd blasted a three-run homer to give his team the lead. It wasn't enough. The Crimson Tide came back with a dinger of its own to retake the advantage, 7–6. With two outs in the bottom on the ninth, Flack strode to the plate with teammate Reid Fronk standing on second. Before leaving the on-deck circle, the third baseman turned back to the bench to make a quick statement: "We're not losing this game." Flack hammered the second pitch that he saw. Two-run homer. Game over. See you at The Blatt.

One year later, Flack stumbled through a brutal junior year, though Coach Fox kept showing faith by unflinchingly plugging him into the starting lineup. Unlike Hollander, he likely would have left for the pros after his junior year, but unlike Hollander his .247 batting average had soured the pro scouts, scared off by the 137-point drop-off from 2006.

But the team still won. A lot. And this time the NCAA's second round came to Chapel Hill. The opponent was border rival South Carolina and again the Omaha-or-home series came down to a third and deciding game. Again the Heels trailed late and again Flack came to the plate with a man on. No Hollywood quotes this time, but he still hammered the second pitch he saw. Two-run homer. Game over. See you at The Blatt. Again.

This third trip in 2008 had been earned without the drama and, quite frankly, without Chad Flack's bat. His hitting stroke had been elusive at best, especially in the postseason. UNC was a perfect 5–0 through the first two rounds of the NCAA Tournament, but their third baseman was hitting a paltry .125 with one RBI. Still, his Chapel Hill legacy was set. He and his classmates had indeed turned their school into Clemson. They had, in fact, displaced the Tigers and South Carolina as the premier program of the Carolinas. Flack was still the starting third baseman, but had taken a gracious, deliberate step back to let his hotter-hitting younger teammates carry the load.

In case Chad Flack had any doubts about his place in the hearts of the Heels faithful, they were erased when, like Michael Hollander at The Box, he received a standing ovation during his final home at-bat.

As the Tarheels and Tigers went through their pregame routines before Game Ten, Flack leaned against the railing of the first-base dugout and chatted with fans.

"Hey, Chad, it's about time to hit one of those home runs, isn't it?"

"That would be nice," he replied with a smile. "But right now I'd just take a hit."

Had Flack looked over his right shoulder, he would have seen the clouds rising from the eastern horizon. At first they looked light and puffy. Then they grew taller. Then darker. Then downright scary. The center-field flags laid limp, they blew north to south . . . then east to west . . . then . . . hell, they blew all over the place. This was bad.

For nearly a week The Blatt had enjoyed perfect weather conditions. Grounds-crew supervisor Jesse Cuevas had pulled out the tarp only once, protecting the infield dirt during the overnight rainstorm that came along after Game Nine to bog up Vicky's Valley.

Other than that, life had been about as easy as ten games in six days could be for Jesse and his crew. He'd started working at Rosenblatt in 1969 at the tender age of ten, walking to work from his home in The Neighborhood (which he still did forty years later) and shagging balls for long-time groundskeeper Frank Mancuso. Cuevas grew up with a rake in his hand and an ear tuned in to endless Mancuso stories. Together, Cuevas and The Blatt had witnessed or heard about more bizarre natural happenings than the Old Testament.

Omaha's inaugural Series in '50 began with temperatures of more than 100 degrees. Five years later the mercury barely made it out of the forties, prompting champion Wake Forest's slugger (and future Super Bowl half-back) Billy Ray Barnes and his teammates to hit local stores in search of new clothes while joking about burning their bats for warmth.

In the '64 Monsoon Series, rain postponed five of the fifteen games and the '68 tournament began under a tornado warning. In 1979, Omaha suffered from the same oppressive heat wave that sacked in most of the United States all summer long. Cal State Fullerton won the championship, the clinching game won by a pitcher named, of course, Dave Weatherman.

When Mother Nature decided to pick on Mancuso, Frank countered with Jesse Cuevas and his preteen pals from The Neighborhood, aka Frankie's Urchins. The kids hit the field with snow shovels to clear the base paths for an early spring game. They once scooped out and replaced all of the dirt around home plate to offset nearly three inches of early morning rain so the O Royals could play. Their mouths hung open as they heard stories of Mancuso bringing in a helicopter in 1964, to hover three feet above the pitcher's mound, its blades whomp-whomping away the wetness of a huge overnight rainstorm. Then their jaws hit the turf when he did the same again before a Major League exhibition game in '68.

"Pretty sure they wouldn't let us do that now," Cuevas said, speaking barely above a whisper while leaning against the green foam padding behind home plate, padding still saturated by the previous night's soaking. Rain, snow, ice, hail, frost, drought, bugs, goose crap—Cuevas believed he had seen it all.

"But I have no idea what the story is on this," he said as he walked out to the grass halfway between the mound and home, motioning with his hand in a slicing movement to draw an imaginary line from baseline to baseline. Almost imperceptible were sixteen footprints from roughly a size-ten shoe, running eight one way and eight back. "You can't even really see them until you get up on top of them. But they're there. Been there all week."

The question was when and how and by whom were the tracks laid down? With round-the-clock security on duty throughout the Series, no one had an explanation. But Cuevas had a theory: "It's the ghost of Frankie Mancuso. Back to check up on my work one last time."

On the day of Game Ten, as always, Cuevas spent as much time staring at the weather radar as he did at his field. Typically, bad weather rolled in from the west. But anyone who bothered to look out toward Council Bluffs knew that today wasn't going to be typical.

"None of us expected to be weathermen when we grew up," said home-plate umpire Bill Speck, making note of the cloud of dust being stirred up from the casino and shopping-mall parking lots on the other side of the Missouri. "But umpires, coaches, stadium personnel, NCAA officials, after all these years in baseball any one of us could probably teach a meteorology class by now."

When Game Ten finally started there was no rain, but there was a flood of trouble for Coach Paul Mainieri and his Tigers. UNC hitting machine Dustin Ackley, who trailed only The Pick with a .404 batting average, *tinked* the evening to a running start with a bounding single just right of Michael Hollander's diving glove.

His parents parked and in their seats, left fielder Kyle Shelton came to the plate feeling as though he, as Coach Fox put it, was playing for his playing life. Like classmate Chad Flack, he hadn't been drafted. But with a good showing in Omaha he hoped to land in the minor leagues as a free agent. So far, so good, as he was hitting precisely .333 for the year and was 4-for-8 in the College World Series. After being dry-freezed by a wicked inside breaking pitch from LSU starter Blake Martin, Shelton was 4-for-9.

From there, it got a little ugly for the *L-S-U* chanters. Right fielder Tim Fedroff smoked a double to score Ackley. Catcher Tim Federowicz was hit in the back of the head by a wild pitch and second baseman Kyle Seager caught another pitch in the elbow. Then Chad Flack drew a four-pitch walk. It wasn't a hit, but when it pushed in a run it was just as good as one. The Blatt's hot-dog cookers hadn't even warmed up and L-S-U was already down by two runs and staring at a very bleak future with the bases loaded and only one out.

Then, only nineteen minutes into Game Ten, Mother Nature came over the plains looking for Jesse Cuevas. As Blake Martin threw his fifth consecutive pitch out of the strike zone, umpire Bill Speck saw a lightning flash in the distance and pulled the plug on the action, which signaled Cuevas and his crew to pull the tarp. Within minutes, the rains came. Genuine Cornhusker-State-good-Lord-it's-never-going-to-end rain.

From 2011 until the next Ice Age, the people of Omaha will debate whether or not Rosenblatt Stadium should have been replaced by a new downtown ballpark. The traditionalists will continue to argue that the new park lacks The Blatt's charm. The more progressive set will say that amenities outweigh charm. But anyone in attendance for Game Ten of the 2008 College World Series will always agree on one fact when it comes to Rosenblatt.

It wasn't built for rain.

Cuevas spent decades perfecting the playing surface. During its first thirty years, the College World Series had as many games delayed by rain as not, due in no small part to a playing field that was, to put it kindly, not up to big-league specifications.

"That field was so overworked," former city-events planner Terry Forsberg said. From 1977 to '92 he oversaw operations at The Blatt. As a teenager he ran the scoreboard from a press box that was literally thrown up onto the roof of the grandstand. When one of those big Iowa winds decided to blow in across the Missouri, it would buffet around the press box like a mechanical bull. When a visiting school would recruit public-address announcer Jack Payne to help them pipe play-by-play action back home to Los Angeles or Austin, Forsberg slid over to address the game. No matter what the weather conditions, from his seat behind the glass high above home plate, the grass was always greener on the other side, literally. "Frankie had an amazing ability to make sure that field was green for game time. Now I'm not saying he wasn't above *painting* it green . . ."

But since 1980, only six games had been pushed back a day, and only two since 1986. The improvement was courtesy of a field upgrade that was one-part politician and one-part mad scientist. Cuevas combined different types of grasses to strengthen the overused infield and tested different types of water-absorbing dirt. Meanwhile, Forsberg leveraged "another city is going to steal the Series away" rumors to secure monies for field improvements. In 1992, they took advantage of a stadium and dugout overhaul to install a state-of-the-art Major League drainage system, creating a field that Cuevas claims can now withstand nearly nine inches of rain per hour.

Unfortunately, during the great downpour of 2008, the grandstand around that field began drowning after half an inch.

Water collected all along the first row of seats, creating wading pools nearly as deep as the one the neighbors had set up to lure parkers away from Vicky's Valley. Water filled the floor of the world's slowest press-box elevator and made the metal steps to the press box nearly too slick to risk (thankfully the bouncy box was replaced by a new $4-million model in 1996). Rain cascaded from a cracked drain spout directly above the ESPN broadcast booth, tossing down a Bridal Veil Falls–sized stream into the lower-level yellow seats. A concourse built sixty years earlier to accommodate a few thousand fans suddenly served as refuge for more than 15,000, all wrapped in impromptu garbage-bag ponchos, compliments of The Blatt's maintenance staff. LSU fans mingled with Carolina fans who mingled with Omaha locals, all packed into the tiny hallway and looking like the cattle of the Stockyards. After three hours of waiting, the smell had to be pretty close.

The head coaches, Mike Fox and Paul Mainieri, who'd never gotten to talk before this week, sat in the LSU dugout and played the "what coaches do we both know?" game. The Tigers sat around their clubhouse, retelling the story of the Rice comeback in the hopes that it might spark a similar effort once the game was restarted. And the Tarheels, the ones who had been so quiet and so businesslike that their coach had run out of ways to loosen them up, loosened up.

All it took was for someone to put on their clothes upside down.

Pitcher Brian Moran was a Tarheel only because his uncle, former Carolina great and longtime Major Leaguer B. J. Surhoff, had called Mike Fox and asked the coach to let his nephew walk on. In 2008, he'd made his uncle proud by emerging as the team's best shut-down middle reliever and by developing pinpoint control.

His uncle was slightly less proud when the lefty emerged from the dugout during the rain delay with his jersey pulled over his legs, his pants pulled over his head, and his cleats pulled onto his hands. Just by walking out onto the field the sophomore sent his teammates to the damp dugout floor in laughter. The scene even coaxed out some UNC fans into the rain to watch him dance.

Then he did the cartwheel.

"That's the future of Carolina baseball right there," Chad Flack sarcastically said later while watching a slow-motion replay of the cartwheel and resulting sideways crash into the red clay of the warning track. "We're leaving things in great hands, aren't we?"

Coach Fox wasn't laughing quite as hard as his players and staff. He found no humor in the fact that Game Ten had been started even when NCAA officials admitted that they had fully expected the rain to show up. Fox wasn't amused that everyone had to sit around for more than three hours while the inevitable decision was being made to postpone the game until Friday. And there was certainly nothing funny about the momentum of his team's big inning being washed away.

But wearing your uniform upside down and turning a cartwheel?

Now that was funny. And his team, The Favorite, was finally loose.

When Game Ten was finally suspended the team laughed all the way to the bus and all the way back to the suburbs. Clothes upside down. Classic.

When the two teams showed back up on Friday to resume the action, Paul Mainieri admitted that his famous cell-phone speed dial had been in overdrive all afternoon. Why wouldn't it be? When else would he have the chance to ask for advice on how to handle one very crucial at-bat from his father, Skip Bertman, Tommy Lasorda, Jim Hendry, Roger Clemens, and, what the heck, Rudy, on how he should handle a one-out, 0–1, bases-loaded jam. It was the greatest phone-a-friend lifeline ever.

"This will go down as the most overanalyzed at-bat in the history of college baseball," the coach joked as his team took batting practice again. "But look at Hollander over there. One more day doesn't bother him one bit. He'd pay someone to come out here and take batting practice and infield at Rosenblatt Stadium. At least one more day in that LSU uniform. Let's hope it is one more week."

Mainieri's advisers told the coach what he'd already known. Get starter Blake Martin the hell off the mound and give the ball to righty Jared Bradford. Bradford was the only senior on the team not named Michael Hollander, a soft-spoken son of a Baptist preacher from the NASCAR hotbed of Hueytown, Alabama. More important, he was a Greg Maddux–cloned sinker-ball pitcher who made his baseball living forcing hitters into rally-killing double-play grounders.

At 6:09 P.M., exactly twenty-four hours after the original first pitch, Bradford tossed two pitches. The first was a called strike. On the second serving, LSU catcher Micah Gibbs hopped and set his mitt in the center of the plate like it was straight third-strike cheese. But at the last instant, Bradford's right arm dropped as his index and middle fingers rolled over the ball. What UNC designated hitter Garrett Gore saw was a fastball, but what he got was exactly what Bradford was out there for, a pitch that dropped like a shot dove at the very instant that Bradford had committed to swinging. An uppercut designed to lift the ball into left field instead slapped the top of the ball with the bottom half of the metal barrel.

The result was a bounding chopper traveling about three feet inside the third-base line. That's exactly where Michael Hollander was standing: 5–4–3, double play.

New day. New game.

At the bottom of every inning, Michael Hollander ran out to his position at third. At the top of every inning, Flack did the same. For the next four hours, the two seniors combined to put on a clinic of how to live and work on the hot corner.

Hollander's approach was more energy-driven, a constantly moving scene of semicircles drawn with his right foot, small kicks to the dirt, followed by a quick tap of his toes to his back of his pants legs. Right, left, right, left. By the end of the night the areas just above the tops of his cleats were completely dark with dirt. Flack had a much more stoic approach. He dug in at his position and made educated defensive shifts with deliberate steps from left to right.

This was the routine of the night. The two seniors endured another nearly two-hour rain delay sitting on their respective benches. Hollander gravitated toward Bradford, whose playing career was also at its potential end. Flack hung with his fellow seniors as well.

When Game Ten was actually being played, Hollander and Flack crossed paths throughout the night. In the third inning, Hollander was caught between second and third on a fly ball that looked like a single coming off of LSU bopper Blake Dean's bat. Hollander was thrown out from left by Kyle Shelton as he dove back to second, having been lured closer to third than he normally would have wandered thanks in part to an excellent fake-out by Chad Flack, who acted like he was covering third as if expecting a runner to be coming on the base hit.

Three innings later, Hollander returned the favor by shading Flack perfectly, moving to within a few steps of the third-base line and even with the bag. When the Carolina slugger slapped a hard high chopper, Hollander stayed flat-footed, held up his glove, and watched it bounce in for the easy throw to first and the out.

Neither hitter contributed to their teams' scoring efforts, but both served as their dugouts' biggest cheerleaders as the two teams jabbed their way into a 3–3 tie, LSU finally catching up with a two-run blast from first baseman and NCAA home-run leader Matt Clark in the bottom of the sixth.

The tension rose like those storm clouds the day before. Every out tightened the screws just a little bit more. In the UNC dugout, Coach Fox's trademark gray hair suddenly looked a little grayer. On the LSU bench, Paul Mainieri, Mr. Smiles-a-Lot, grimaced as if his pants were too tight. Only one thing could release the valve on a pressure cooker such as this one.

A naked dude.

Jared Potter was an Omaha resident, but as soon as he opened his mouth, everyone knew he wasn't a native. His twang was distinctly Cajun in nature.

Throughout the 2008 Series, he'd been talking LSU smack to his Cornhusker coworkers at the Big Brain Tattoo Parlor in downtown Omaha. He'd also made a comment about streaking, which his tatted-up friends immediately threw down some money on. But the night of Game Ten he'd had to work late and didn't have a ticket to see his beloved Tigers fight for their lives.

"I was headed home," said the twenty-one-year-old. "I thought, well, maybe I can make it out to see LSU next year. Then a buddy of mine called and he was at the game sitting in center field and he had an extra ticket. He said, 'Go put on your tear-away running pants and get out here!'"

Potter arrived in the eighth inning and took his seat with the intention of not staying in it for very long. His timing was perfect. His beloved Bayou Bengals were rallying, but they looked uptight. They needed his help. So off came the T-shirt, off ripped the tear-away pants, and away he went.

Potter, now known only as Naked Dude, appeared over the center-field wall with one out in the bottom of the eighth, mere moments after Chad Flack had nearly short-armed an out throw from third to first. In a tied elimination game that was now in its twenty-eighth hour, this fine American sprinted across the outfield grass and began to zigzag his way around center field, committing the only act capable of out-weirding someone doing cartwheels with his clothes on upside down. Which was, of course, wearing no clothes at all.

He jogged around a bit to make sure that he had everyone's attention, including ESPN play-by-play man Sean McDonough, who violated the network's strict "Don't show or talk about idiot fans on the field" policy when he corrected his original "scantily clad" description with the more accurate, "I think he had on sneakers and socks, and that was about it." Once assured that the eyes of The Blatt were on him, Jared Potter realized that he was out of moves. So he simply kneeled on one knee behind second base as if to give thanks to the god that had granted him with his nakedness.

The Rosenblatt old-timers weren't impressed. They'd seen better. If this guy had any balls (and clearly he did) he would have reenacted what they witnessed in 1973, when a man also donned only in sneakers calmly walked up to the plate and went into his batting stance with a plastic bat. He then proceeded to run the bases backward and bolted up the Blatt stairs toward the exit. Security didn't catch him until he'd made it all the way to the parking lot. Stunned into a rare loss for words, Jack Payne leaned into his public address microphone and stated to the crowd, "There he goes."

As the Streaker of 2008 went into his one-knee stance, Nick McCoy, a member of the Cuevas Crew, was building up a head of steam, barreling in from the third-base side of the ballpark. Jared Potter never saw it coming as McCoy laid him out. From the stands it looked like a hit worthy of entrance into the archives at NFL Films. Turner said that in reality it was more of a glancing blow. It didn't matter.

Ice broken, everyone started to laugh.

Everyone but Michael Hollander. He was too honed in, already thinking about his next at-bat.

As Potter was dragged off by security, laughter turned to chuckles, which was replaced by the returning tension. As Game Ten finally entered the final frame, the chants returned.

L-S-U. L-S-U.

Somewhere deep within the Rosenblatt grandstand, Omaha's adopted team stirred up the purple and gold ghosts that Hollander had saved from that old box of videotapes. LSU superfan Anita Haywood, "The K Lady," brought the road-hardened Tigers fans to their feet. A chemical salesman name Chris Guillot, a man some refer to as the "Human Megaphone," who proposed to his wife Sherry at Alex Box Stadium, began some sort of Bayou voodoo chant designed to rattle opposing pitchers. Even LSU legend Skip Bertman joined the cheers, having traded in his heart-healthier press-box digs for a seat down in the crowd.

With two outs in the top of the ninth, Michael Hollander stood at third base and looked over at the people with whom he'd grown up. *His* people. The extended family that helped raise him in Section L2 and now cheered him as one of their own. So many times he'd watched them rattle an opponent to the point of literally sweating and shaking.

But this opponent was different. This was The Favorite.

UNC rubber arm Alex White, perhaps the best raw college pitcher in the nation, had shut the Tigers down in Game Four for the win. Now he was the pitcher of record again, having left three LSU runners stranded in the eighth, each of whom had represented the go-ahead run.

Now Tim Fedroff, perhaps the best hitter in the nation, was standing on first. Dustin Ackley, perhaps even better than Fedroff, was on second. Ryan Graepel, perhaps the best number-nine hitter in the nation, was on third. Like Hollander, he had taken notice of the rowdiness in the stands to their right.

The Carolina fans, sensing an imbalance in the decibel level, came to their feet with an impromptu "U-N-C, U-N-C," as the team leaned on the railing of the dugout.

Catcher Tim Federowicz, who liked to joke his name was Tim "I'm Not Fedroff" was at the plate. A native of Apex, North Carolina, he'd signed with the Tarheels for the chance to play with North Carolina high-school legend Chad Flack and the others in the class ahead of him. Like Flack, he was without a hit on the night. Like Flack, he was in a rut, hitting only .200 with the bases loaded on the season. Three pitches later, he joined Flack as a home-run-hitting blue-clad Carolina hero.

When Garrett Gore stepped to the plate at the start of the night, he hadn't had time to adjust to a breaking ball that snuck up on him. Federowicz adjusted just fine, thank you. He tracked LSU reliever Louis Coleman's breaker to the last possible instant. The pitch broke, but not soon enough or low enough.

Boom.

Michael Hollander made a slow-motion turn from his post at third base to watch the ball sail ten miles over his head. When it landed ten rows deep in the left-field bleachers, he simply looked up at the giant scoreboard that loomed over the fans now fighting for the first CWS grand-slam ball in seven years. Then he watched the "4" pop up in the ninth column on the line score and the "7" that followed it.

UNC 7, LSU 3.

Twice during the 2008 season LSU had faced certain elimination. They'd scored five runs in the ninth against Cal-Irvine in the second round of the NCAA tournament. They'd scored four in the ninth against Rice in Game Seven. They would need at least that much to see another day. Anything less meant the end of the year, the dream, and for the seniors, the end of everything.

With one out and a man on first, Jerry Michael Hollander III walked to the plate with the look of an athlete who had quite literally left it all on the field. The backs of his pants legs were filthy. His knees and the front of his jersey were stained in Rosenblatt mud. The top button, just above the bold purple TIGERS had come undone, exposing the gold T-shirt beneath, the one that looked just like those magical gold jerseys of those magical teams on those crusty old tapes.

He laid back for ball one, letting everyone know that he wasn't nervous, just patient, steady, and ready. Ready to hold the rope, get on base, and let hard-hitting Blake Dean get his ass back up to the plate to hit a grand slam of his own.

When the 94-mph fastball left the fingers of Alex White, Hollander's mind instantly registered, "You can drive this pitch."

He swung hard, but topped it, nearly coming out of his shoes to make something happen at the last instant.

The ball took a first high bounce and had eyes on finding a seam between short and second, but Ryan Graepel had Hollander shaded perfectly in the hole at short. He took the low hop off the Jesse Cuevas grass and flicked it to Kyle Seager at second who paused to let runner Ryan Schimpf slide under him, then rocketed an all-arm throw to first.

Michael Hollander's career at LSU ended at 10:33 P.M. in Omaha, Nebraska, arriving at first base one fraction of a second slower than the throw that ended the game. That career ended as it should have.

At full speed.

As Chad Flack joined his teammates for a round of high fives at the mound, Hollander came to a stop twenty yards down the baseline, pulling off his batting helmet, and leaning into his knees in disbelief. As he made the slow walk across the diamond, he never looked at the Tarheels as they formed two congratulatory lines. He disappeared into the clubhouse where, alone, he tossed a chair and took out a season's worth of emotions on a water cooler. It all went unnoticed by his coach, as Paul Mainieri sat on the bench with his arm around the team's other senior, Jared Bradford. "I know your last out stings," the coach later recalled telling the kid who had pitched so well. "But wouldn't you rather it sting here at Rosenblatt Stadium than anywhere else?"

Soon the Tigers gathered in foul territory, huddling up for the final time in 2008. As their fans applauded, the team stopped their meeting, realizing that their third baseman, their heart, was missing.

"Where's Holly? We're not doing this without him . . ."

A member of the training staff found number 7 sitting alone in the clubhouse, crushed that he'd let his team down, unreasonably believing that the game had come down to his season-ending double play. "C'mon, man, they're waiting on you."

When their red-eyed leader emerged, the team opened their circle and held out their arms to draw him in. His shirttail now hanging out, Hollander never smiled—how the hell was he supposed to smile?—but he stepped in as the team surrounded him, spoke words that only a team gets to hear, and then broke the huddle.

For the final time, Michael Hollander left the field to the chant, that simple little song that had served as the soundtrack of his entire life.

L-S-U . . . L-S-U . . .

In Lot A, for a tortuously long half hour, the Tigers were forced to sit on their bus and marinate in agony while watching through their windows as the Carolina players and their loved ones hugged, laughed, and recounted every big play of the night.

As the buses finally pulled away at 11:23 P.M., the Sheltons descended the hill down to Fourteenth Street, where Linda Willis was waiting in a Carolina blue T-shirt to congratulate them. Their boy was going to get to play at least one more day.

Two blocks north, Vicky's Valley was empty, as was the Nike Fieldhouse. Even the soft-serve machines at Zesto had powered down for the night. But over at Starsky's the party was just getting started. At least a dozen people milled through the crowd in the overpacked beer garden, bragging about the fact that they had tickets to Game Ten, but chose to stay here at the eighty-six-year-old bar and drown themselves instead. Another dozen boasted about the fact that they hadn't missed a College World Series in years, but had never actually been inside the stadium. They preferred to watch the games here, only a couple hundred yards across the street.

But only one man, a nose-ringed tattoo-parlor employee, stomped around Starsky's claiming to be the Streaker.

"Bull . . . *shit!*" cried a nonbeliever over the wailing sounds of a local cover band rifling through the greatest hits of the 1980s.

"Look here!" Potter yelled as he pulled what appeared to be an official Omaha Police Department citation from the pocket of his . . . what were those? . . . tear-away gym pants? When told about the Streaker of '73, Potter took pride in carrying on a legacy. Sneakers-Only Guy #1 was The Blatt's first streaker. Perhaps Potter, Sneakers-Only Guy #2, would be its last. He would take so much pride in his place in history that within days photos of the incident were displayed proudly for all to see on his Facebook page. One month later he appeared in court and walked away with only a $50 fine. Turned out a local defense attorney was in the stands that night and thought Potter's jaunt was hysterical. She tracked him down, offered to represent him free of charge, and negotiated the nominal penalty.

"That's the Rosenblatt family, man," Jared Potter, the Naked Dude, said with a Cajun chuckle. "We look out for each other."

EIGHT

THE INSURANCE MAN AND THE POPE

Saturday, June 21
Game Eleven: Georgia vs. Stanford
Game Twelve: Fresno State vs. North Carolina

Walk up to any American on the street and ask them to reveal the first thought that pops into their mind when you say the word "Omaha." The three most likely answers will be:

College World Series.

Mutual of Omaha's Wild Kingdom.

Steak.

The great old Omaha steakhouses are scattered haphazardly throughout the city like cattle feed scattered to the wind. Some occupy palatial brick buildings, complete with giant fiberglass cows standing watch on the roof. Others are harder to find, hidden in the middle of neighborhoods built long before zoning laws or tucked in behind an office building or a warehouse park. Some fall into the "Traditional Omaha" category while others are labeled "Italian Steakhouses." No matter what the style, their names unfailingly end with an apostrophe "s."

There are Piccolo Pete's, Gorat's (*Derek Ventura now appearing in the lounge!*), and Johnny's Cafe, which has sat on the edge of the old Stockyards site for nearly eighty years with a veteran waitstaff that look as though they must have been there since day one. At Angie's, the parents of players dined on T-bones alongside university presidents. If you were looking for Skip Bertman or pretty much anyone else from LSU they could be found at the Drover, standing in line beneath the wagon wheel facade over the front porch or sitting beside the steer skull fireplace.

Hidden between the churches of Tenth Street was the low-profile facade of Cascio's, with shiny Mylar baseball-shaped balloons floating out front to lure CWS visitors. This place was strictly an Italian steakhouse, sitting at the crossroads of what used to be Little Italy. The neighborhood was once ruled by the Salerno brothers, Joseph and Sebastiano, who founded the local Bank of Sicily and convinced hundreds of Italians to move from the Mediterranean Sea to the Missouri River. Little Italy became the center of the city's bootlegging operations, horse betting, and even had its own branch of the mob, headed by Tony Biase, an associate of New York's infamous mafioso, Vito Genovese.

For a century, South Omaha was the place to go for illegal liquor and gambling.

In 2008, visitors come looking for a rib eye and a house salad.

Larry Cascio greeted these visitors with a handshake, guided them to their tables, and then went back to filling out his racing forms at the host stand. This was his sixty-second year on the job. He started working for his father and uncle, Al and Joe, after they opened the place in 1946, boxing pizzas for a quarter an hour. Four years later the Series came to town and Larry can't remember a June when at least one team didn't come in on the prowl for dinner. In 1999, when the restaurant fell into financial difficulty, Larry dug up $500,000 of his own money to save it. Ten years later he was already looking forward to handing it off to his kids and eventually to their kids.

"I get people every summer telling me about the first time they came here," he said as he pulled out a red leather upholstered chair for a patron, a seat that looked like it had been stolen from Don Corleone's office. "They came to their first College World Series in the 1960s as a kid and here they are again. Hopefully the food is still as good."

It should be. Other than adding carrots to the salad ("It needed some color"), the menu hasn't changed much since Texas won the first Omaha Series in 1950.

Just as everyone has his or her favorite CWS moment, team, or player, they also have their favorite steakhouse. Trying to convince an Omaha resident or regular visitor to trade in one for another is as futile as trying to convince a Democrat to become a Republican or vice versa. And while unknowing patrons have broken bread in their favorite dark wooden dining rooms, the backrooms of the great steak establishments have been home to more political maneuvering than either of these parties has ever managed to accomplish at a convention.

The fate of early Omaha may have been shaped by guns and nooses, but its modern direction is determined over grain-fed beef and cabernet sauvignon.

The direction of the city's signature event is no different.

Management of the College World Series is a uniquely complicated yet simple public/private business experiment with no peer in American sports. There are no less than four different parties involved, each bringing different perspectives, ideas, and agendas to the same table at the same time. Amazingly, they always end up rowing their oars in the same direction.

The first is the NCAA, four letters with the ability to simultaneously excite and frustrate everyone from fans to student-athletes to college administrators. Though a longtime target of critics for the route that it takes to get where it's going, the governing body's success cannot be questioned.

Next, is College World Series of Omaha Incorporated or CWS of Omaha Inc., a group of local business leaders including corporate CEOs, bank presidents, and store owners. Everyone is a volunteer. Many of its members are multigenerational, a proud ladder of last names that have steered, and frequently saved, the Series for more than forty years.

Player three is a relative newcomer, the Metropolitan Entertainment and Convention Authority, which is shortened to what *Omaha World-Herald* columnist Robert Nelson describes as the "accidentally cool acronym" of MECA. Like CWS of Omaha, it is a civic board formed to determine the direction of city events, specifically those at the still-new Qwest Center arena, the soon-to-be next-door neighbor of the Series. In 2008, the Center was five years old and MECA was only eight.

Finally, there is the Mayor's Office, which plays ball with the other three even while it frequently resents the power they possess, an especially difficult compromise to stomach while one is being booed in the produce section of the supermarket.

The good news about this four-corner relationship involving dozens of people is that no decision is made without every angle being discussed and every potential scenario being forecast. The bad news is that those dozens of people also bring dozens of titanic egos, each much more accustomed to telling someone what to do than being told what to do.

Enter The Insurance Man and The Pope.

They are longtime friends, sometime enemies, and de-facto brothers. Their versions of the steakhouse meeting have rescued and undoubtedly nurtured repeatedly the event they both hold so dear. But you'll never get either one of them to admit it.

John D. Diesing Jr.—Jack—is the president of CWS of Omaha, Inc., an Omaha native and member of the board since the mid-1980s. Like so much of corporate Omaha, Diesing is in the insurance business, but don't mistake that statement with a guy on the corner pushing supplemental life policies. He's the local chairman for the Aon Corporation, the world's largest insurance brokerage firm. His dialect is classic Midwestern as are his manners, a father of three and grandfather of three more who arrives to the ballpark for each CWS game with a look of relief that says, "Enough with the B.S., let's watch some baseball."

Dennis (Dennie) Poppe—pronounced "Pope"—is the NCAA's Managing Director for Football and Baseball and has overseen every Series since 1988. A Missouri native, he lettered three years with the University of Missouri Tiger football team, playing in the 1970 Orange Bowl to cap off an All-Big 8 and All-Academic campaign as a safety. He joined the NCAA in 1974, and every autumn since has been filled with endless phone calls from perhaps the most overinflated personalities outside of Hollywood—college-football coaches. Championship management, rules changes, and legislative decisions all fall to committees formed under Poppe's watch, putting him in the unenviable position of being the targeted messenger of a lot of decisions that he didn't make. His ability to survive the minefield of coaches, athletic directors, and college presidents, not to mention his ability to remember everyone's names and biographies, has earned the respect—no matter how reluctant—of everyone involved.

"Dennie has the ability to walk into a room full of very angry people and make everything seem okay," explained former Georgia A.D. and football coach Vince Dooley. "He has that great Midwestern smile and that tone in his voice that never wavers, never rises, even if everyone is trying to push his buttons. Next thing you know we're all in agreement with something that we were determined to blow up and he's left the room. You're like, 'What just happened here?' A lot of people enjoy criticizing the job that he does, but I can tell you this: Nobody wants his job, either."

It is hard to find anyone who dislikes Diesing or Poppe, almost as hard as it is to find someone who completely agrees with them. But in the end, none of what the College World Series has been or will become would have happened without them and their relationship.

When the bureaucrats, politicians, and corporate suits have left the room, The Insurance Man and The Pope always stay behind. It's when the two of them are alone together that the battleship is turned, the College World Series equivalent to the secretive back channels between Washington and Moscow that kept the world from coming apart at its Cold War seams.

Every few years the NCAA would start making noise about leaving and CWS of Omaha would counter with improvements to Rosenblatt. Whenever the NCAA made a fuss about their share of the financial take, CWS of Omaha countered with an increase in the league's portion of the pie chart. Everyone would yell and scream and get their feelings hurt. Then Jack and Dennie would figure out a compromise.

"We're almost like brothers," Diesing said, quick to point out that brothers fight as much as they play. When Jack's wife Linda had shoulder surgery, Dennie called from Indianapolis wanting daily updates. When Dennie's wife Donna battled breast cancer, it was Jack who made the constant calls. They've spent holidays together, vacations, and the Diesing children refer to the Poppes as Uncle Dennie and Aunt Donna.

"Our children have grown up together over the last twenty-plus years and we, the adults, have grown up together as well. And as a result he and I can almost tell what the other is thinking before it's said."

Then Diesing caught himself and smiled with one eyebrow raised. "Well, almost."

When the Georgia Bulldogs arrived for Game Eleven, it was their first appearance at The Blatt in five days. They had become the victims of their own undefeated success, a one-day delay for rain, and a new ESPN-friendlier CWS schedule that had games spread out further than ever before. A win today meant Stanford would be gone and the Dawgs would be playing for a national championship. Lose and there would be a rematch the following night; Georgia's first back-to-back games in two weeks.

For five days they sat around the Embassy Suites. Five days of watching movies, playing *Guitar Hero*, and eating out. They'd been shopping. They'd made it out to Rosenblatt for a game or two. They'd even played Marco Polo in the hotel swimming pool. "It's like those people in *The Shining*," third baseman Ryan Peisel joked. "We can't get out of the hotel."

It didn't hurt that their hotel draw was the best of the eight teams . . . or the worst, depending on your palette and point of view. The Embassy Suites was directly across the street from the Old Market, the bustling twenty-block center of Omaha nightlife.

Every eating establishment in the city did whatever they could to lure CWS out-of-towners, from the eighty-four-year-old Bohemian Café's big screen (which was, thankfully, not eighty-four years old) to the seven team flags that flew over the door of Kurt & Clyde's. (Said the bartender, "I know, we're missing Fresno, but where the hell do you get one of those?") Even the Nebraska Shakespeare Festival at Elmwood Park used baseball in its marketing to try and sell the Bard as a compliment to The Blatt.

But the epicenter of every night was found in the middle of the Old Market. Most of the old brick warehouses were constructed in the latter part of the nineteenth century, when chaos still reigned on the brick-paved streets, Buffalo Bill Cody's Wild West Show stampeded through town, and "perpetual mayor" Cowboy Jim Dahlman (aka the "Wettest Mayor in America," thanks to his love of green-lighting new saloons) was coaxing millions of visitors into his city with a double-whammy of the Tran-Mississippi Exposition and the Indian Congress. MECA would be so lucky.

The cavernous buildings sprung up all along the northern ends of Tenth and Fourteenth streets to handle and store the thousands of tons of goods being loaded and unloaded from the endless trains running through Union Station. There was Baum Iron, Bemis Bags, Skinner Macaroni, and the Windsor Hotel. Every building was trimmed with beautifully dark redbrick loading docks and proscenium archlike entrances, the shouts of produce dealers and buyers constantly echoing off the walls.

In 2008, these docks were covered with tables and tourists, now the front porches of restaurants and bars such as The Underground, Mr. Toad's, and a Dawg favorite called Old Chicago. Every establishment was plastered with CWS-friendly signage screaming, "Drink here, free shuttle to Rosenblatt," and one bar featured a carefully positioned street sign, strategically placed so that the Bulldog players could see it from their rooms.

HEY GEORGIA. BORED? THE GIRLS ARE OVER HERE.

UGA head coach David Perno didn't lock up his team in the hotel for fear of party burnout, but there was a standard bed check each night to keep his guys focused. That concern was certainly not unique to Perno. For the 2008 Series at least one school had requested to be assigned to one of the three suburban hotels located several miles west of downtown and away from the allure of the Old Market and THE GIRLS ARE OVER HERE.

In the 1950s, it wasn't uncommon for coaches to request hotels outside of town to avoid "accidental" contact with any "innocent" coeds who happened to be in town for the games. One major exception came in the grueling '64 Series when rain delays stretched the six-day event into eleven. Sensing restlessness within the team, Minnesota coach Dick Siebert told his boys there would be no more curfew, but they had better be ready to play. The Golden Gophers were more than a little thrilled, as they'd already befriended some local girls from a Catholic school.

They also won the national championship.

For decades the first person each team saw when they got off the plane in Nebraska were local girls known as the CWS Sweethearts, dressed in pink jackets, red dresses, and high heels. The program was overhauled into the more politically correct Ambassador program in 1992.

"As soon as we saw the Sweetheart, the coaches were like, 'Now leave that girl the hell alone,'" recalled former USC masher Dave Kingman, who won a CWS title in 1970. "We'd tell them, don't worry about it. We're here for business."

Now, finally, with the arrival of Game Eleven, Georgia could get on with business as well.

"We came to Omaha to play," all-world shortstop Gordon Beckham said as his team strolled into the stadium for their first game since Monday. "I like Omaha, but I don't want to get sick of it. We've got to play some baseball or we're going to kill each other. We almost got in a big fight at practice yesterday."

Stanford had caught a break with the one-day rain delay, giving them a chance to rest their arms after playing three games in six days. The biggest beneficiary was staff ace Jeremy Bleich, who was penciled into The Mastermind's lineup as the Cardinal's Game Eleven starter. This was precisely one of the reasons that the NCAA had devised the new spread-out schedule, to help the one-loss teams gather up enough strength to compete. The fact that Georgia and Fresno State had to sit and wait a little longer was a sacrifice the winners would have to make in the name of parity.

"It isn't the first sacrifice we've made this year for parity's sake," Coach Perno said during a practice at Bellevue during the team's downtime. "It's just the first time we've had time off because of it."

Perno's comment was a not-so-veiled jab at Poppe's NCAA Baseball Committee. The 2008 season had brought a sweeping new set of rules aimed at closing the gap between the sunbelt schools and those above the "warming line" that cuts across the nation from the Carolinas through the Texas panhandle and ultimately through the center of California. Teams above that line didn't just fail to win the College World Series, they rarely even made the trip, an imbalance credited to earlier practice schedules and longer regular seasons in the warm-weather states.

The committee and its outgoing chairman Larry Templeton had formalized the once-loose baseball calendar by setting the specific practice start date of February 1, and not allowing teams to play games before later that month. In the past, warm-weather teams were playing ball weeks before their northern counterparts. There were also new restrictions on fall practice, new school-transfer rules, and future restrictions on how each school could distribute its scholarships through its soon-to-be downsized roster.

The reaction of the coaches was, to put it kindly, irascible. They were already a sensitive bunch, angry about their sport playing second, third, or even fourth fiddle to football, men's basketball, and—*snarl*—women's basketball. They believed the new restrictions did nothing to help that. The most vocal opponent was Templeton's coach in Starkville. During the 2008 season Mississippi State head coach Ron Polk announced that he would be retiring at season's end, exasperated over the committee's new policies, and writing a vicious open letter to the NCAA as a parting salvo.

His former assistant was more discerning in his assessment of the situation.

"Thankfully, I'm good at math," Dave Perno joked as he went through his plan for dividing his 11.7 scholarships among a roster of thirty-five players in 2008, thirty in 2009, and twenty-seven in 2010, all in mandated 25 percent slices. "If I wasn't good at math I'd have to go find another job. But just as big of a challenge as sorting out scholarship money has been navigating the schedule."

The newly compressed calendar meant teams had to play the same number of regular season games—fifty-six—in a smaller period of time, which meant two or three games during the week followed by three-game weekend sets. "At first, you think you're going to be okay because in Georgia in the spring you're going to get some rain, right? We couldn't buy a damn rainout. By the time we got to May we'd been playing five games a week for three straight months. Now all of the sudden we're sitting around in the hotel for five days. I'm not complaining, because it's a much better position to be in than the other seven schools. Bu it's an adjustment, there's no doubt about it."

As the two teams stretched their legs for their elimination game, Dennie Poppe watched from his customary pregame position on the field, standing to the left of the batting cage with his arms crossed, just a few steps right of the third-base dugout. He chatted with both head coaches and wished them both luck. He chatted with ESPN producers and on-air talent. And he chatted with his staff of fifteen-plus, a group that would grow to more than twenty for the championship games. The fastest-moving of that bunch was Randy Buhr, Associate Director of Championships. It fell to Buhr to make sure that every game went off according to the minute-by-minute plan, from calming down nervous national-anthem singers to making sure the green *Star Wars*–ish homing beacon tripod thingy was in place to perfectly execute the occasional Air Force pregame flyover.

"When I first came here in 1988, we had three people," Poppe said. "I remember (former NCAA media director) Jungle Jim Wright sitting on his hotel room bed with his legs crossed, going through a box of media credentials and tickets, and handing them out to people as they came by his room to sign in. Thank goodness we've improved things since then. Now, when the game starts I'm the last line of defense. They only bother me when something either has the potential to be seriously wrong."

Like the rain two nights earlier?

"Yes, sir."

As the rain continued to fall on the first attempt at Game Ten, the two head coaches had Larry Templeton surrounded. They were wet, mad, and ready to express their feelings that the game should have never been started in the first place. They launched on Templeton, Buhr, and anyone else who happened by with an NCAA badge clipped to their shirt. When Poppe eased over to join the conversation, they started to launch on him as well. Then he did whatever it is that he does that Vince Dooley was so in awe of. Within a few minutes everyone in the huddle was shaking hands and the game was postponed to the next day.

"Everything seems a little more urgent at the time that it's happening," Poppe said when asked to recall the conversation, which took place on the field in plain view of anyone still hanging around in the wet. "But we have a bunch of smart people in this sport and they all come around to do the right thing in the end. Everyone knows that whatever is decided is what's in the best interest of the student-athletes."

As a kid growing up in the Middle of Nowhere, Missouri (his words), Poppe learned his back-up-and-take-a-look-at-the-bigger-picture approach from his father, the kind of quietly strong farmer that today can only be found in books and old movies. In the late afternoon Mr. Poppe made young Dennie hop onto the family tractor and start plowing, usually just as storm clouds were beginning to brew off in the distance.

The kid would ride one mile out and one mile back. As he approached the house at the end of each lap he would look for the signal from his father to shut it down and come in before the rain. If the signal didn't happen he'd have to make the turn and head back out again. Finally, after miles of riding back and forth, his father would give him the "come on in" sign, and inevitably, just as Dennie parked the tractor, the rain would start.

Fifty years later, Poppe reflected on that experience nearly every time he stood on the field at Rosenblatt. As painfully boring as those tractor rides had been, they'd also taught him patience, not to get too worked up about an oncoming storm until it actually got there. "And it taught me how to predict rain," he said with a wink as he pointed to the skies with the antenna of his omnipresent radio. "You can't be in this business and not be part weatherman."

It also helps to ride out those thunderbolts from the coaches, not to mention critics and columnists.

"Yes, sir."

The Bulldogs and the Cardinal picked up right where they had left off in Game Six, by hitting the ball very hard and very often. Each team was the perfect representative for its region. Stanford had long been the epitome of classic West Coast "small ball," though the old-school coach had certainly adjusted his team's style to fit with the home-run-powered times (a fact that goes largely unnoticed by anyone other than those who played for him).

Georgia was a classic MLB-style big-basher Southeastern slugging squad. On their recruiting boards back in Athens they listed needed positions as:

LH Pitchers
RH Pitchers
Middle Infielders
Outfielders
Catchers
Bangers

Under perfect skies, the Bulldog bangers played Game Eleven like men happy to be let out of their cages, even if those cages were suites. First baseman Rich Poythress and designated hitter Joey Lewis, each six-foot-four, looked and swung like a couple of lumberjacks, jumping all over Stanford's rested pitching staff for a combined six hits, including two doubles, and six RBIs . . . and that was just through the first four innings.

By the fourth, well-rested starter Jeremy Bleich was getting more rest on the bench, chased by six runs on eight hits. Bleich was relieved by suddenly human Drew Storen, who gave up three more runs over one and two-thirds.

When Austin Yount took the mound in the sixth, some in the press box viewed the move as a surrender flag. In truth, The Mastermind was executing two psychological maneuvers at once. First, he needed someone to come in and stop the bleeding, to stabilize his increasingly disconsolate bench. Yount did that, retiring seven of the first eight batters he faced. Second, he wanted Yount to enjoy a strong Omaha outing to erase the nightmare of Game Six, when the righty had taken the loss against Georgia.

It was the second goal that meant so much to Larry and Gail Yount, the pitcher/third baseman's parents. Gail was watching the game from where she always did, in the photographer's pit as the official team shooter. Larry sat in the stands with the rest of the Cardinal parents. His entire life he'd been known as "Robin Yount's brother," and he'd never been ashamed of that, just as he'd never been ashamed by the thoughts of what could have been for his own big-league career. In a scene straight out of an overwritten sports movie, Yount was a twenty-one-year-old pitcher in the Houston Astros organization and on September 15, 1971, started warming up in the Astrodome bullpen for his Major League debut against the Atlanta Braves. But during the warm-ups tosses, his right elbow began to stiffen up. By the time he reached the mound, his arm was too tight to throw and he walked off the field to the trainer's room before throwing a real live game pitch. He never made it back to the big leagues.

Since Larry Yount was announced as the pitcher of record, he is credited with a big-league appearance in the Baseball Encyclopedia. "The Yount brothers played in 2,857 big league games," said Larry, the successful real-estate developer. "Robin played in 2,856 and Larry played in one."

As soon as the 2008 Series was over, Austin Yount started working on adding to the family tally, reporting for minor-league duty with the Los Angeles Dodgers.

Yount held Georgia to only one run in nearly four innings pitched, but entering the bottom of the ninth, the Dawgs led Stanford 10–4.

Making matters even worse, they once again sent in Josh Fields to close out the game. The deeply spiritual righty's soft-spoken manner belied the sickest breaking ball this side of, well, no one knew where. They just knew that it was sick, twelve o'clock–to–six o'clock–in-a-fraction-of-a-second-right-over-the-corner-of-the-plate sick.

As Fields tucked his long hair behind his ears and began to fire in his warm-up pitches, his designated catcher Jake Crane did what he always had to do, turning and warning home-plate umpire Frank Sylvester not to bail when it looked like a Fields pitch was going to pull a "Nuke LaLoosh" from *Bull Durham* and sail into the netting of the backstop. "They never listen," Crane said, shaking his head. "They say, 'Yeah, all right, thanks. But I've seen a curveball before, jerk.' Then Josh throws it and the umpire ducks to keep from being hit in the head and misses it when it breaks back over the plate. Then they're left guessing like the ump in *The Naked Gun*. Um, strike?'"

Fields wasn't supposed to be here. He'd been so dominant during his sophomore season, Georgia's last visit to Omaha, everyone assumed that he'd be just as good during his junior year, get drafted in the first round, and take the first plane to The Show.

But his junior year was abysmal. After earning fifteen saves in 2006, he earned only seven in 2007, while his earned run average ballooned to nearly 5.00, giving up thirty-four hits in thirty-eight innings pitched. The coaching staff and his teammates were too nice to point fingers, but his inability to close the door wasn't a reason they'd gone from first to worst in 2007, it was *the* reason. He was drafted by the Atlanta Braves but ultimately decided to return to campus when the two sides couldn't come to financial terms. On February 27, 2008, the Bulldogs played their annual exhibition game against the Braves at Turner Field. After seeing the Josh Fields curveball in person, Braves manager Bobby Cox went straight upstairs to see his bosses in the front office. "Why the hell didn't we get this kid signed?!"

Luckily for Dave Perno and the UGA faithful, Fields returned as the 2006 Jekyll and not the 2007 Hyde. The coach said his closer had rediscovered his groove by refocusing and not overthinking or overthrowing. The closer said it was because he'd found his lucky necklace, a cheap one he'd bought in a trinket store at Myrtle Beach. He couldn't find it during the entirety of the 2007 nightmare. Then, just as the 2008 season began, there it was, lying in the bottom of his locker. Suddenly the ball started breaking off the table again.

"Whatever he says," the coach said when asked about the necklace. "Whatever it took to make him confident again I'm all for it. Just in case you needed a reminder that we're still dealing with kids here, there it is."

When first baseman Brent Milleville, the number-five hitter, started the ninth by going down swinging to a 95-mph Fields fastball, everyone assumed the game was over. But, of course, here at The Blatt, it wasn't. He walked designated hitter Randy Molina. Then center fielder Sean Ratliff singled, the first hit off of Fields in the Series so far.

In the Stanford dugout, Coach Marquess started pacing.

After left fielder Joey August struck out, Marquess sent in freshman Colin Walsh to pinch hit. Why not? The kid may not get another chance to play in the College World Series. He stroked another single. UGA 10, Stanford 5.

The Mastermind picked up the pace, marching back and forth behind his players on the dugout rail. Fifteen steps up, fifteen back. He thought about the reaction when equipment keeper Matty Ritson had delivered the news of the LSU comeback against Rice four days earlier. The coach's reaction that day suddenly became his rally cry as his clapped his hands together and shouted.

"Hey, guys, *why not?*"

He sent Ben Clowe, another freshman, to the plate. Hey, Walsh had gotten a hit and he was a freshman. Why not Clowe? The kid worked a full count. It looked like Fields was overthrowing again.

Tink.

Home run. Only the third dinger off of Fields all year. UGA 10, Stanford 8.

"Why not?"

Marquess stopped pacing. He plopped down atop an empty bucket at the opening in the center of the dugout rail, staring at Josh Fields, whose empty expression gave up nothing about his emotions. Georgia coach Dave Perno had no such poker face and looked as though he would bite through his bottom teeth.

The only reliever in the nation as revered as Fields had been Rice closer Cole St. Clair, the kid who'd blown the lead in the LSU comeback. But Fields wasn't going to pull a Cole St. Clair . . . was he?

Now the top of the Stanford order was up. Second baseman Cord Phelps took ball one . . . and ball two . . . which brought out Georgia pitching coach Brady Wiederhold for a little classic arm-around-the-waist sports psychology. *Point out the obvious.* "All right, there's two outs. We're still up two. There's no one on base." *Rebuild his confidence.* "Look at me, Josh. Now do what you know you can do. Put it in play. Whatever. One out and we're done."

Ball three.

"Why the heck not?!"

Fastball. Fastball. Fastball. Fastball. Two takes, two fouls. Full count.

Fields threw one more fastball, this one with an extra grunt and a body motion so violent that it pulled the closer's shirttail out from his beltline. It was right over the heart of the plate. Cord Phelps made contact, but sky-balled it for the third out.

The Georgia Bulldogs would be playing for the national championship.

As the two teams went through the postgame handshakes, Gordon Beckham stopped to hug only one of the opposing players. Cardinal catcher Jason Castro, never one to show a lot of emotion, had the same shell-shocked look that had already been displayed by Yonder Alonso and Michael Hollander. His college career had ended at 4:42 P.M. Omaha time, standing on deck—the potential winning run—praying for a chance to win it in the bottom of the ninth. "I'll see you later, man," Beckham said to his fellow first-round draft pick. Like Buster Posey and Alonso five days earlier, these two were perhaps already looking ahead to an Astros–White Sox interleague matchup down the road. The two had played together on that same Yarmouth-Dennis team in the Cape Cod League, a team that, with Posey, boasted three of the top ten picks of the MLB draft.

"You, too," the Stanford catcher said back. "Go win it."

For Stanford coach Mark Marquess, the reality of going home started to set in after the handshakes, destroying his charts, and wading through the postgame press conference. Just as the bus closed its doors to head back to the Hilton, he fingered the small "KW" patch on his right sleeve and thought about his late assistant, how she wouldn't be there when he got back.

Finally, it was time to go home and mourn.

When Johnny Rosenblatt's ballpark became a reality and the College World Series had become his stadium's cornerstone event, the dairy salesman convinced the city's political and business leaders to join a committee that would ensure the big blue stadium did what it needed to in order to keep the CWS in town. The marriage of the fast-growing city and even faster-growing NCAA was annually extended only by year-to-year contracts, agreements that were reached at the close of each June's tournament, usually drawn up in, yes, a steakhouse.

In 1964, the same year that Municipal Stadium became Rosenblatt Stadium, an energetic department-store manager named Jack Diesing Senior, father of Jack Junior, took over the mayor's CWS committee when Blatt pioneer Ed Pettis, his coworker from Brandeis Department Store, passed away. Almost immediately he realized that the casual looseness of the partnership wasn't going to be enough to keep the event in Omaha for the long haul. Over its first fifteen editions, the CWS had only averaged about 3,000 fans per multigame session, and the event had lost money nearly every year. Sensing shaky legs, other cities were asking the NCAA about hosting the Series. The biggest early threat came from a power-packed group of Los Angeles businessmen that included Walt Disney and California governor Pat Brown.

"You know who headed up that deal? You won't believe it," Diesing Sr. recalled with an octogenarian mind sharper than anyone could ever wish for, invoking the name of none other than the most successful coach in

CWS history. "Rod Dedeaux of all people, the coach from USC that won all those championships right here in Omaha. He felt like the event wasn't growing as quickly as it should have and needed more promotion behind it. That lit a fire under some people. But Dedeaux? It's hard to imagine the man who became the face of the College World Series in Omaha thinking it should have been somewhere else.

"I don't think I'm going out on a limb when I say this," he added with a laugh, "but I think after all those championships he finally came around to Omaha."

In '67, Diesing formalized the city side of the Series-NCAA marriage, separating the CWS decision makers from the muddiness of city politics by forming a not-for-profit corporation known as College World Series of Omaha, Inc. He recruited twenty city business leaders, real Nebraska men who took pride in their city as if it was their country. Almost immediately, the event moved into a higher gear.

"We didn't have a lot to leverage to get people activated," Diesing explained. "We preached civic pride. This wasn't just another event. This was *our* event. Once people felt that way, they'd do anything to protect it."

He appointed new leaders to reorganize ticket sales ("Best thing that ever happened," says Eddie Sobczyk) and took whatever money was made and put it into a reserve fund to make improvements for future years. He replaced that money, which had previously been distributed to local charities, by devising the service group ambassador plan, which allowed those groups to sell general-admission ticket books to support their own local causes. And he also did away with the steakhouse year-by-year renegotiations with the NCAA, drawing up a contract that automatically renewed unless one of the two parties canceled by the end of summer.

"It was really the beginning of local sports commissions," explained former Rosenblatt Stadium manager Terry Forsberg. "Every city, every state, every bowl game, they all have teams of local business leaders who work to attract or keep sports events in their city. Before Jack Senior, no one had even thought of that."

Attendance in the 1960s was twice what it had been in the '50s. In the '70s, it doubled again. By the 1980s and the arrival of ESPN, total attendance topped more than 100,000 at more than 12,000 per game. Even as the NCAA's share of the profits continued to grow, CWS of Omaha, Inc. still pocketed enough coin to start sinking millions into stadium improvements.

Diesing, along with everyone else on his committee, received no pay for their positions. They even paid for their tickets. With the exception being an event-planning company, a ticket sales director, and an accountant, everyone involved were volunteers. As of 2008, nothing had changed.

"Yeah, I pay for these seats," Jack Jr. said as he headed back to his front-row seat alongside his family, including his five- and eight-year-old grandsons. "Everyone does."

Almost everyone.

From Suite A, Dennie Poppe could see and hear everything that he needed to.

He watched every game simultaneously through the window of his sky box high above third base and on the TVs installed in front and above him. From a tiny black speaker he could hear the ESPN production truck and from his walkie-talkie he could be summoned by anyone from the field about any issue, though they bothered him rarely if ever.

In the middle of it all, he shook hands and slapped backs with visiting VIPs, whether they were college presidents, conference commissioners, or just old friends stopping by to say hello. And at least once per every Series, he did all this while keeping an eye on his own young grandson, the same boy who had the entire press box in stitches over his nightmare-inducing close encounter with a King Kong–sized gorilla over at the zoo.

"You think about Jack Senior and Jack Junior coming to these games when Junior was a teenager," Poppe said with a nod to his friend's seats. "Then here he is with his grandkids. I used to bring my kids here when they were little. Now my grandson is up here running around. Jack's daughter used to babysit all our kids when we had to go to late-night functions or be over here for games. We got back one night and they were all crawling all over the roof of Jack and Linda's house. It wasn't funny when we found out, but it's a great memory now."

In the end, those memories are what kept the College World Series in Omaha, spurning more lucrative overtures from San Francisco, Minneapolis, and Indianapolis. "Plenty of cities could throw more money at the NCAA," Senior said. "But our equity is in the people, the service clubs and the bus drivers, and their hospitality. The relationships and friendships built over the years, like Dennis Poppe and my son."

Poppe, being the athlete that he is, is also not one for showing a lot of outward emotion. But he is hopelessly romantic about the city, the Series, and the vision of the multigenerations moving its turnstiles. So is Diesing, who was initially distracted by the action during a midgame interview, but became very locked in to the conversation when it came to addressing the future in the new downtown ballpark.

"What is most important to Dennis is what is most important to me. That's fighting to keep this family spirit alive no matter where we play the games. A lot of people are worried about it becoming too corporate downtown, becoming like the Super Bowl or the Final Four where the real fans can't get a ticket and families can't afford to go together. If we took that away, we'd also be taking it away from my family and the Poppes. We won't let that happen. It is very personal for us."

That's why Diesing worked so hard for so long to keep up-fitting The Blatt in an effort to keep the NCAA happy. It's why his feelings were a little dinged when, after he believed that both sides were near another agreement to upgrade the old stadium, the city received the now infamous "New Stadium" letter in March 2007. Realizing that the new park had to be built, Diesing moved on from romanticism to reality, even when it meant standing with Mayor Fahey to be verbally tarred and feathered during those Claim Club–style public hearings in the spring of 2008.

The Insurance Man and The Pope quietly worked with all parties to hammer out the groundbreaking twenty-five-year agreement, a contract that ensured the Series would remain in Omaha until Poppe and Diesing were both gone, if not from Earth then certainly from office. They graciously took a step back to let Fahey and NCAA President Myles Brand give the speeches and have their pictures taken at the announcement of the new deal in the parking lot of the Qwest Center.

One week later, in the middle of the 2008 Series, they reminded everyone whose deal it really was. They circled the wagons on Fahey after the mayor made a power play to have MECA chairman David Sokol, an old political rival, removed from his job. (The official reason: Sokol wasn't a registered voter in Nebraska, but rather in Wyoming where he owned another home.) After a few phone calls to the city's heavyweight business leaders (including Warren Buffett) and no doubt some terse steakhouse conversations, Sokol was back at his post, Fahey issued an apology, and everything was back on track.

It wasn't throwing chairs and breaking noses on the State House floor, but it was close enough.

An hour after eliminating Stanford and earning a spot in the 2008 championship, Georgia head coach Dave Perno sat in the Hall of Fame Room doing a live TV interview with WGCL-TV, the CBS affiliate back in Atlanta. Just in case he'd wondered if maybe his team's success had transformed Athens into a baseball town, the second question snapped him back into the real world: "Coach, do you feel a lot of pressure to win because of the success of Georgia football?"

He simply smiled and rolled out his standard why-the-hell-are-you-asking-me-about-football response: "They certainly set the bar pretty high, but you know iron sharpens iron."

As Fresno State and North Carolina went through their pregame warm-ups for Game Twelve just a few hundred yards away, the second inevitable question piped through Perno's earpiece: "Who would you rather see on Tuesday night, the Bulldogs or the Tarheels?"

In his mind, the question was much more specific than that. Who would he rather play for the national championship, The Underdog or The Favorite? What he said was, "It doesn't really matter to me. We just have to take care of our business, no matter who we play."

What he meant was, "Go Fresno."

Like Georgia, the "other" Bulldogs had been held prisoner in their hotel, fittingly, Seavey's Jailhouse. When they arrived at The Blatt for the first time in four days, they nearly jumped off the bus before it came to a stop.

This would be only their third game of the Series and their second against North Carolina. But this one felt different. If anyone had accused

The Favorite of taking The Underdog lightly in Game Eight, they wouldn't be able to do it in Game Twelve, even if those Dogs looked so relaxed they could have flopped down on the grass and taken a nap.

After another rain delay ("Are we doing a rain dance or something and don't realize it?" asked UNC assistant coach Chad Holbrook), the Heels and Bulldogs put on the sharpest display of baseball seen yet.

Freshman starter Matt Harvey was starting his second game in as many days and had warmed up for the third straight day, thanks to the twenty-eight hours of Game Ten. In the first inning, Fresno did what Fresno does. A walk, a fielder's choice, a base hit from red-hot second bagger Erik Wetzel, and another from the captain, Steve Susdorf.

Underdog 1, Favorite 0.

For three hours and three minutes, the two teams put on a baseball-fundamentals clinic. Justin "Pack of Marlboros" Wilson, on the mound again because teammate Clayton Allison hadn't been able to loosen up a stubborn pitching shoulder, delivered huge strikeouts in the first, third, and fourth innings. Harvey answered with five Ks of his own.

Carolina assistant coach Scott Forbes huddled over his notebooks, signaling in every pitch to Harvey and catcher Federowicz. (Most, if not all, college pitchers receive their pitches from the bench.) Fresno received their signs from Coach Batesole, who may have been recruited by Mark Marquess, but couldn't have been more different. While The Mastermind stomped and stalked, Coach Bates lurked in suspended animation behind the old metal fan mounted in the back corner of the dugout, his elbow propped up on a ledge so casually he almost looked as if he was thinking about movies, or the beach, or anything other than the game, though that certainly wasn't the case. He only left his post when it was time to grab a cup of water from the cooler, duck down the steps to the clubhouse bathroom, or pull a player aside for some one-on-one adjustment tips.

When UNC third baseman Chad Flack stepped to the plate for the first time of the night, it was his sixty-seventh career College World Series at-bat. Two more trips to the plate would break the all-time mark. He yanked a 2–2 pitch along the ground for what should have been a hit. But the ball was snared by the other third baseman, Tommy Mendonca, with a one-kneed stop and throw, handful of dislocated fingers and all.

Unlike his fellow residents of the hot corner—Flack, Michael Hollander, and Ryan Peisel—Mendonca hadn't arrived in Omaha with a lot of pre-Series hype. He certainly wasn't the leader of his team; that job belonged to Steve Susdorf and the other seniors. Other than the strikeouts, Mendonca wasn't known for much outside his own clubhouse. But his homer against Arizona State in the second game of the NCAA Super Regional had kept his team alive and Batesole gushed whenever asked about his glove, declaring the sophomore "the best defensive third baseman in the country." In the Fresno State media guide the player declared his baseball hero was Ty Cobb.

What twenty-year-old says "Ty Cobb"?

In the top of the fourth, Mendonca dug in at the plate with one on. First baseman Alan Ahmady had already reached on a two-strike, two-out opposite-field single (*work the count . . . two-strike hits*). So far Mendonca hadn't struck out, but he had grounded out to start the second.

Actually, he was tired of hearing about the strikeouts. Why not swing hard and swing early, he figured, just in case he hit it? That philosophy had earned him a team-leading fifteen home runs. The first pitch from Matt Harvey was barely out of the righty's hand when Mendonca was already launching into his maybe-I'll-hit-it cut.

Make that sixteen homers.

Fresno 3, Carolina 0.

In the bottom of the fourth, Flack lofted a hard double safely over Mendonca's head. In every inning UNC had left men on base. Not this time. Two singles later, Flack scored his team's first run, having been moved over by a single from DH Garrett Gore and driven in by a single from center fielder Seth Williams. By the end of the inning, the Heels had scored again.

Fresno 3, Carolina 2.

All evening long, the two teams traded punches.

Back in the third, Fresno's Alan Ahmady had sprinted from first to snare a long foul ball as he slid into the rolled-up tarp, popped up, and fired a strike to third to catch Ackley.

In the seventh, North Carolina's Alex White, the starter-turned-reliever, made his third appearance of the Series in an impossible situation, the bases loaded with one out. He struck out two batters with a basket full of 90-something-mph fastballs.

"Is this not some great shit?" Fresno head football coach Pat Hill slapped his hands together and high-fived the Red Wave fans that were thrilled to be sitting around him. The gravel-voiced coach was revered throughout the San Joaquin Valley for his handlebar mustache and his willingness to build the football program with a "we'll play anyone anywhere anytime" philosophy that made his team an ESPN weeknight staple.

When he phoned Mike Batesole to congratulate the coach on Fresno's first two wins, Bates threw down the gauntlet by replying, "See? I knew you wouldn't come out here."

A pissed-off Hill hung up and drove straight to the local airport, walking up to the ticket counter and barking, "I need a ticket to Omaha."

"Right now?"

"Yes, ma'am."

"The next flight out is going to cost you $1,500."

"Fine." And he plunked down his credit card.

When the football coach landed at Eppley Airfield, he grabbed a rental car and drove until he found Rosenblatt. Not realizing the game wasn't sold out (far from it) he bought a $20 ticket for $100. It was worth it, the scalper promised, because the seat was "behind the dish."

The football coach had no idea what that meant.

He walked inside and tracked down an usher for help finding the "dish," whatever the hell that was. The very polite man welcomed Hill to The Blatt, but was sorry to inform him that his seat was at least 400 feet away, somewhere in the vicinity of center field.

"A Fresno fan recognized me and they got me straightened out over here," Hill said from his location with the other Bulldog loyalists behind the visiting dugout, dressed in his Batesole-style short-sleeve Windbreaker. "But Mike knows I'm here. That's what matters."

Across the diamond, in the exact same seat on the first-base side, Roy Williams also clapped his hands in support of his school. While Hill and his wallet barely made it to Nebraska, Williams had essentially been commuting between The Blatt and Chapel Hill all week. Back home on

Franklin Street the basketball coach could be lifted and carried from meeting to meeting like Cleopatra if he so desired. But here, during his third consecutive visit to Rosenblatt, he could exist as close to anonymously as he wanted to . . . as long as he was outside of the UNC cheering section.

Earlier in the day Williams stood in line with everyone else at Zesto for a cheeseburger and a milkshake. He'd almost made it to the counter without being recognized when a young man slurping on a soft-serve cone ID'ed him. "Hey Roy! Where's your Kansas sticker?" He was referring to the coach's decision to wear the logo of his former employer on his shirt at April's Final Four after his Heels had been eliminated. Back in Chapel Hill, the fans were not amused. Now Williams was not amused. He waved and turned back to look at the menu over the door.

The hoops coach had been in town for the CWS opener and then flown back to Chapel Hill for work. Now he was back once again, but would have to return home that night in the hopes of catching another flight for the championship series the next week. Williams went to all this trouble because he loved his school. He also loved Jennifer Holbrook, wife of associate head baseball coach Chad Holbrook and Williams's administrative assistant.

When the Holbrooks' two-year-old son Reece was diagnosed with leukemia in 2004, it was Williams who led the Carolina faithful to rally for the kid's support. He told Jennifer, pregnant at the time, to stop coming into the office and to stay at home where she was needed. They followed Reece's treatments on the Internet, including video updates posted by the family on YouTube. They even organized the Reece Holbrook Golf Classic to raise money for the family and the cause.

During Game Twelve, Roy Williams sat behind Jennifer, Cooper, and yes, Reece Holbrook, now six years old and as healthy as he could be. Perhaps a little too healthy judging by the youthful damage he'd done to the Tarheel dugout earlier in the week.

"Don't tell any of my basketball friends," Williams said with a handshake, "but this is more fun than the Final Four. Well, unless we're playing in it."

Williams had been there the nights that Chad Flack became a Tarheel Diamond god. He sat with then-new football coach Butch Davis in the 2007 Super Regional and all but kissed him on the mouth as Flack's second milestone homer left Chapel Hill's Boshamer Stadium.

As the Carolina third baseman approached the plate in the bottom of the eighth, Williams did the same as everyone else in the old ballpark. They cheered only sparingly, more nervous than excited. With shortstop Kyle Seager standing on second, Flack looked down at third base to head coach Mike Fox, who always stood at this post when his team was on offense. The coach looked over his glasses and sent the signal.

Bunt, Chad.

It was a good plan, especially with no outs and the tying run already in scoring position. Plus, Flack's struggles were all over him again. He hadn't had a homer in a month. But the sacrifice had to be scrapped when Flack fouled off the first attempt. He showed bunt twice more, but didn't get a good pitch to slap down.

Okay, Fox signaled in, *to heck with bunting.* Flack worked the count full.

Bulldog pitcher Justin Miller and catcher Ryan Overland got their sign from assistant coach Matt Curtis in the Fresno dugout. Curtis was an all-WAC catcher at Fresno and the only alum on the coaching staff. He signaled in for a breaking ball, inside corner. *Let's make him chase it and miss or at least force a groundout.* Another grounder to Mendonca at third would have been perfect because it would also hold the runner at second.

Flack looked over at Coach Fox, who touched the Carolina Blue lettering across his chest, grabbed the bill of his cap, tapped both hips, his right shoulder, both elbows, his cheek, and then his right wrist and elbow. It was a very elaborate dance that meant one thing:

Swing from your gonads.

Miller whipped out the pitch, which wanted to break. It really, really wanted to break. But it hung nice and fat and slow as if it were dangling off a string.

Two-run homer. Game over. Carolina 4, Fresno 3. See you tomorrow night.

Whenever a game entered its final inning, Dennie Poppe left Suite A and headed down to the field. He bypassed the world's slowest press-box elevator and took the stairs, always pausing as he hit the highest landing. From there he could see the fans flowing in and out of the front gate, hear the music rising off of Thirteenth Street, and smell the smoke from the Omaha Steaks grill in the courtyard below. Would he miss this at the new ballpark? Without a doubt.

As Alex White blew through the final three Fresno hitters in twelve pitches, Poppe was in his customary end-of-the-game spot among the coaches and season-ticket holders that occupied the lower level yellow seats. As the teams lined up for handshakes, he darted down the handful of stairs that led to the padded gate behind home plate and onto the field.

Before shifting back into diplomat mode, he turned to his right and saw the Diesing family standing to leave their seats. With a small wave and a smile Uncle Dennie and the Diesings acknowledged one another and went about their business.

It had been another great game, and another great memory to chew on over a steak.

NINE

THE GRIND

Sunday, June 22
Game Thirteen: North Carolina vs. Fresno State

As the Saturday-night clock struck midnight and the College World Series entered its second week, nearly everyone involved was beginning to look and act a little punch-drunk.

After Georgia's Game Eleven win over Stanford, an Atlanta television anchor got into a shouting matching with a San Francisco newspaper photographer because one of them had accidentally walked into the other's shot. Who? That depended on who you asked. A radio reporter repeatedly referred to "Cal State Fullerton head coach Mike Batesole" during a live interview with the Fresno skipper. In the parking lot the Professional Tailgaters were running out of food and the souvenir business on Thirteenth Street had slowed to a trickle since five of the eight teams were now dead flamingos.

What's worse, The Blatt's attendance numbers may have looked good on paper, but the stands were visibly emptier than usual. Way emptier. Some blamed soaring gas prices and the roller-coaster economy, others pointed to the lengthened schedule, especially locals, who were still perturbed at the NCAA for moving the first two games from Friday to Saturday, claiming that it had upset their natural Omaha rhythm. In years past, the championship series would have already been under way by now. This year there were still three teams alive.

Even Mike "Bulldog Man" Woods, aka The Guy with the Dog Painted

On His Bald Head, had thrown in the towel and gone back home to Georgia, despite having generated more media coverage than any of the UGA players. "I'm out of money," the retiree exclaimed as he posed for photos beside The Road To Omaha statue. "See you during football season!"

At one point the Rosenblatt grounds crew had to come back out and redo the chalk line that marked the batter's box because they had accidentally used the template backward. "It's amazing they aren't doing more stuff like that," groundskeeper Jesse Cuevas said as he stood among his bleary-eyed team. "They've been working fourteen hours a day for two weeks."

When someone suggested that the arrival of the championship series would be a light at the end of the crew's tunnel, Cuevas cut his eyes and pointed to an Omaha Royals pocket schedule lying in the bed of his John Deere Gator 4X4, a subtle reminder that the home team would be back on Friday.

"My tunnel is a lot longer than yours."

The long days and short nights were becoming particularly tough on the foul-ball girls. In a Rosenblatt tradition dating back at least twenty-five years, a team of crew members were selected to snag foul balls as they slid down the backstop netting and back onto the field. Make a great catch off the net and the crowd rewarded it with gracious applause. Let it hit the grass and prepare to receive a rain of boos that Nebraskans typically reserved for the Oklahoma Sooners football team.

"When you do it for the Omaha Royals, it's no big deal because no one's here," said Kathleen Brown, a seven-year net vet and also the softball coach at Patrick Henry Community College in Martinsville, Virginia. She grew up in Omaha and still came back for the Series. "But the first time you get booed at the Series it scares you because there's 20,000 people. Some people tell me that they come just to watch us and not the game."

Throughout the Series, Brown and her three teammates made in-game fielding adjustments no different than if they were an outfielder playing the Green Monster at Fenway Park. They learned to factor in the speed of the ball, its trajectory, and where it hit the cables that supported the net. When ESPN starting mounting robotic cameras on those cables, it made balls more difficult the judge, thanks to a tighter net and longer bounces out toward home plate. "The best is when people watch on TV and they've never been here. They have no idea about any of this, they just can't figure out why the crowd keeps cheering or booing when nothing's going on in the game."

"I'll get about four hours of sleep tonight," Brown said with a what-are-you-going-to-do shrug, pointing to her muddy shirt from a ball-saving dive into the warning track. "If I get any funny bounces tomorrow my reaction time isn't going to be much help."

In the food court just inside The Blatt's entrance, concessionaires calculated their inventories and cup counts for the ninth consecutive night. From the Famous Dave's BBQ booth a woman shouted over to a friend who was cleaning out an onion blossom/funnel cake fryer, "Did you ever see the movie *Groundhog Day?*"

"Yes," her friend said back, waving an oil-covered rag as if it were a surrender flag. "Tomorrow I'm bringing a cot so I can just sleep under the counter between games."

"Excuse me, sir?" BBQ girl called to a sportswriter on his way out for the night. "Who won tonight? I have no idea."

Welcome to The Grind.

Two hours after earning his third win of the 2008 College World Series, North Carolina pitcher Alex White slipped into the cool waters of the indoor swimming pool at the Regency Lodge. He'd retired all eight Fresno hitters he'd faced, striking out five. He had four pitches in his arsenal of an arm, but had fired only one breaking ball and thirty-three fastballs to earn the win.

The nineteen-year-old laughed when he was told that he'd already tied the record for pitching victories in a single College World Series. When he returned to Omaha for his second trip he'd certainly expected to start a couple of his team's games, but not three of the four with perhaps four more games to go. Back in the day it wasn't unusual for a pitcher to stand on the mound at The Blatt until his shoulder came apart, but in this era of MLB–style specialization, pitch counts were monitored by coaches, trainers, scouts, opposing teams, and the press box. Of the eight other hurlers with whom he now shared the mark, only one, John Hudgins of Stanford, had accomplished the hat trick since 1989.

As White swam alone under the watch of Greg Gatz, UNC's Director of Strength and Conditioning, his mind swam with possibilities with what could happen over the next twenty-four hours and beyond. He might have to return in relief again Sunday night, despite the fact that he was admittedly a little tired. Coach Mike Fox had been reluctant during the postgame press conference to answer questions about the chances of trotting him back out, but everyone could tell he was considering it. Even if White didn't pitch in Game Thirteen that meant he'd likely start one game in the championship series. Nobody had ever gotten four wins, had they?

The art of mapping out one's pitching rotation during the time-space madness of a College World Series has long befuddled coaches, no matter what their level of postseason experience. When the great Texas coach Cliff Gustafson was asked to write about his personal process behind setting up a rotation for the postseason, he rambled for four pages about tournament seeding, lefty-righty matchups, and familiarity with each umpire's strike-zone tendencies. When asked to paraphrase that explanation in a sentence, he growled, "I don't know, just go with your gut."

This from a man with two CWS rings.

The first player to win three games in one Series was Jim "Shuffles" O'Neill of 1952 champion Holy Cross (yes, Holy Cross). The Crusaders played seven games in six days and five of their six wins came on the arms of only two pitchers, righties O'Neill and Ron Perry, both in school on basketball scholarships. Perry was a gregarious local kid from Somerville, Massachusetts, who also won a national basketball championship two years later alongside future Boston Celtic Tommy Heinsohn. O'Neill was a tall, quiet kid from Columbus, Ohio. Perry was pumped full of emotion; O'Neill's expression rarely changed. Each hailed from different American universes, but both threw hard until someone told them to stop.

Their coach was Jack Barry, a slick-as-ice infielder with the Philadelphia A's and Boston Red Sox from 1908 to 1917. He played in five World Series, four times on the winning side. In Philly he was part of manager Connie Mack's "$100,000 Infield" and played alongside Frank "Home

Run" Baker. In Boston he was player-manager for one season, teammate and coach to Babe Ruth, Tris Speaker, and Smoky Joe Wood before joining the Navy in World War I. He once picked on Ruth so badly that he made the Bambino cry.

It doesn't get more old school than that.

"Barry didn't believe in pitch counts. Back then, nobody did," Perry recalled from his desk at Holy Cross, where he served as athletic director for twenty-six years, and as of 2008 still kept an office in the field house and still started each morning by doing laps in the pool at the age of seventy-six. "There were no relief pitchers. If you started a game you were going the distance. Every game we pitched in the College World Series, really all year, was a complete game."

The team played in twenty-four contests during the '52 season and their top two hurlers accounted for sixteen of the twenty-one wins, combining to throw nearly 170 of the 227 innings played. O'Neill earned his second win of the Series on just two days' rest and his third, the title-winner, after only one day off. Perry's two wins came over three days. Unfortunately, keeping their arms warm was not a problem.

"It was so hot the whole week and the hotel where we stayed did not have air-conditioning in the rooms. I think maybe the coaches had it, but that was it. There was a park across the street, so at night we would walk over there and sit out and relax to try and cool off. Guys tried to sleep over there instead of their rooms."

The sleep-deprived Crusaders were iron men all the way around. Coach Barry carried only fifteen players to Omaha and played only eleven. No substitutes, no pinch runners, no bullpen. All the way to the championship.

"I don't know how the hell he did it. You sure couldn't do it now." As Perry stated the obvious he mourned the passing of 1952 Series MOP O'Neill nearly a decade earlier, but was proud to say that the living members of the team, all of eight of them, continued to stay in touch and reunite whenever possible. "You couldn't do it like that today. The Labor Department might come after you."

Ohio State hurler Steve Arlin managed to out-iron O'Neill and Perry in 1965, when he made three starts in four days, including a fourteen-inning shutout effort against Washington State in an elimination game. He returned in '66 to start five of the Buckeyes' six games. Like O'Neill, he was named Most Outstanding Player with two wins (both over USC) and a save.

"Can you imagine even suggesting that today?" asked '65 MOP Sal Bando, whose Arizona State team denied Ohio State the title that they came back and won a year later. "You think Milwaukee Brewer fans were mad when I traded Paul Molitor (as Brewers GM)? Imagine if I had all our pitchers throwing three times in four days."

Fifty-six years later, Fresno's Mike Batesole didn't want to employ the Holy Cross–style roster-minimalist plan, but he had no choice. Injuries and disciplinary action had whittled his roster down to twenty-four, one player less than the CWS roster limit of twenty-five. His number-eight hitter, right fielder Steve Detwiler, had reinjured his thumb diving for Kyle Seager's eighth-inning double. The image of Detwiler's face wincing in pain had kept Batesole up all night, worried that he was pushing the kid into a lifelong injury. The number-nine hitter was Jordan Ribera, the *designated* hitter that was lugging around a .189 batting average. "If they would let me send only seven guys up there, I would," the coach told ESPN during their pregame meeting. "But I have to have nine, so that's what we have."

In three games he'd thrown two starters, Justin Wilson and Justin Miller. What's more, he'd thrown both against Carolina in Game Twelve, which meant neither would be available for what could be the last game of the season. Not even O'Neill and Perry could pull that off.

In a perfect world Batesole would send Clayton Allison to the mound and lose no sleep over the decision. The smooth six-foot-five, 230-pounder had just the kind of easygoing manner that was custom made for a game like this one. He'd honed his already laid-back demeanor with a literal trial by fire, spending the summer of 2007 battling forest fires in Oregon's Umpqua National Forest. ("It got a little dicey a couple of times.") Only two weeks earlier he'd thrown a masterpiece, going pitch-to-pitch with University of San Diego ace Josh Romanski and outdueling the best pitching staff on the West Coast with a complete game five-hit shutout in the first round of the NCAAs. But since that night Allison had developed a weird tightness in his pitching shoulder.

Dammit, Batesole would allow himself to think for a few minutes, *imagine if we had the twin tower starting pitchers of Tanner Scheppers and Clayton Allison bookending Wilson and Miller.* For that matter, what if he had North Carolina's pitching staff? Adam Warren, their number-two starter, was fully rested and apparently Alex White's arm was made out of pool chlorine and flubber.

No, Fresno had two guys they couldn't use, a bunch of exhausted middle relievers, Scheppers sitting in the stands, and Allison's mysterious ailment. All week Allison had worked that shoulder with soft tosses, hard throws, anti-inflammatory medicine, ice, electrical stimulation, and endless pulls of a bungee tether tied to the chain-link fence at Bellevue East. During the team's last visit to the high school, he pulled and grunted over and over as his teammates gathered around him.

"Well, dude? You gonna throw this week or be a candy ass?"

When the coaches asked how he felt, the twenty-three-year-old senior said he was ready to go. Of course he did. When the coaches were asked by the media if he was ready to go, they said they had no idea. Of course they did. Even if they thought he was ready (and they didn't), why not pull a Coach Marquess and make the other teams sweat a little bit while they waited on the lineup?

In the postgame press conference the night after Game Twelve, Batesole was asked about the obvious plight of his pitching situation. He reacted by curling his bottom lip to feign surprise, saying flatly, "I think we're in great shape."

No one believed him.

On Sunday morning at Dietz United Methodist, Reverend Stephanie Ahlschwede thought she recognized a young visitor as he and his family slipped into the back of the church, but she couldn't recall where she'd seen him before. Soon the congregation was buzzing and someone told the pastor that she was recognizing him from ESPN. When she called on Fresno State All-American Steve Susdorf and introduced him to the church, they applauded and lined up to shake the Bulldog outfielder's hand. Some told him how impressed they were he'd even bothered coming to church on the morning of such a huge game, a game that would either end his college career or put him in the championship. He grinned as he replied.

"It can't hurt."

That afternoon the pickings were slim at the Fresno State souvenir table in the Hilton Garden Inn lobby. A couple of alums joked that it was either a good sign (people were buying a lot of their stuff) or a bad one (no one expected them to be around the next day). The UNDERDOG TO WONDERDOG T-shirts that fans had scoffed at on Father's Day were now the biggest sellers on Thirteenth Street. They'd become such a hot property that Fresno associate A.D. Paul Ladwig had scrambled to have the design officially licensed and pounded the pavement of The Neighborhood to have bootleg shirts removed and replaced.

Standing between the souvenirs and the lobby restaurant was Buddy Allison. If pitcher Clayton Allison was curious as to what he might look like a couple of decades down the road, he needed to look no further than his father. Same smile, same large piercing eyes, same very intimidating build. But even their shared even-keeled manner couldn't mask the increasing strain that The Grind was placing on Buddy and most of the other Bulldog parents.

"This trip is starting to get expensive!" The construction worker from Visalia, California, never hesitated when it came time to make the trip to Omaha; none of the parents had. However, they hadn't expected this. No one would admit to believing that the trip would be a short one, but the group of predominantly blue-collar moms and dads were also realists. Don't misunderstand what they were saying here. No one was going home until the job was done, but at $200 a night hotel rates plus meals and whatever else it took to pass the time, The Grind was starting to grind away savings accounts and credit ratings.

"If we could do it all over again we wouldn't have bought those round-trip tickets," Buddy Allison said with an eyebrow raised. "Clayton's mother is handling the finances on this trip. When she says we have to go home, we'll go. I just hope I still have my job when I get back." He was only half joking.

When asked about his son's shoulder, Buddy said his boy was ready to go. Of course he did.

Behind the counter at Zesto, it felt much like it must have in the Holy Cross hotel rooms back in '52. "Dammit!" one employee yelled as she pounded balls of ground beef into hamburger patties. "It's so hot I would stick my head in the ice-cream machine if I wasn't so sick of looking at ice cream." With every minute that marched by on the way to the first pitch of Game Thirteen, the crowd of customers gathering outside the two-story building at the corner of Thirteenth and D streets became more and more swollen. There was always one line and it always moved as fast as manager Sue Trumble could make it, filing in through the glass door on the right and led to a pair of permanently frazzled order takers. Malted shakes with chocolate fudge. Ice cream swirls from an endless number of flavors. Sundaes, fries, and cheeseburgers, cheeseburgers, cheeseburgers, wrapped up so tightly that everyone sitting out front on the scattered wooden picnic tables licked the melted cheese from their aluminum foil without shame.

Zesto looked and felt like an establishment out of the 1950s. This was no accident. During the *American Graffiti* heyday of the drive-in burger joint, the popular chain exploded out of its home in Atlanta, throwing up franchises all the way to Seattle. But when the '50s ended, so did the reign of Zesto, with only a handful of restaurants kept alive by their local owners.

"People don't know any of that," Trumble said as she stood out back burning a cigarette. "If you ask anyone about Zesto anywhere in the country, they immediately talk about this one."

Fifty weeks out of the year, the store was staffed with a handful of family members and teenagers, serving up the goods for Omaha Royals fans, visitors to the zoo, and the occasional out-of-towner anxious to have a taste at the place they'd seen on ESPN every summer. The other two weeks, these two, Trumble employed nearly twenty people and sold 1,500 cheeseburgers a day, grilled fifty at a time.

"Those other two weeks are crazier than crazy," Trumble said between shouts into the kitchen to pick up the pace. "Half of our revenue for the year will come from these two weeks. My husband Ron, he's the one that just ran by us with the tool box. We live right there in the house next to the store. The one that overlooks the beer garden."

The burger stand added the party tent to its D Street parking lot in 2001, the closest brew in proximity to The Blatt, where no alcohol is allowed or sold inside the gates. On the Thirteenth Street curb beside the kitchen, where tables sat during the slower weeks, the Zesto owners leased retail space to Lids, the national baseball-cap retailer. Burgers, beer, ice cream, and ball caps. One-stop shopping in a space smaller than the Rosenblatt infield, and business that had long lured broadcasters, ball-players, and Final Four basketball coaches to come stand in line beneath the big blue letters: NATIONALLY KNOWN . . . ZESTO. Now Trumble and her bosses hoped that those same folks wouldn't forget about them when the College World Series moved downtown.

"We'll see," she shouted over the garbled barking of orders via the in-house P.A. system. "We've gotten permission to keep the beer garden open all summer and we're looking at adding a drive-in. The zoo is supposed to expand into the area where the stadium is now, so that will bring more people. Who knows?"

Then she threw down her Marlboro, took a breath, and looked back into the chaos.

"Man, we were getting people through here a lot quicker during lunch. Our best ice-cream machine has been acting up all week. Most people are pretty patient, though. The people who have been here before understand that we're not a fast-food restaurant. We make it when they order it and they know it will be worth it. Sorry, I gotta go."

Back to The Grind . . . and the ground beef.

Much was made in the media of the mental conditions of the Bulldogs and Tarheels as they left The Blatt after Saturday night's roller-coaster Game Twelve. The image of Chad Flack's UNC teammates crowded around home plate to welcome him in was slapped onto the front pages of sports sections and Web sites from Chino to Chapel Hill, while writers and reporters described the faces in the Fresno dugout as "stunned" and "the look of a team that has used up its magic."

ESPN led off its Game Thirteen telecast by statistically confirming what everyone had already suspected. Carolina's Mike Fox had used his bullpen more than Fresno and Mike Batesole, but Fox also had the nation's deepest pitching staff so the effects of The Grind would be minimal. Meanwhile, Batesole had a bunch of relievers that no one had ever heard of.

The lone exception to that was reliever Kris Tomlinson, who was now known throughout Omaha not because of his arm, but his hair. The junior's 'do had become The Underdog's good-luck charm. Before every big game his mane was sculpted into a newly horrific hairdo. As long as his hat was on, everything looked normal, with long hair out the back and over his ears, garnished with a goatee stolen from a second-rate Civil War reenactor. However, removal of the hat revealed the "Skullet." His mane was shaved on the sides and in the front, but two-thirds of the way around his head dark brown hair suddenly flowed. It looked like a dead squirrel had been stapled to the back of his skull.

Earlier in the day Tomlinson's family offered to take him out for lunch, but only if he agreed to keep his hat on. When he removed that cap for the singing of the national anthem, a woman sitting behind the third-base dugout let out a reactive, "Oh my God."

If Fresno was wound tight because of the elimination game, they had a hell of a way of showing it. The team gathered, as always, into a loose circle by the coach's box at third base, where DH Jordan Ribera began leaping around and ricocheting off of his teammates, who loosely let out a series of *woos* and *woops*.

Coach Batesole had calmed any nerves by calmly laying out the plan.

Allison, you just gut it out and get us to the seventh and we'll bring in Sprague and Burke. Just get us to Sprague and Burke.

Hitters, work the count, make those one-pitch adjustments.

During batting practice, Coach Bates was back at his post, instructing his hitters to swing as if there were already two strikes. He quietly repeated over and over: "Two-strike adjustment. Two-strike adjustment."

. "Just another game," assistant coach Mike Mayne repeated, still trying to feign his surprise as he shook his head, wishing he was young enough to do some leaping around of his own.

As Fresno jogged onto the field for the fourth time, they did so to the smooth sound of a 1935 Hammond Organ, electrically powered harmonies that felt like they were oozing out of the steel and concrete of the old ballpark.

In a glass booth on the first-base side of The Blatt's press box, Lambert Bartak's eighty-nine-year-old fingers danced and flicked and danced some more, his hands occasionally and reflexively fiddling with pages of the sheet music that looked older than the Constitution, though he knew every song by heart. Every inning was punctuated with a three-song medley. "It's a crutch," he shouted slightly over the machinations of his instrument, never slowing down. "I don't even know what I'm playing half the time. I just play."

Let me call you sweetheart . . .
You are my sunshine . . .
If I can (bomp) make it there . . .

The routine was the same tonight as it had been for something in the neighborhood of fifty years (he won't disclose the exact number), always in a knit shirt, a blue hat that read cws staff and his totally unnecessary credential hanging around his neck. He slipped off his shoes (it's easier to work the pedals in sock feet), flipped on the organ with a whirr, and put everything in its place. Bowl of goodies—peanuts, M&Ms, whatever was in the press-box cafeteria—sitting on the left side of the organ, the bottle of water on top, while sheet music and playlists were scattered all over the place.

Bartak grew up on a farm in Norfolk, Nebraska, about one hundred miles northwest of Omaha, and on his fifteenth birthday his parents gave him an accordion. During World War II, he hauled that squeezebox all over Europe to entertain the troops. When he came back home, he played at weddings and at funerals, performed live on radio station WOW, serenaded diners at Mr. C's Steakhouse, and even hit the road as an accompanist to a childhood friend.

"It would be just me and Johnny Carson. We'd be at a Moose Lodge or an Elks Club and I'd sit in the back and play whatever just to fill the space while Johnny did card tricks. Just background noise to the action. It's really not much different than this when you think about it."

For decades Bartak and his organ sat on the roof of The Blatt's grandstand, only partially protected from the elements or the birds that liked to use Bartak's box as an outhouse. Now they were both on display like a pair of museum pieces, encased in their custom-designed glass room, surrounded by a half-dozen young computer wizards who operated the stadium's frenetic 1,550-square-foot video board, cranking out stats, hitting charts, computer-generated games, and trivia questions. For a large part of the game they also spun canned music, from classic rock to hip-hop. When the time came to turn back the clock, one of the young bucks tuned and gave Bartak a hand signal to start playing.

"He's done it so long that his built-in body clock is more accurate than any stopwatch in the world." Public-address announcer Bill Jensen pointed through the succession of glass walls that separated his booth directly above home plate from the one that housed Bartak's aged yellow organ to his right. "The organ actually blocks his view of home plate, but it doesn't matter. As soon as it is time for me say something or just as a manager gets back to the dugout after visiting the mound, no matter what he's playing he hits the last note at exactly the right moment. Every song has an end, it doesn't just stop cold in the middle, and he can play any song by ear. Give him a couple of notes and he just takes off with it."

Bartak played songs that most knew as classics, but which he still remembered as radio hits. And during baseball's summer-long 2008 celebration of the one-hundred-year anniversary of "Take Me Out to the Ballgame," it was hard to imagine that anyone had played the song more than Lambert.

But his best-known tune is one he played only once: the theme from the old Mickey Mouse Club television show. It happened during a 1998 argument between Omaha Royals catcher Larry Owen and umpire Angel Hernandez, on his way to becoming one of the great blue agitators in Major League Baseball. As Royals manager Glenn Ezell joined the shouting, the crowd began to laugh as they recognized the notes coming from the press box.

M-I-C . . .

K-E-Y . . .

M-O-U-S-E . . .

Hernandez's umpiring crewmate Tony Maners was not amused, pointing to Bartak high above the field and ejecting him from the stadium. It was only the second time in baseball history that an organist had been tossed. "Not my finest moment," the organist said as he threw one leg over the other to sit in a manner few eighty-nine-year-olds would dare even try. "But in my defense, it was not a great call on the field."

The four-man umpiring crew of Game Thirteen was spared such controversies, thanks to another cleanly played baseball game between two fundamentally sound teams.

North Carolina's struggles to score runs early had to end or the season would end with them. So Coach Fox shuffled his lineup, moving up designated hitter Garrett Gore from seventh to second in the batting order, sliding the previous night's hero, Chad Flack, back into the cleanup spot, and moving struggling outfielder Kyle Shelton from second to seventh. Fresno right-hander Clayton Allison and his shoulder started the game facing a rhythm-killing lefty-righty-lefty-righty-lefty-righty lineup.

The first pitch Allison threw was sent sailing into center field for a double by first baseman Dustin Ackley, who was now hitting a cool .432 for the Series. Ackley had scored in five of the first eight innings he'd played so far in the NCAA tournament and now he was standing on second and looking for more. But a vacuum catch by Tommy Mendonca at third got rid of Gore, Allison got Tim Fedroff to fly out, and Flack and Kyle Seager weren't able to bring in Ackley from third. So much for the new UNC lineup producing an early run.

In the second inning, second-base umpire Jim Garman had to do a complete lap around the bag on a throw down to second, when UNC catcher Tim Federowicz caught Mendonca napping. Shortstop Ryan Graepel dropped the throw, but masked the bobble well and stealthily scooped it up while pleading with Garman, "I've got it! I've got it!" To which Garman replied with a smile, chuckle, and a safe signal, "No, you didn't have it."

Other than that fleeting moment of confusion, Game Thirteen was crisp baseball played by a bunch of kids so exhausted no one would have blamed them if they'd been sloppy.

Through three innings Allison and his bum shoulder had cruised. Adam Warren and his well-rested arm had not.

The confidence that had carried the UNC junior to his much-ballyhooed 22–1 record seemed to vanish in the Omaha air. He'd taken the loss in Game Eight against Fresno, and on this night he looked stressed nearly from the moment he left his dugout. Was it the pressure of being The Favorite, the stress of The Grind, or something else entirely? We'll never know. What we do know is that he didn't give up a run in the first two innings, but tried his best with four walks and a wild pitch. With one out and the bases loaded in the second, he was lifted for teammate Brian Moran. Thanks to a diving stab by Ryan Graepel at short and his heady double-play toss to second, the Heels escaped.

Whatever Coach Mike Fox's plan had been, this wasn't it. What was it Texas Coach Cliff Gustafson said? To heck with the pitching plan and go with your gut? That's exactly what Fox had been reduced to doing. Forget being set for the championship series. Lose tonight and there wouldn't be a championship series. Proaction had been officially replaced with reaction, with perhaps a pinch of panic thrown in.

When Moran returned to the mound in the third, he, too, was gassed. The strain of his fifth appearance in five games was apparent in hurry. Facing the middle of the Fresno batting order, he gave up a single to Erik Wetzel, a double to Steve Susdorf, and a two-strike two-run single to Tommy Mendonca.

Mendonca had looked terrible on the first two strikes, watched two should-have-swung balls and then roped Moran's ninth pitch of the at-bat for a hit. *Work the count, one pitch adjustment.* Fresno 2, UNC 0. Moran was out of steam and would not return for the fourth inning.

Mendonca, however, was not out of steam. Here, in the seventy-fourth game of the year, he and his bag of dislocated fingers were just beginning to hit their stride. In the first he played a high chopper from Carolina DH Garrett Gore beautifully, with a running catch, a look to second to freeze the runner, and a missile throw to first. In the second he had an eyes-closed snare of a shoe-top laser beam from Kyle Shelton. Now he had a hit and two RBIs. In three innings he'd already had a game's worth of highlights.

Like his fellow CWS third basemen—Hollander, Flack, and Peisel— Mendonca hadn't really considered doing much else with his childhood or young adulthood than play ball. He grew up on a hundred-acre dairy farm in Turlock, California, the heart of the San Joaquin Valley and eighty miles north of Fresno. When he was only three, his father Ray would come home from a day of milking cows and mother Tami would toss her husband a glove, her arms covered in seam-shaped bruises. "I've been pitching to him all day. It's your turn."

Tommy played baseball under the watchful eyes of his father and some very involved uncles. "All he wanted to do was play baseball," Ray said while driving from his current job as a water-distribution operator to his nighttime softball game. "Some people are blessed scientifically or academically, but Tom was just born to be an athlete. He's always had one speed. Go, go, go."

In high school Tommy laid out hits at free safety and laid the wood at the plate, hitting .429 as a senior. Colleges from Southern California and the Pacific Northwest all came calling with scholarship offers, but in the end he decided to attend Fresno State because he didn't want to be too far away for his parents to see his games. Plus, he liked Coach Batesole, he liked his intensity. This was the kind of guy he could play for.

As soon as fall practice started, he realized that maybe that intensity wasn't such a good thing after all. Batesole rode the freshman's ass throughout fall practice and into spring. It wasn't just Mendonca. Coach Bates was hard on every first-year player, but Mendonca's all-or-nothing approach at the plate drove Mr.-Work-the-Count-Two-Strike-Plan through the clubhouse roof. In his freshman year, Tommy struck out seventy-two times versus sixty-eight hits. When he started out at his record K clip in 2008, their coach-player relationship certainly didn't improve. Mendonca shrugged it off, laughed it off, and went to work.

With a month to go in the 2008 season, outfielder Blake Amador, the team's other Turlock resident, came to Ray and told him, "Mr. Mendonca, I've been talking to Tommy and we've decided that he's going to go for 20–100 this season." In normal baseball lingo, 20–100 meant twenty home runs and one hundred runs batted in. "No," Amador clarified. "We mean twenty homers and one hundred strikeouts."

Tommy came close.

"He just loves to play," Dad said proudly. "He's always been hurt a lot because he played so damn hard. But that's when he's always done his best work, when something's wrong."

Perhaps that's why Tommy Mendonca and Clayton Allison got along so well.

As the shadows grew longer, Allison kept chugging through his aching shoulder and through the North Carolina hitters. *Just get us to Sprague and Burke.* He showed signs of wavering when he started the fourth by giving up a run, but ended the inning with a strikeout and two groundouts. Fresno 2, UNC 1. From there, Allison trudged his way through the two-time defending national runners-up, Batesole's leash tightening with every pitch as he clocked the big righty with a stopwatch. The longer he took to make his delivery to the plate, the coach's hook inched a little farther out toward the mound.

The fifth inning ended on another great snag by Mendonca and a whip throw to second. In the sixth, Allison stumbled with two wild pitches, but came back to end the inning with a swinging strikeout of UNC outfielder Seth Williams with two on. *Just get me to Sprague and Burke, baby.*

Meanwhile, the Carolina pitching carousel kept turning. Fresno hit Colin Bates in the fourth and chased Rob Wooten in the fifth. When Alex White took the mound in the sixth, his Heels trailed 4–1, three RBIs coming off the bat of, yes, Tommy Mendonca.

Unfortunately, the healing waters of the Regency Lodge were all used up and not even the unflappable right arm of Alex White could fend off The Grind of pitching three nights in a row. Wetzel singled. Susdorf doubled. They each moved up on a fielder's choice, a phenomenal play by Chad Flack when he dove to grab a smack by Alan Ahmady and nearly threw Wetzel out at the plate, missing by half of a step. Fresno 5, UNC 1.

Up came Mendonca, who reverted back to his swing-in-case-you-hit-it ways. One pitch. Single down the right-field line. Another run batted in. Fresno 6, UNC 1.

When the North Carolina bench got into a shouting match with home-plate umpire Mitch Mele about his strike zone, the Fresno players looked to their left and right, and started simultaneously nodding their heads. It was official. The Underdog had set up camp inside The Favorite's head.

As the middle of the seventh arrived, Lambert Bartak's smiling face popped up on the video board in left and he started into his ten-millionth rendition of "Take Me Out to the Ballgame" to thunderous applause. The Bulldogs smiled for a whole other reason.

This sumbitch was over.

The University of North Carolina's greatest class of baseball players, the Class of 2008, played their final futile innings with the same dirt-covered effort that they'd used to turn around a long-dormant program. When they came to Chapel Hill, the stadium was a picturesque yet antiquated little facility where the classic architecture masked the facts that there was little or no attendance at UNC games and the home team had no air-conditioning in their clubhouse.

But by the time the Class of 2008 was finished they had convinced the school to construct a new $14-million stadium with suites and season tickets that were sold out before construction was even finished. They played 271 games together, winning 206, an ACC championship, and an unprecedented three consecutive trips to Rosenblatt.

Sadly, Game Thirteen of the 2008 College World Series would be their last game together and loss number sixty-five.

Chad Flack turned in a handful of spectacular defensive plays at third and extended his UNC career records for at-bats and hits. His 328th and final hit came via a single in the fourth inning.

Pitcher Rob Wooten hadn't had the kind of exit he deserved, lasting only one-third of an inning, while fellow hurler Mike Facchinei spent the game on the bench, and Tyler Trice was sent out to finish the game in the bottom of the eighth.

In the end, the greatest class in Diamond Heel history was epitomized by a play from its least-heralded member. Kyle Shelton's dream of playing in Chapel Hill had caused him to ignore offers from other schools as he set offensive records at Charlotte's South Mecklenburg High School.

When he told Coach Fox that he wanted to come to Carolina no matter what, the coach explained to him that he might not get to play much as a freshman or even as an upperclassman. Shelton proved the coach wrong, earning a starting spot by his sophomore year, then disappointed Fox by slumping terribly his junior year. In 2008, he had bounced back to have his best season offensively and defensively.

"All Kyle has ever done is exactly what we've asked him to do," Fox said as he watched the left fielder shag flies during practice at Boys Town. "And we've asked him to do a lot."

In the crucial fourth inning Fresno had already scored a run and was threatening to blow open things with two men on and Steve Susdorf's WAC-Player-of-the-Year bat at the plate. When he fouled off a 90-mph fastball deep down the left-field line, everyone in the stadium gave up on it as a foul ball.

Everyone except Kyle Shelton.

The senior ran with total disregard for anything but the location of the baseball. He sprinted from his post in straight-up left field toward the third-base bullpen. When his peripheral vision realized that the green grass below him had given way to red dirt, he instinctively went into a one-knee slide, his eyes still locked skyward.

All at once he caught the ball, adjusted his slide to avoid the rise of the bullpen mound, and snapped his head down to calculate the proximity of the thinly padded wall. He never saw it, at least no more than a bug sees the windshield before he hits it at 65 mph. Shelton's face, chest, thighs, and still-extended left arm slapped the green wall flush with a nauseating *thwap*. His right knee, the one he slid in on, fit perfectly beneath the gap in the padding just above the dirt, making sure that the knee received some very painful contact with the concrete behind it.

Third-base umpire Mike Conlin, already running out to watch the play, immediately signaled for the UNC training staff with one hand . . . but paused with the other . . . wait . . . did he . . . yes . . . the batter's out!

For a couple of minutes Shelton laid on the dirt, surrounded by teammates and the Carolina coaching staff. Some 350 feet away Terry and Linda Shelton's phone rang with friends watching on ESPN seeking any information on their little boy. Over on Fourteenth Street Linda Willis, keeper of the Sheltons' car, got a sick feeling in the pit of her stomach. *Get up . . . get up.*

He did get up. Then, as it should be, Kyle Shelton received a standing ovation as he finally stood and ran like hell back across the diamond to the first-base dugout. North Carolina fans cheered, as did Fresno fans and the good people of Omaha. Nothing eased the pain of The Grind like a true grinder playing his heart out for, as his coach had described it, one more day in his baseball life.

When Fresno closer Brandon Burke forced Garrett Gore into a game-ending double play, Mike Fox made a beeline for the other head coach, Mike Batesole. He shook the coach's hand and offered up just one piece of advice from a man who had been in his position, playing for the national championship, each of the previous three summers.

"Good luck, Coach. Enjoy this."

As he walked back to his own dugout, Fox was suddenly overcome by a familiar ill sensation that crawled down his spine. The same heaviness that had settled in on him on this very field thirty years earlier. That little voice that says, "It's time to turn in your uniform, kid. It's over."

He stopped and stood at the entrance to the dugout, greeting each player he could grab as they came off the field from postgame handshakes. "Great game . . . you played your guts out . . . what an amazing season . . ." Coach Fox said whatever came to mind, but what do you say to someone whose dream just ended?

By the time he finally turned and stepped into the dugout, most of the team had already ducked into the clubhouse. Kyle Shelton hobbled off the bench, his pants down around his ankles and a pound of ice taped to the parts of his right knee that hadn't been left stuck to the left-field fence.

The last Tarheel remaining on the bench was big number 34. Chad Flack sat alone and sobbed. No one had to tell him this was his last day in uniform. He already knew it. Fox sat down beside his leader, the one he'd visited at his home in Forest City to tell him that he could be the guy that forever shifted the balance of baseball power in the Carolinas. He wanted to tell Chad that he'd done it. He wanted to tell Chad that he'd turned

LEFT: Chop's Bowling greets drivers on Thirteenth Street with a familiar theme for everyone living and working around Rosenblatt Stadium. *(Courtesy of Ryan McGee)*

CENTER: Rosenblatt Stadium is packed for the 2008 Opening Ceremonies. *(Courtesy of Ryan McGee)*

BOTTOM: The plaza in front of Rosenblatt before game time—the crossroads for every resident, fan, and hard worker in the Neighborhood. *(Courtesy of Ryan McGee)*

TOP: The line for general admission seats starts forming hours before each game, especially when LSU is in town. *(Courtesy of Ryan McGee)*

CENTER: Welcome to the reality show life of Florida State catcher Buster Posey, aka "the Pick." *(Courtesy of Ryan McGee)*

BOTTOM: The kids of Bellevue, Nebraska, do whatever it takes to track down a long ball. *(Courtesy of Ryan McGee)*

TOP: Fresno State assistant coach Mike Mayne celebrates Father's Day with his grandson Noah. *(Courtesy of Ryan McGee)*

CENTER: The Boudreaux Thibodeaux party on Bob Gibson Boulevard. *(Courtesy of Ryan McGee)*

BOTTOM: The Blatt at night. *(Courtesy of Ryan McGee)*

TOP LEFT: Miami's Yonder Alonso's college career has just ended. *(Courtesy of Ryan McGee)*

CENTER RIGHT: Stadium View Sportscards, the heart and soul of Thirteenth Street. *(Courtesy of Ryan McGee)*

CENTER LEFT: Stanford head coach Mark Marquess actually sitting still with his charts and his legendary briefcase. *(Courtesy of Ryan McGee)*

BOTTOM: World Famous Zesto . . . not Zesto's. *(Courtesy of Ryan McGee)*

LEFT: If your school's flamingo has been hooded, that's bad. *(Courtesy of Ryan McGee)*

CENTER: No grass? No horseshoes? No problem. Let's play Washers. *(Courtesy of Ryan McGee)*

BOTTOM: The citizens of the Neighborhood lost their battle, but cling to their battle cry. *(Courtesy of Ryan McGee)*

TOP LEFT: Every NCAA championship trophy is handmade just a few miles away from Rosenblatt. *(Courtesy of Ryan McGee)*

TOP RIGHT: NCAA baseball director Dennis Poppe chats with WAC commissioner Karl Benson. *(Courtesy of Ryan McGee)*

BOTTOM: Eighty-nine-year-old Rosenblatt Stadium organist Lambert Bartak. *(Courtesy of Ryan McGee)*

TOP: Jesse Cuevas has kept watch over the Rosenblatt grass since he was eight years old. *(Courtesy of Ryan McGee)*

CENTER: No one knows what Fresno State head coach Mike Batesole is thinking but Batsesole. *(Courtesy of Ryan McGee)*

BOTTOM: "The Road To Omaha" statue greets fans and teams to Rosenblatt Stadium. *(Courtesy of Ryan McGee)*

TOP: LSU's Michael Hollander walks off the field for the last time. *(Courtesy of Eric Sorenson Ryan McGee)*

BOTTOM LEFT: Fresno State third baseman Tommy Mendonca, the CWS Most Outstanding Player for 2008. *(Courtesy of Eric Sorenson)*

BOTTOM RIGHT: Georgia head coach David Perno has turned the doormat of Southern baseball into an annual visitor to Omaha. *(Courtesy of UGA Sports Communications)*

his school, Fox's alma mater, back into a baseball school. He wanted to offer him a chance to come back and work as a student-coach in 2009.

But instead of jabbering away, Mike Fox simply put his arm around his third baseman and let the kid know that he was there.

Fox knew the feeling firsthand. Even now, thirty years later, he hadn't come up with anything to say.

In the Hall of Fame Room, the media peppered Coach Fox with questions about the smaller-than-normal crowds, wanting him to compare the enthusiasm level in the Rosenblatt grandstand to what he'd seen in his three previous experiences. He politely answered the first few inquiries and then bowed his jaw.

"Listen," he said, making sure he had everyone's attention. "Even when you lose, this is still the greatest place on earth."

Coach Batesole's turn at the big blue table was dominated by one simple, familiar question: Who in the world are you going to put on the mound tomorrow night? When he gave the media members nothing, they scrambled back upstairs to the press box and turned their attention to see who could crank out the most ridiculous pre-championship series headline between the Fresno State Bulldogs and the Georgia Bulldogs:

IT'S A DOGFIGHT.

CWS: A DOG EAT DOG WORLD.

A DOGGONE GREAT SERIES.

As Batesole walked toward the exit for the bus outside he was intercepted by the same group who had grabbed him in the hotel lobby on the way to the bus on Father's Day morning, led by beaming A.D. Thomas Boeh. "My phone has been texting and ringing off the hook all night. They're getting buses together back home to bring in fans for the championship series."

No response.

"Well, Coach, go get some sleep. Maybe you can dream up a pitcher."

As run after run had crossed the plate that Sunday night, Aaron Dean and Shawn Tremble were 1,300 miles away, jumping up and down as if they were the ones scoring at The Blatt. Soon, everyone around the two young men was celebrating with them. By the time Game Thirteen came to a close, the two infectious fans had recruited nearly every person on the floor of the Caesar's Palace sports book into the Fresno Red Wave. They'd even convinced the floor manager to put The Blatt on the big screen, dropping the usual horse races onto the smaller screens for a couple of hours.

When Dean and Tremble's beloved Bulldogs lost Game Twelve to North Carolina, the pair jumped in the car and drove east out of the San Joaquin Valley toward Nebraska in the hopes of making it to Omaha in time to support their team in person. Now they'd made a pit stop in Las Vegas. Hey, it was on the way, right?

No doubt some of the enthusiasm in the immense room came from those who'd been brave enough to lay some coin on The Underdog over The Favorite in the elimination game, but the sight of the two kids in red jumping up and down and leading cheers had created believers out of folks who likely hadn't even known that college baseball was an actual sport.

The send-off they received as they left the casino for Omaha was a vision worthy of a Roman Emperor whenever he departed a conquered city, as Dean and Tremble received a line of high fives from their new best friends whom they would never see again. They jumped back into the car, turned onto The Strip, and continued their eastward push toward Nebraska.

In less than twenty-four hours their Bulldogs would be playing for the by-god national championship, starting pitcher or not.

TEN

THE STATEMENT

Monday, June 23
Championship Game One: Fresno State vs. Georgia

The area of South Omaha that was once dominated by the Stockyards was now an endless succession of nondescript warehouses and industrial parks. Behind extraordinarily plain walls residents of O Town were busy making, storing, and delivering goods that Americans can't live without.

At the William H. Harvey Company, they manufactured plumbing specialty items such as washing-machine hoses and toilet-bowl gaskets. At Tab Construction they cranked out heavy highway needs, including guardrails.

In between those two businesses, hidden at the bend of the road where F Street became South Sixty-seventh, was a low-rise faded brick building, plainly identified in highly generic lettering: MIDWEST TROPHY MANUFAC-TURING. From beneath the aluminum roof came the unmistakable sounds of woodworking. Saws, sanders, and air hoses. One step inside the door was a step into the permanent smell of sawdust and lacquers, soaked into the walls after fifty years of crafting plaques, awards, and trophies.

Here, barely six miles west of Rosenblatt Stadium, is where every NCAA championship trophy is born.

"Hard to believe, isn't it?" rough-mill manager Mike Johnson said as he stroked his beard, looking at coworker and location manager Frank Pankowski, who held a tall dark maple trophy emblazoned with the NCAA logo and a plaque reading MEN'S COLLEGE WORLD SERIES PARTICPANT. "All of those people cramming into the stadium all these years to watch teams fight for one of these. And no one has a clue that we make 'em ten minutes down the road."

While nearly every citizen of Omaha knew the story of how the Series had transformed The Neighborhood and The Blatt, no one outside of Mike, Frank, and their eight employees realized that the NCAA had also saved an Omaha factory. In the 1970s the building was home to nearly two hundred people, an assembly line that crafted awards and certificate frames for Fortune 500 companies throughout the United States. That plaque your grandfather has on his wall for Best Scissors Salesman of 1974? Chances are it came from this building.

By the '90s, companies stopped giving awards in lieu of stock options and digital goodies. The factory on Sixty-seventh changed ownership over and over, each new parent shedding more and more of the building's headcount. Then the current owners, Oklahoma-based Midwest Trophy, signed a five-year deal with the NCAA, who hoped to update their classic wooden monoliths.

"We went from sitting around looking for something to do to working fifteen- to sixteen-hour days," Pankowski said, adding the classic warning: "Be careful what you wish for."

The new contract required Midwest to crank out nearly 15,000 NCAA awards per year, covering every team and every student-athlete that participated in all eighty-eight championships, from skiing and rifle to basketball and lacrosse. The crew of ten (plus some hired help) shaped, constructed, and shipped the awards to colleges and championship venues all over the country. One half of the building was filled with cardboard boxes, all packed with trophies ready for delivery to everywhere from Collegeville, Pennsylvania, to Rumford, Maine. Rowers, runners, riders, and volleyball players all spend their entire young lives in the hopes of one day opening a box from Mike and Frank.

"We didn't have to ship the College World Series championship trophies," Johnson explained as he watched thirty-three-year employee Charlie Trout meticulously connect the wooden base and glass middle insert of a 2008 Division II Heptathlon trophy. "I drove them over to the stadium in the van."

The guys down at Midwest liked to make fun of the old plainer version of the NCAA championship trophy. Johnson said that whenever ESPN showed archival footage of teams hoisting that brown monolithic panel of wood, it gave him nausea.

Not David Perno.

Every day the Georgia head coach came and went from his office in Athens, he looked at the brown award that read 1990 DIVISION I BASEBALL CHAMPIONS. Right next to it was that time warp of a team photo, with twenty-two-year-old Dave sitting on the third row. Next to him was Brian Jester, the team's All-American and offensive leader, now the Bulldogs' director of baseball operations.

Since the summer of '90, the Dawgs had been back to Omaha four times, three with Perno at the wheel. Four times they came back with one of those maple trophies, each reading PARTICIPANT instead of CHAMPIONS.

For the better part of 120 years, Georgia baseball was the doormat of southeastern baseball, including the decade that followed the CWS title. No one knew that fact better than Perno, an admitted history buff who liked to pepper conversations with Bulldog-baseball pop quizzes. Whenever he did, it was always to underline one common central point—they had all worked too hard for too long to settle for another PARTICIPANT award.

On Sunday night the coach started watching Game Thirteen from the press box, where he made an appearance in the ESPN booth with commentators Sean McDonough and Barry Larkin. He watched the middle innings during dinner somewhere in the middle of the Old Market. Then he caught the final stanza from his hotel room, where his analysis of the Fresno victory was the same as everyone else's, though he might have been the only person who would actually say it out loud.

"I just don't get it," he said, pointing to the rosters, Carolina's pitching staff, and Fresno State's M*A*S*H unit collection of players. "I mean, I do. When a team starts to believe, there's not much you can do about it. But if a sportswriter got it out and just looked at the matchup on paper, it makes no sense."

With that, he pulled out the sleeper sofa in the den area of his room at the Embassy Suites. His wife Melaney was in town now and she would have the bedroom all to herself. He knew, as she knew, that the coach wouldn't be sleeping tonight.

Around 1:00 A.M., he found a replay of Georgia's Game Two comeback victory against Miami on ESPNU. "Man, what a huge game," he whispered to himself, not wanting to wake anyone. Then his cell phone buzzed with an incoming text message. It was Ryan Peisel, his third baseman, anchor player, and unofficial assistant coach.

U UP? MIAMI GAME IS ON

While Perno and Peisel texted back and forth, Mike Batesole had his DVD player cranked up again. He wasn't worried about no Tanner Scheppers, no Justin Wilson or Justin Miller, or the fact that Brandon Burke and Holden Sprague could barely drag their arms down the hallway to their rooms. He was, as usual, not worrying about the stuff he couldn't control and focusing on what he could: offensive strategy, defensive positioning, and whatever else might suddenly reveal itself on the television screen. He started to take note of Georgia's overaggressiveness at the plate when they got way up or way behind. He didn't see anything in the UGA pitching rotation that scared him much. But man, did Gordon Beckham scare him. There was no way, no matter what it took, that Fresno could let the Georgia shortstop beat them.

Bates should have been just as exhausted as Perno, but instead he was suddenly riding a new wave of energy, a jolt that he'd received when he returned to his hotel room and saw the little red message light blinking on the phone. "Michael," the recording said with a voice that would send a chill down the spine of any college-baseball coach. "This is Augie Garrido . . ."

The winningest coach in college-baseball history had called to say that he was in town for the championship series and he'd be at The Blatt not as the greatest coach ever, but as a Fresno State alum and a supporter of Mike Batesole. He said he was proud of the coach for what he had accomplished and for sticking to his beliefs when everyone around him, even his players, thought he was screwing up.

"From here on, anything can happen."

Damn right it could.

———

As Championship Game One approached, Garrido arrived at The Blatt in a nonworking capacity for the first time in his near-seventy-year life. He certainly would have preferred to be there with his Longhorns, but they had fallen to Rice in the first round of the NCAAs. Garrido had participated in no less than fifty-five College World Series games, five as a player and fifty as head coach. The last time he'd been here in Omaha, he entered and exited through the dugout, leaving with his fifth championship trophy. Any other Series game he may have attended over the years was with a clipboard and a stopwatch, scouting a future opponent.

All those trips to Omaha and somehow he'd never done it like this before, handing someone a ticket at the turnstiles, and then sitting in the grandstand with nothing to do but cheer for his alma mater. Then again, the ticket-taker had likely never welcomed a five-time national championship coach.

He walked through the plaza and up to the gate with his old friend Stan Benes, whom he'd met when Benes was the stadium manager at The Blatt. Their relationship started when the coach needed to score some tickets and a hassle-free entrance for his friend, Cal State Fullerton alum and Hollywood's all-time greatest baseball icon, Kevin Costner. Like so many relationships between Series competitors and Omaha citizens, Benes and Garrido were baseball associates who had become great friends of more than twenty years.

Before Coach Garrido walked through the gate, he nonchalantly strolled over to the left side of the Road to Omaha statue, pausing to stand at the same spot where he always paused during each and every visit to Omaha. The first time he'd occupied that space was on June 17, 1959. He was a twenty-year-old right fielder with the Fresno State Bulldogs, who were making their first CWS appearance. The team had slugged its way to within one game of playing for the national championship and their best hitter was Garrido, who led the squad with a .336 batting average.

But the magic ran out in the semifinal game against eventual champion Oklahoma State, losing 4–0. Cowboy pitcher Dave Baldwin shut down Garrido and everyone else, allowing only two hits and striking out ten. Making matters worse, the kid also hadn't had his best game in the field. Unfairly, but typical of Garrido's highly competitive and even more highly emotional approach to the game, he blamed himself for the loss (paging Michael Hollander). While his teammates loaded up their big yellow school bus, young Augie sat down on the curb outside of Rosenblatt Stadium and cried his eyes out.

Five decades later, the curb was gone, flattened to create the bustling thoroughfare around the front gate and the statue. That didn't stop him from strolling over and having his traditional moment with the most heartbreaking spot in Omaha.

"In 1979, I came back here as the head coach at Fullerton and we were very much like Fresno is this year," said the Longhorns skipper. "No one expected us to win but us. And when we did I walked out there to that curb, it was still there then, and jumped up and down on it and said, 'I gotcha!'"

On June 9, 2003, he doled out one more gotcha. When the Longhorns' defeat of Florida State earned Garrido his eleventh trip to Omaha, it also handed him the record for most wins by a head coach with 1,428. During the postgame celebration he paused to point at the heavens and delivered another proclamation of revenge:

"I told you so."

August Edmun Garrido Jr. was born February 9, 1939, in Vallejo, California, son of August Edmun Garrido Sr., aka He Who Was Being Told So. Augie's father was one part salt, one part fruit, and all parts realist. He worked alongside wife Lois picking peaches and plums at a quarter a box, managed a parts warehouse in the Mare Island shipyard, and found happiness in the little things to ease a life permanently scarred by the Dust Bowl.

Augie Senior didn't have a high school diploma and neither did Lois. They hadn't come close. Everything they had, everything their three children had, had been earned by shutting up and working hard. Augie Senior wasn't a bad guy, far from it. He worked all day at the shipyard and then worked all night running the community center of their government-projects neighborhood, taking on the Josh Gibson–like task of coaching and officiating every sport supported by the center. At first, little Augie was the batboy for his father's baseball team, watching his old man coach and catch. As he grew older, his father became his coach, and Senior was particularly hard on his son in both arenas, though his intentions were pure at heart.

Senior could talk to anyone anywhere about anything. He just didn't want to talk with his son anymore about going to college and becoming a baseball coach. They didn't have the money to pay for college and they needed Augie to work, so Pops lined up a job for him, sifting through nuclear submarine parts at Mare Island. Besides, he said to his son, no one ever made a decent living as a coach.

Junior wanted no part of that settle-for life. He loved his father, but not enough to become his father. So he applied his parents' work-hard philosophy to something—everything—other than simply trying to pay the bills. He worked on his swing, glove work, classwork, his diplomas, and a six-year stint in the minor leagues. Then he worked on becoming a teacher and a coach, moving up the ladder and thoroughly fascinated by the psychology of it all—individuals, teams, fans, how they all played a part in success or failure on the field. He dove into the books of the Bible and then into the books of John Wooden. He took psychology classes and blew through three marriages. He also moved through the coaching ranks at San Francisco State, Poly San Luis Obispo, Illinois, and Fullerton. It was as if had he dared to slow down, he would suddenly be beamed back into the Valley to pick cherries and take rudder inventories for the rest of his life.

"People are motivated by fear," he explained. "Not fear like 'I'm going to beat you up if you don't do this,' but fear of failure. It's the great internal battle every athlete and coach has to fight. On one side you have expectations and the other you have failure. Which do you allow to push you in one direction or the other? The fear of expectation, or the excitement of expectation? Does the fear of failure motivate you to do whatever it takes not to fail, or does the fear cause you to fail? I'm talking about baseball here. But I'm also talking about life."

As Garrido took his seat behind the first-base dugout for Championship Game One, he watched the two teams as they hit the field for warm-ups, looking for signs that would tip him off as to which way each squad was leaning in that expectations vs. failure struggle.

It was too early to tell for sure, but both teams looked loose. The truth would be revealed soon enough.

Before Championship Game One, Mike Batesole stood in his customary spot behind the batting cage, quietly repeating the night's mission statement to his hitters. *Two-strike adjustments . . . but be aggressive when the time calls for it . . .*

As Bates watched his batters, David Perno approached, hand extended. The two coaches hadn't had a chance to talk up to this point, nor had they ever, and the Georgia coach sought to break the ice like all good coaches do. "Coach, congratulations on a great season. You know, I think you know a friend of mine . . ."

Batesole was pleasant, but clearly not interested in any kind of chitchat, not even a game of connect-the-coaches. Perno, realizing that the small talk was going nowhere, cut the conversation short, offered up a second handshake and wished the other coach luck. They wouldn't speak again until the Series was over.

That went well, Perno sarcastically thought to himself.

It could have been a lot worse.

In 1962, Michigan Wolverine head coach Don Lund walked over to chat with Texas coach Bibb Falk before their Game Two matchup. Falk greeted Lund with an immediate dismissal and screamed, "We're going to kick the shit out of you!" Michigan won 3–1.

In 1981, Falk's successor Cliff Gustafson drug his Horns back to The Blatt for a noon game after playing in a fifteen-inning affair that ended at 2:00 A.M. the night before. When he arrived eight hours later for batting practice, Arizona State coach Jim Brock offered up his sympathies and also volunteered a pep talk to get Texas ready for their elimination game with the Sun Devils. Remembered Coach Gus: "Brock said he would start his speech by saying, 'I know you guys are tired and I know you didn't get but two hours of sleep and I know it's going to be tough to play this game because you are so, so tired . . .'"

Gustafson laughed and declined the offer. He also lost 12–3.

Now, in 2008, the coaches led their teams through what should have felt like just another Omaha pregame ceremony, but this one was undoubtedly different. There were MLB World Series–style player introductions. The crowd, though still smaller than organizers would have liked, was bigger than the games before it. The Air Force conducted a jet fly-over, timed perfectly with the end of the national anthem. There were six umpires instead of four, two ESPN field reporters instead of one, and whatever family and friends that hadn't made it for the first thirteen games were surely here now.

What's more, the threatening skies that had hung around all afternoon suddenly parted as the first pitch approached, and the sun now washed over the thick, green infield.

"You wouldn't think that it would feel different after being here for a week and a half," said Georgia designated hitter Joey Lewis, looking sky-ward to the brightening sun. "But this definitely feels different. It feels more important. A lot more important. It should, you know. Because it is."

Had Bates and Perno had an actual conversation they likely would have dis-cussed and agreed that what they were about to experience was one of the best ideas ever put forth by Poppe and his Baseball Committee. Since 2003, the College World Series champion had been determined by a best-of-three series, ending a fifteen-year experiment with one winner-takes-all title game, an idea designed to appease then-TV partner CBS Sports and their desire for a guarantee that the champ would be crowned on their air waves.

Prior to that, the title was decided for decades by a de facto best-of-three matchup, with a true double-elimination "winners" and "losers" brackets. The team with one loss had to win two games to take the title; the team with no losses needed only to win once.

Now, as it had been for six years, both teams hit the Reset button and set a simple goal. Win two games and collect one of Midwest Trophy's finest wood pieces.

"Best-of-three is how it should be," Perno said as he stood on the top step of the home dugout, constantly staring straight ahead to glean what-ever last-minute information that could be taken from Fresno's BP. "When we won it in 1990, it was one game and we certainly benefitted from that. But the nature of the game, especially the college game, is life lived in three-game series. It's what we do all season, so that's how it should be."

It's also how it was in that very first College World Series sixty-two years earlier, when only two teams were invited and they played best-of-three. It was the completion of a six-decade circle that connected Jackie Jensen and Poppy Bush to Tommy Mendonca and Gordon Beckham.

But wouldn't it have been funny to put the Golden Boy and his mates in a time machine and delivered them to stand along the baselines with the Bulldogs and the Bulldogs for the national anthem? Imagine the comments crusty Cal coach Clint Evans would've had about Kris Tomlinson's Skullet? Envision hard-ass Jack Barry's reaction to Beckham's postgame ritual of hammering out the speed-metal drumming of British band Dragonforce and their song "Through the Fire and Flames," a tune he discovered while playing *Guitar Hero*.

The six clean-cut, spic-and-span teams of 2008 now all had hoods over the heads of their flamingos. All that was left was two gangs of unkempt dirt dogs. Georgia hadn't even made its own conference tournament in 2007 and now it was trying to become the first team in CWS history to win the title one year after posting a losing record. Fresno was ranked eighty-ninth out of 296 teams in college baseball's mathematically deduced power index rankings. No matter which team won, they would set a record for most losses by a College World Series champion.

And remember all those Hall of Fame coaches who sat at the head table in Hall of Fame Room on Friday the thirteenth? They were gone, too. The two coaches left were the two youngest in that room, the two that no one really had any questions for.

It was all so beautifully ugly.

"Hey, it doesn't matter how you get here. It just matters that you're here."

As Nolan Ryan said it the all-time strikeout king waved and was hustled down the hallway of The Blatt's press box to his suite over home plate, the same room that had housed Skip Bertman and his mending ticker.

On the field, the grounds crew and ESPN cameramen buzzed about the energy coming off the two teams. In the stands, the fans murmured as, was that . . . no way . . . it is . . . Augie Garrido took his seat down the first-base line. And in the press box, the modern-day knights of the keyboard were sticking their heads out into the hallway, ogling like fans on the red carpet at the Oscars, eager to catch a glimpse of the Ryan Express and the man who had invited him to come out for the game.

"That's him?" one writer asked.

"You mean Jimmy Buffett?" someone replied sarcastically, reminding his friend of his mistaken ID of the jersey in the Hall of Fame Room.

"Yeah, yeah, okay. But seriously, do you think if I touch him my arm will turn to gold?"

The Richest Man in the World strolled into Rosenblatt Stadium looking less like a billionaire and more like someone's favorite uncle. Warren Buffett was dressed in a plain blue knit shirt and entered with a smile as he paused to sign a baseball for Ernie the security guard, who'd manned the door of the press box all Series long (and by his own admission had "every page of the *World-Herald* memorized by now"). Once finished with Ernie, the Oracle of Omaha looked at the media horde with their faces pressed against the glass and waved.

This was a big deal. Buffett simply didn't come out to see Series games anymore. Sure, it was nothing to see him down at Gorat's (I'll have the T-bone, rare, hash browns and a Cherry Coke) with board members from Berkshire-Hathaway. It wasn't uncommon to see him over a neighbor's house—back in the day he was a regular at Jack Diesing Senior's—playing bridge and sometimes even bringing a surprise playing partner such as Bill Gates or Martha Stewart. And it certainly wasn't a huge deal when he came to Rosenblatt to watch the O Royals, seeing as how he coowned the team. He used to show up in uniform once a year for his annual shareholders night (he'd turned more than 15,000 Omaha residents into millionaires), where he tossed right-handed pitches to annual invitee Ernie Banks, warning the Hall of Famer, "I throw a premature sinker. Bring your shovel."

But Warren Buffett at a CWS game? It rarely happened anymore. He attended his first College World Series in 1951, the year of the Oklahoma upset, and the twenty-year-old was anxious to see Princeton pitcher Dave Sisler, little brother of St. Louis Cardinal Dick Sisler. These days he thought the game moved too slowly, with too many pitching changes and too much overmanaging from the dugouts. However, the chance to watch baseball with Nolan Ryan was more than enough to coax him out of his modest home in the Dundee neighborhood, a house he bought in 1958.

So, was he planning on offering up any investment advice to the newly appointed president of the Texas Rangers? "No," the Oracle said as he, too, was escorted down the hall. "Mr. Ryan seems to be doing just fine without any advice from me."

Had someone asked Ryan for advice to help Fresno's depleted pitching staff, his response would have been the same. They were doing just fine without him. He wasn't sure how, but they were.

When Batesole looked at the arms he had available, he decided to go with Sean Bonesteele as the starter. Yes, the same Sean Bonesteele who'd pitched so sparingly he'd been the source of "he doesn't need a jersey" jokes one week earlier. But Bates, as always, had thoroughly thought through the decision. The big six-foot-five righty had thrown the final two innings of the Game Three blowout of Rice. That meant the twenty-year-old had already been on the mound at The Blatt and had used up any nervousness he would have felt had he been heading out there for the first time . . . which was probably going to be the case for everyone else Fresno sent out to pitch. Just in case, he didn't inform the sophomore that he was starting until about two hours before it happened (which was yet another reason Garrido liked Batesole—he used the same last-minute strategy in '84 with oft-nervous pitcher Eddie Delzer, waiting until a half hour before he started and won the title game for Fullerton).

Above all, Batesole knew that Bonesteele would throw strikes. At this point, that was as good as the team could hope for.

In 1953, Missouri was in a similar situation, facing elimination in the quarterfinals and totally out of arms. Head coach John "Hi" Simmons sent unheralded Norm Stewart to the mound, a kid who described himself as "not a pitcher, but a thrower," and a member of the Tigers only because his roommate had dared him to try out. He took the mound against Oklahoma A&M with the words of Coach Simmons still rattling between his eardrums: "Just throw the goddamn ball over the goddamn plate!" Missouri won 7–3 and three days later won the title over the '53 edition of The Underdog, tiny Rollins College of Florida.

From his first pitch of the game, Bonesteele would have made Hi Simmons proud. He threw only thirteen pitches in the first inning, eight of them in the strike zone. Batesole's hunch had been right. Georgia came out way too aggressive, way too early. Third baseman Ryan Peisel led the game off with a double, but was nearly stranded when the next two batters—including Beckham—jumped on early pitches and quickly recorded two outs. Finally, first baseman Rich Poythress, hitting .475 in the Series, drove Peisel in to take a 1–0 lead.

Still, they'd let Bonesteele off the hook.

When the Fresno lineup had been posted on the UGA dugout wall, the team and coaches reacted with, "Who the hell is Sean Bonesteele?" All the hitters saw was the big fat 6.75 earned run average printed next to his name. The resulting overanxiousness to jump on his midrange stuff had them hacking at first and second pitches and cost them a chance to put the game away early. Even when they did hit it hard, someone like Mendonca was waiting to suck the ball out of the air, capped by a Brooks Robinson–like dive and steal of a shot by second baseman David Thoms.

In the dugout, Perno did not get out of the throttle. He sensed a chance to punch this win out in a hurry, big-bopper SEC-style. But again, the team wasn't able to convert swings into runs. In the second inning, Bonesteele threw only eight pitches. In the third, he tossed seven. Georgia hit hard, but after three innings still had only one run to show for their cuts.

On back-to-back plays in the third, left fielder Steve Susdorf ran down a David Thoms shot to his right and then robbed Peisel with a one-knee slider of a catch.

"They are doing it again," an ESPN producer Scott Matthews told his play-by-play team in their earpieces. "They hung around against North Carolina with defense and they are hanging around tonight with defense."

Georgia was being aggressive with the bat and Fresno with the glove. Mike Batesole wanted to do the same on the base paths, but every time he tried to drop the hammer, it bounced off the nail. In the first, second, and third innings they got the leadoff man aboard and immediately went to work West Coast style, attempting to move the runner with bunts, sacrifices, steals, and hits behind the runner. But like Georgia, they couldn't convert.

In the press-box bathroom, Fresno A.D. Thomas Boeh stood in line with everyone else between innings, waiting his turn to wash his hands.

"Thomas," the shout came from inside a stall. "You get any sleep last night?"

"No," he replied, splashing a little water onto his face. "But the kids did, that's all that matters. I just wish they could make this a little easier on the rest of us!"

Count Trevor Holder among those getting a hard time from Fresno. The Georgia starter threw a lot of pitches—106 over seven innings—and gutted out a line drive off his shin in the third. He gave up homers to Jordan Ribera, whose average had now skyrocketed to .198, and Steve Detwiler, whose torn-up thumb, the one that had Mike Batesole sitting up all night with worry, had him grimacing on every swing. But like Bonesteele, Holder got some vacuuming defensive help, including a homer-robbing grab off the wall by left fielder Lyle Allen.

Bonesteele's big 6.75 earned run average gave way to freshman Jake Floethe's 8.51, which handed off to Tomlinson's 6.75, and Jason Breckley's 7.54. Every pitch looked bigger than the next, but Georgia's anxiousness to hit one into the Missouri River kept the big inning from happening.

As Holder walked out to the mound for the seventh inning, the dog fight was locked up 3–3. Peisel ran out of the dugout to walk with him, asking the starter, "How we feeling, Trev? This is your night, brother. You know it is!"

The pitcher never responded verbally. Instead, he merely looked at the grass below his striding cleats, nodded his head, and gently pumped his fist.

High above the tension on the field, no one was enjoying the night more than Nolan Ryan and Warren Buffett. They laughed, ate peanuts, and laughed some more. They especially enjoyed what was turning out to be a rough night for Kathleen Brown and her ball-shagging teammates. Fouls were taking strange caroms off the netting all night, forcing them to twist and dive. One of the girls unwillingly reenacted Kyle Shelton's face-plant in plain view—and to the boos—of the 19,559 in attendance.

"Tough crowd," Ryan said to his billionaire buddy.

Sitting in that crowd was Lauren Massanari, wife of Georgia catcher Bryce. Over the last week Mrs. Massanari had received more TV airtime than Erin Andrews, Buster Posey, or even Bulldog Head Guy. It never hurts to be beautiful.

"I have to admit," said Beckham, pointing to the catcher before the game, "Mass has got it pretty good. It's even more impressive when you consider he's really not what you would call a pretty man."

The former Lauren Scyphers was used to being the center of attention. Any former Miss Nevada and top fifteen finisher in the Miss USA pageant knows what it feels like to be stared at. One month earlier she was seen on the silver screen in the blockbuster *Iron Man* (she's the brunette standing next to Robert Downey Jr. when Terrence Howard finds him at the craps table blowing off an awards dinner), but she still hadn't seen it. She was too busy raising—and now sharing the spotlight with—Marley, the couple's not quite two-month-old daughter. Ever since Marley had arrived, the junior catcher had looked very tired, thanks to juggling books, baseball, and bottles, but it hadn't been all bad. "This is my baby girl," he said with a nod toward the infant dressed in a UGA onesie. "We haven't lost many games ever since she got here."

The day Marley left the hospital she was immediately taken to Foley Field in Athens, where her Pops stroked the game-winning hit against Ole Miss. Over the next month he hit .410 with six homers and twenty-nine RBIs, powering the Dogs into Omaha. So much for sleep deprivation. "Maybe I should have started changing diapers a long time ago," he said with a chuckle. "If I get in a slump next year I'll start looking for babies in the stands."

Some people accuse Omahans of being too romantic about the College World Series, but Rosenblatt has long been a surprisingly frequent garden of warm feelings and love affairs. An informal poll of past and present stadium employees turned up a least a dozen stories of marriage proposals or love at first sight.

Jerry Buechler of Bellevue came to The Blatt looking for baseball and ended up with a wife when he spotted his future bride-to-be selling T-shirts. In 1960, Minnesota players Larry Molsather and Ron Caulston missed the first two games of the College World Series to have their already-planned weddings and then spent their honeymoons in Omaha winning the national championship.

In 2003, between Games Three and Four, a stretch limo pulled up to the Zesto beer garden. When the driver opened the door, Jennifer and

Aaron Mann stepped out, the bride in her stunning white dress and the groom in his tuxedo, followed by their best man and maid of honor. As natural as if they were in flip-flops and tank tops, the newlyweds purchased two Coors Light longnecks and sucked them down in the blazing sun. "We're on our way to the reception," said the groom. "Why wouldn't we stop? It's the College World Series, man!"

In 2007, Benji Johnson took that sentiment to a whole new level.

One year earlier the Tarheel catcher was warming up the UNC pitchers before their Game Six matchup with Clemson. That's when he heard a female voice coming from the grandstand above the third-base bullpen.

Senior Airman Michaela Ammerman was at The Blatt not because she wanted to be, but because she had to be. Stationed at Offutt Air Force Base, she was "volunteered" for duty at her squadron's concession stand for the opening weekend of the Series, trading in her dress blues for an extra-large Rosenblatt Stadium T-shirt and "a visor that was beyond ugly." During Game Five she'd grilled up hamburgers and Philly cheesesteaks, so by the time she and a friend wandered into the stands for some fresh air between games, she looked and smelled like she'd been grilled herself.

That didn't stop Johnson from coming over when the blonde linguistics specialist took a chance and asked for a baseball. "We actually tried to get the attention of the Clemson players first," the twenty-three-year-old San Jose native recalled. "But they totally ignored us, so we walked around to the Carolina players."

There, at roughly the same spot where teammate Kyle Shelton would one day try to knock down the wall with his face, Benji and Michaela fell in love at first sight. When she got back to the base, she looked him up on MySpace ("It's embarrassing, I know") and soon she was back at The Blatt, this time of her own volition, sans the grease and fried onions, and with the ball in hand. "I needed an excuse to approach him again, so I said I wanted an autograph on my baseball."

During an off-day for the team, they went on a date. Then another. And another. "Thank God they made it all the way to the finals that year. It kept Benji in Omaha for more than a week. They went home on a Tuesday morning, and the next Friday I was on a plane to North Carolina. We did that for almost two years."

When the Heels returned for the '07 Series, Benji asked Michaela to come out for the first day of workouts and suggested they meet up by the bullpen to take a picture where they'd first met. When she arrived, he strolled up with the entire team in tow. Then he reached in his pocket and pulled out a ring. On the dirt of the Jesse Cuevas warning track and to the rousing shouts of his teammates, catcher Johnson asked Airman Ammerman to be his wife.

As the 2008 College World Series unfolded, Johnson watched his former teammates on a clubhouse TV at State Mutual Stadium in Rome, Georgia, home of his new team, the Class A Rome Braves. Michaela watched from the Johnsons' home in Pittsboro, North Carolina, where she was busy planning her October 11 wedding, complete with a groom's cake modeled after Rosenblatt, ring bearers with mitts instead of pillows, and an Atlanta Braves garter around her thigh.

Take that, Jennifer and Aaron Mann.

Now, just a few months before the Johnson nuptials, Massanari was writing a love letter to his wife and child the only way a catcher knows how—with his bat. In the fourth inning, he singled with two outs. Two batters later, he bolted from second just as banger Joey Lewis banged a single through the ride side. Mass, who had long since surpassed the 215 pounds listed in the UGA media guide, lumbered his massive frame down the third-base line and scored on a hooking slide around Overland to temporarily hand Georgia the lead.

He popped up, slapped fives with his teammates and then looked into the stands for his girls, Lauren waving furiously while Grandmother held Marley up in the air to see what was happening.

Love, baseball, and The Blatt. There's nothing overly romanticized about that.

To a true baseball fan, there are few visions lovelier than a 3–3 tie game heading into the eighth inning, and that's exactly what we had in the first game of the 2008 championship.

Holder had gotten Perno's team through seven and now the game was in the hands of Alex McRee, a very large and very intelligent sophomore from Gainesville, Georgia. In 2009, he was expected to become the ace of the UGA staff. But in 2008 he was the anchor of the bullpen, the get-me-to-Josh-Fields setup man. He'd already made three CWS appearances and been lights-out in all three, jokingly complaining to ESPN producers that they kept editing him out of the late-night game re-airs the team liked to watch in their hotel rooms. (The producers suggested he give up some runs so he couldn't be edited out.)

But from the first warm-up pitch of the evening, the biology major knew something wasn't right. His elbow was stiff. As a result, his fastball wasn't snapping and his breaker wasn't breaking. He thought he knew why. After throwing two shutdown innings against Stanford in Game Eleven, the six-foot-six lefty had received his regular low-pulse electric simulation treatment to his pitching arm. However, as soon as the switch was thrown it shocked the hell out of him. After the power was decreased, everything was fine. Until now.

He walked Wetzel on five pitches and gave up an RBI double to Susdorf, a solo homer to suddenly the greatest baseball player who ever lived, Tommy Mendonca, and plunked Ryan Overland in the butt. Just like that, McCree was gone. His replacement, Justin Earls, brought his Fresno-ish 6.14 ERA to the mound, and immediately gave up a long RBI double to Detwiler.

Fresno 6, Georgia 3.

From there, the chess game was on.

Earls was a lefty and Detwiler, a righty, had just taken him for a ride. So Batesole pulled the number-nine hitter, lefty Jordan Ribera, for righty catcher Jake Johnson. Perno pulled Earls and replaced him with right-handed pitcher Will Harvil. So Batesole pulled Johnson and replaced him with lefty pinch-hitter Justin Wilson. As in pitcher Justin Wilson. At this point a sportswriter in the back of the press room took it upon himself to make an announcement to his coworkers: "In case you were wondering if Fresno was out of moves, they are now officially out of moves."

Wilson, hitting .294 on the year with seventeen at-bats, bounced the 2–2 pitch to second for the inning's final out.

Georgia trailed 6–3 entering the eighth. They needed a hero.

Before the game started, long before his electrocuted shoulder had been shelled, Alex McRee had leaned on the railing of the Georgia dugout and laughed with his bullpen mate, Fields.

The nation's best closer had taken a page from the Stanford fun manual and grabbed a piece of white athletic tape. He scribbled something on it with a black marker and carefully stuck it to the front of his white baseball cap. Now, alongside the big flat G were the letters O-R-D-O-N.

"You haven't heard?" McRee said, pointing to his friend's lid. "They're going to change the name of our school to the University of Gordon is Awesome."

As in shortstop Gordon Beckham.

Beckham looked like Patrick Swayze with Beatles hair. Like Fields, he'd come to Athens undrafted out of high school, but with plenty of local buzz from the Dawg fans who'd seen him play quarterback and shortstop for Atlanta's Westminster School. He was also considered to be one of the best polo players in the southeast. (Yes, the one where you ride the horses.)

Like Posey, the stories about Beckham were so Paul Bunyan-esque that it caused Perno to jump in the car and ride out to see him in person. He only played two innings and committed an error, but the coach had seen all he needed to. He'd carried himself the right way, approached the people around him the right way. It was like Mike Martin said—you know it as soon as you see him.

Beckham hit .280 his freshman year with a dozen home runs and the Dawgs went to Omaha. Down 5–3 to Oregon State in the ninth with two men on, Beckham grounded into a 6–4–3 double play that ended the game and the season. Two-and-'cue. The coach ran past everyone else as they left the field and put his arms around the nineteen-year-old. "You did not lose this game. You forget about this, because you're going to lead us back here one day. I know it."

Two years later, Perno was scrambling to help his team forget another bad memory—the entire 2007 season. When he met with his team leaders to discuss how they were going to do it, Beckham was among them. He gave Gordon the same speech he'd given the other seniors and standout juniors. *If you have your best year, we can't lose.*

Beckham responded by not only having his best year, he had the greatest year of any athlete who had ever put on a Georgia baseball uniform. The regular season numbers were something straight out of a video game: .394, 23 homers, 57 RBIs. Then the postseason arrived.

In the regional round of the NCAAs, Georgia was down three runs to Louisville and facing elimination. Beckham hit a game-tying three-run homer in the seventh and Georgia won. One week later, with a trip to Omaha on the line, Beckham homered again, this time amid a standing ovation for his final at-bat at Foley Field. By the time he made his coach's promised return to Rosenblatt, he'd boosted his 2008 stats to .401–26–72.

Welcome to the University of Gordon is Awesome.

When he saw Fields and his G-ORDON hat, Beckham scoffed. Fields shot back with, "Hey, All-American, when are you going to hit another home run?"

Beckham smiled. "When we need one."

As he walked up to the plate in the eighth inning of the sixty-ninth game of the season, they most certainly needed one. With no outs and a man on, Batesole began a walk to the mound that made Wayne Graham look like Jesse Owens. Breckley was gone and Brandon Burke, who was admittedly exhausted, came in for a six-out save.

Burke was not a power pitcher and never claimed to be. Two-inning saves were nothing unusual for him and neither were stressful men-on-base, too-long half innings. But much more often than not, games ended with a win when he was on the mound.

But at this moment, for whatever reason, he decided to go after Gordon Beckham with his second pitch, a fastball that was supposed to be down and in, but instead rode high and over the plate. Beckham had come to the plate waiting on a fastball, but figured he wouldn't see it until the third or fourth pitch of the at-bat. Still, he choked up after the first-pitch strike and waited for it. When it came sailing in on the second pitch, he actually, almost imperceptibly, curled his lips into a little smirk.

Tink.

Fresno 6, Georgia 5, no outs.

Burke followed the ball over the fence and broke out into a huge smile.

He knew exactly what he had done. He'd been guilty of what everyone else on the field had done all night. He'd been too overly aggressive, overthrown, and missed his mark.

"Rice!" After Beckham returned to the dugout after what couldn't be described as a home-run trot, but rather a home-run *run*, he shouted to Matt Cerione. The outfielder stood on deck and turned to hear what Gordon had to say.

"Rice, he's got a slider and a curveball. Be ready for the slider."

Rich Poythress reached on a walk (high breaking ball, more overthrowing) and Cerione came to the plate. In his last game the center fielder had experienced one of the worst nights that not even the oldest scribes in the press box could remember seeing before, striking out swinging five times. Tonight he was 1-for-2 with an RBI. He saw one pitch . . . on the outside corner . . . with a blue button sitting on the lower left corner of the ball . . . there it was . . . a slider. *University of Gordon is Awesome.* Rice sliced it into left for a double as Poythress beat Susdorf's throw home. Tie game. Joey Lewis, hitting better than .450 for the Series, then doubled with a ball that ricocheted off second base for an RBI.

Georgia 7, Fresno 6. Bring on Josh Fields. Zing. Zing. Zing. Game over. The Statement had been made. *We're the SEC champions and we'll see your asses tomorrow night.*

Peisel gathered his team on the third-base line, taking lead of the huddle just as he always did.

"That's how you do it! That's how you lay it out there! Look at Trevor . . . he gets hit with a line drive and what did he do? He laid it out there! That's right, that's a champion, baby! Give me a Dawgs . . ."

DAWGS!

As the Dawgs celebrated, the UGA dignitaries spilled onto the field to offer up their congratulations. Athletic Director Damon Evans, a Nebraska native, offered up handshakes, with an Omaha native in tow, none other than Georgia head football coach Mark Richt. There was even message-board chatter that Uga VI, the iconic Bulldog, was also going to make the trip, but so far he hadn't shown.

"The bandwagon's started to get heavy, Coach!" The shout to Perno came from Craig White, the associate A.D. and baseball administrator.

"Yeah," Perno said with a smile as he shook hands. "Good things happen when you win."

It was good to be the new version of The Favorite. Now he had to ensure his team didn't suffer the same fate at the original. That meant at least one more sleepless night on the pull-out sofa at the Embassy Suites.

As the final out was recorded, Ray and Tami Mendonca jumped up out of their seats and all but ran to the Fresno team bus in Lot A. "C'mon, babe," Ray said. "We're going to have some work to do with these kids."

They arrived with their Augie Garrido psychiatrist game faces on. Thing was, the kids were fine, calmly helping driver Chris Clark throw their equipment bags onto the bus, though they had easily set the 2008 CWS record for fastest clubhouse-to-parking-lot clear out.

"They were laughing and grab-assing like they'd just left practice," Mendonca said, still shocked at the sight weeks later. "And it wasn't a deal where you felt like they didn't care. That wasn't it at all. They just weren't worried. Burke had just given up a damn bomb and he was like, well, we'll get 'em tomorrow night. Tommy goes, 'What, Dad? We're fine.'"

What was that, Coach Mayne?

"Just another game."

Later that night, the Red Wave was not feeling fine. They were drowning their sorrows at Farrell's, a sparkling new sports bar one block east of the Hilton Garden Inn. Red-and-blue-clad fans and athletic department employees were slumped into big leather recliners facing a wall full of plasma TVs. Some of Pat Hill's football staff had come in, as had former Bulldog lettermen. Even assistant coach Pat Waer was in the group, waiting on a call from Batesole that might come tonight or maybe not until tomorrow morning. All he knew was that the coach was already back in his room watching film. Just like Perno, he'd be watching all night.

Every television in the joint was tuned into some sort of ESPN something. On ESPN the Original, *SportsCenter* led with "yet another comeback win for Georgia." On ESPNEWS, the highlights of Championship Game One were shown every twenty minutes, complete with dagger-in-the-heart analysis from Orel Hershiser, "Fresno probably lost their best chance to win the national championship." On ESPNU, they were showing a replay of the game itself (this time McRee made the cut). As Beckham walked to the plate, the group shouted to Burke, "Don't throw it!" But Beckham hit it out again . . . and again . . . and again . . . on every screen in every corner of the bar over and over into the wee hours of the morning.

Across the river in Council Bluffs, Aaron Dean and Shawn Tremble were having midnight breakfast at Ace's Diner, a twenty-four-hour pancake place located in the lobby of the Harrah's Hotel and Casino. They were holding a one-sided conversation with a man covered in Nebraska Cornhusker gear who had certainly had more to drink than orange juice and coffee.

Dean and Tremble had driven through the night from Vegas to make it in time for the first game against Georgia. Just in time to witness the missed opportunity that now made their bacon and eggs taste like road gravel. "We need rain," Dean explained to their new inebriated friend in the booth beside them. "We need rain bad. Rain pushes the third game to Thursday and Thursday gets us to Justin Wilson on four days' rest. And Wilson on four days' rest won't lose to these guys."

"We need rain," Tremble repeated. "But I looked at the weather forecast. There's only a thirty-percent chance."

"To rain," the drunk toasted, holding aloft his bottle of Miller Lite, which apparently went well with his French toast. "I love the goddamn rain."

ELEVEN

THE STORM

Tuesday, June 24
Championship Game Two: Fresno State vs. Georgia

The rain started at 5:00 A.M., a gully-washing, heavy-clouded, stay-away-from-Vicky's-Valley kind of rain. All day long, it felt like a rainout. It had to be a rainout. Fresno players, families, and fans filed in and out of their hotel while the Georgia party did the same. One by one, every single person affiliated with each team took their turn walking outside, leaning out to look at the sky and trying to make some sort of meteorological judgment.

A century earlier, on these very streets, this was the kind of day that turned the Big O into the western world's biggest, nastiest, smelliest municipal mud bog. On March 13, 1868, a writer at the *Omaha World-Herald* even put it into poetry:

> *Some towns are famed for beauty,*
> *And others for deeds of blood,*
> *But say what you may of Omaha,*
> *It beats them all for mud.*

Since it was founded in 1868, until way too far into the twentieth century, the streets of Omaha were in whatever condition the skies above would allow. What began as pleasant long grass roadways were trampled into dirt paths by horse hooves and wagon wheels. During summer that dirt became airborne clouds of lung-choking dust. During winter it became a permafrost-hardened ice rink. But when it rained—really, really rained—that's when the fun started.

In 1868, at the corner of Twelfth and Douglas streets, in between the 2008 location of the CWS championship series team hotels, a mud hole became so deep and so notorious that a resident painted up a sign that read: NO BOTTOM! TRAINS LEAVE DAILY FOR CHINA AND INTERMEDIATE POINTS.

At noon, Randy Buhr and Bob Thomas drove down those same roads—now, thankfully, paved—and arrived at The Blatt a full six hours before the scheduled first pitch of Championship Game Two.

If that game was going to happen it was up to Buhr, Bob, and Jesse Cuevas. Most fans knew Cuevas by face if not by name after watching him grow up right before their eyes, from one of Mancuso's Urchins to the Hybrid Grass Master.

But little if anyone knew anything about Randy Buhr. They'd surely seen him as he frantically crisscrossed the field three hundred times before every game, never stopping to take a breath until the first pitch was thrown and the night was safely in the hands of the umpires.

Even fewer folks could tell you who Bob Thomas was, despite the fact that anyone who'd ever played any sort of organized sport at any stage of their lives certainly had known some version of Bob somewhere. You know the guy. There's always a guy. The guy that takes care of the stuff that no one realizes is even being taken care of. At your local high school field, it's the guy who painted the lines on the football field. Bob's been that guy. At your local small college, it's the guy who makes sure the scoreboard is working properly or there are basketballs pumped with air and ready to bounce. Bob's been that guy, too.

He was a high-school teacher back in Wisconsin for twenty-eight years, coaching every sport you've ever heard of. Then he moved on to the University of Wisconsin–Stout, where he was wrestling coach and organized the nation's second largest high school wrestling tournament.

The schedules that everyone lived by—every coach, A.D., NCAA worker, and grounds crew member—were kept on schedule by Bob and Randy. Umpires march at 5:57 P.M., national anthem at 5:58, umpire/coaches meeting at 6:02, home team takes the field at 6:06, first pitch 6:08 . . . not 6:07 and not 6:09. The only adjustment came if ESPN requested one, and the only adjustment available to them was to start everything two minutes earlier.

"People hear about this guy who has always run such a tight ship," Buhr said while turning down the volume of his incessantly chattering walkie-talkie. "But then they meet Bob and he's literally the nicest person you'd ever meet. Without him we'd be lost."

That's precisely why one of Buhr's top priorities when he became the NCAA's associate director of championships was to call Bob and have him write down everything he did before and after each CWS game.

"Hard to believe no one had ever asked me for that before," said the officially titled "on-field liaison" as he carried what he described as a "box of stuff" to the umpires' locker room. "I'd never actually written it down. If for some reason old Bob hadn't been able to show up, no one would have known what to do, I guess."

Like deliver the baseballs. Bob was responsible for the 130 dozen balls used for games and distributed to the teams for practice. He recruited a few members of the Cuevas Crew to rub down six dozen for every game with genuine St. Louis–brand Mississippi River mud, though this year he'd been a little frustrated with the quality of the balls. "You want them to have that shine right out of the box," he said, figuring he's handled about half a million brand-new baseballs over the years. "But I've had two this year with a rubbed spot on them. Those rubs just suck up that mud and make a terrible brown spot. I know it doesn't sound like a big deal to most people, but that's the kind of thing that will drive a guy like me crazy."

So did a day like today. Rain fouls up everything. It ruins baseballs, runs off fans, and makes everyone move a little slower than normal, which begins to stretch the boundaries of Bob and Randy's time sheet.

"Rain is why we have six dozen balls per game. We used five for a while and then one year we had a bunch of rain delays and had to add a couple of 'if necessary' games and next thing I know I'm sending someone to Wilson (the former baseball supplier, in 2008 it was Rawlings) to beg for two cases of balls! And they weren't monogrammed with the Series logo. It was a mess. So we went back to six dozen."

These are the kinds of problems that keep a man like Bob up all night and at the stadium all day. Without him worrying, we'd have nothing to watch. Unless you like your games played with no schedule, umpires, or equipment.

For six hours, Bob, Randy, and Jesse watched the field, the stadium, and the Doppler radar. If this game was going to happen, it would be up to them.

At the Hilton Garden Inn, Coach Mike Mayne was back in the Seavey Room, eating lunch and talking baseball. This time the pupil was closer Brandon Burke, the only Fresno pitcher to play in Championship Game One with an ERA below 6.00 and also the only one to leave The Blatt with a loss.

Like everyone else, Mayne had seen Burke start laughing when Gordon Beckham launched his second pitch into the general-admission seats. That was good. It meant he was okay mentally. But the walk he surrendered to the next batter, the one that became the tying run, was what bothered the old ball coach.

"You tried to get it done too soon," he told his closer. "You let the best hitter in the game take you out of what you do. You let him talk you into trying to blow it by him and that's not what you do. You're not going to beat Beckham with your best stuff against his best stuff. You can beat him, but you have to beat him with your head. Then, you kept overthrowing trying to get the game over and that walk ended up costing us the game."

They talked about what that meant, about pitching instead of throwing. About doing what Bonesteele had done so well, exploiting Georgia's overaggressiveness at the plate. Stop trying to get six outs with one pitch. One pitch at a time. Then he reminded Burke that life in the pros was going to be all about nights like the last one and how he responded the next day, a day like this day.

"But you're our guy, Brandon. When we win the championship, you'll be the guy on the mound when it happens."

Before Fresno had even left the hotel, Georgia was already at the ballpark. In the morning meeting with ESPN, Gordon Beckham was uncharacteristically fidgety, telling the broadcast team, "We just want to get out there and play. It's time to put this away."

That's how the entire team felt, no one more than Dave Perno, who had explained to his team, alums, ESPN, and anyone else who would listen that tonight's goal was simple: "End this now. Don't let Fresno hang around another night."

Officially sick of the Embassy Suites, the coach rounded up his team quickly and had them at the ballpark nearly a full half hour early. As the coach stood in the dugout, looking skyward into the downpour, his team moved down to the indoor batting cages located behind the third-base grandstands. For an hour Georgia *tink-tink*ed away in three side-by-side batting nets to the country-music sounds of Alan Jackson, himself a Georgia native.

"Hey, Gordon." Right fielder Matt Olson sat on a bench against the wall, leaning his head out the door to watch the raindrops drip off the awning above. "What do you say I hit the first pitch I see to the damn zoo and let's get out of here tonight."

"Dude," the University of Gordon replied, "that would be fine by me. But I don't think we're playing."

Actually, they were. Bob, Randy, and Jesse were sure of it. But there was no way it was happening on time. Soon, Dennie Poppe and Larry Templeton stepped onto the field looking for an update. No one wanted to say it aloud, but they *really* needed to get this game in tonight. Not only was the griping about the new, longer schedule getting tiresome, but the U.S. Olympic Swimming Trials were beginning in three days and the good people at the Hilton Garden Inn and the Embassy Suites, while very accommodating, didn't want to have to tell Michael Phelps that they had no rooms available and he was going to have to sleep in his rental car.

But the news from Cuevas was good. The rains were about to lift and his team was about to pull the tarp off the field.

"How long before the field will be ready?"

"Twenty-five minutes."

"That's it?"

"That's it."

"Randy and Bob, you ready for that?"

"Yes, sir, here's the new schedule and we've got extra baseballs ready to go."

"All right, let's go."

As the tarp came off the field to the cheers of the crowd, the teams began to fill the dugouts, and they did so once again under the watchful eye of Texas coach-turned-Fresno-cheerleader Augie Garrido. It was a fascinating perspective for the eagle-eyed coach, who was usually so caught up in his own team that he never had the chance to back up and really observe the players on both sides of the field.

He watched their body language as they ticked off the now-delayed minutes before the game finally started. Georgia stalked and stomped, uncharacteristically quiet as they were clearly focused on winning tonight and getting the hell out of Nebraska. Meanwhile, Fresno looked like they always did. One player used a piece of white tape to stick a POWERade cup on top of his teammate's head without him knowing it. Brandon Burke, who'd had a far worse night than the one that left Young Augie sobbing on the curb in '59, was standing on the top step of the dugout to watch the fans file in . . . more specifically to watch a group of girls come in.

"It's a beautiful thing not to be worried," Garrido said, harkening back to his '79 Fullerton Titans. "We got killed in our first game against Mississippi State. Then, with our lives on the line, we won five straight games and won the national championship 2–1 with Dave Weatherman on the mound, who threw the game of his life. The freedom of nothing to lose is a great feeling. It's euphoric."

The flip side of that euphoria is the nightmare. Garrido had been there, too.

"The 2004 Texas came in with so much hype. We'd been put on such a pedestal by our fans and the media and everybody that they expected us to beat the 1929 Yankees. Then in the first game of the championship series our first baseman drops a ball thrown right to him, and there you go. The fear of failure swept through the team and we never recovered. We lost two games and lost the championship."

Who'd you lose it to?

"Who else? Cal State Fullerton."

As the chalk lines were laid down it was obvious that Fresno wasn't going to get the rainout that so many of its fans felt they needed, but Mike Batesole wasn't worried. Justin Miller was ready to go. He'd pitched one inning three days ago, but hadn't started a game since Game Eight. Plus set-up man Holden Sprague was available for some long relief if needed. Past that, Bates didn't want to go to the whip with Burke's tired arm and potentially damaged mind-set. But if he had to he had to.

Across the diamond, Georgia was going with Nick Montgomery, a senior righty whose college career had been made up primarily of middle-relief appearances. During the debacle of 2007, he'd gone down with a blood clot in his throwing shoulder, but had recovered nicely from the surgery that followed.

Here, in the fifteenth game of the College World Series, no one knew what to expect or how it would unfold. Well, almost no one.

"Buckle up tonight," Fresno assistant Mike Mayne said as he emerged from the tunnel behind the third-base bullpen and turned for the dugout, the last of the batting-cage *tinks* echoing up the tunnel. "It'll take double digits to win this game tonight. Trust me."

Double-digit runs, yes. But thirty-five runs? Probably not. That was the combined total posted by Southern Cal and Arizona State in the 1998 championship game. The pinnacle and eventual cause of death for what the Omaha locals like to call Gorilla Ball. At the center of Gorilla Ball lies an axis of metal that has long divided baseball lovers into two camps when it comes to the College World Series and college baseball in general.

"It's hard for a lot of people to stomach the aluminum bats." As ESPN's Robin Ventura said it, he realized how ridiculous it must have sounded from someone who posted some of the gaudiest numbers in collegiate history, including that fifty-eight-game hitting streak that everyone liked to remind him was ended on the very field where he stood. "But these bats aren't like they were twenty years ago. They were just goofy back then. Trust me." (Here, it must be noted that Ventura did just fine with wooden bats, thank you, whacking 294 home runs and making two All-Star teams during sixteen years in the big leagues.)

The first aluminum bat was swung across the plate at Rosenblatt on June 7, 1974, whipped into action by, of all schools, Harvard. Coaches had pushed the NCAA to let them use the metal clubs with the argument that it would help them cut costs. One aluminum bat would last ten times longer than the increasingly expensive wooden models. Instead of thirty players hauling stacks of personal bats, the entire team could use four or five total. Of course, they'd also figured out that balls tended to pop a little more off the hollow barrels. The NCAA relented, allowing the bats to debut during '74, the same season that the designated hitter was added to collegiate batting orders.

Aluminum had some impact on the '74 Series—three teams posted double-digit scores—but the explosion wasn't immediate. For the next decade the bat companies—Worth, Easton, Louisville Slugger, and the like—slow-cooked recipes of different alloys, fibers, and barrel diameters. Anxious to ignite sales throughout the lucrative youth- and high-school ranks, an arms race began to see who could bring the biggest stick of dynamite to amateur baseball's biggest stage.

In 1984, Oklahoma State lost to Arizona State 23–12, came back to beat Texas 18–13, only to lose to Fullerton 10–3. "You still had to put the ball on the bat," Fullerton coach Garrido said. "But it was becoming a lot easier to make it do something happen."

The pinnacle, and the breaking point, came fourteen years later.

"All you need to know about the 1998 Series is this," Skip Bertman recalled, reaching back into a brain filled with more statistics than the *Baseball Encyclopedia*. "That year our LSU team set records for most home runs hit in one game with eight and most home runs in a Series with seventeen in eight games. And we finished third."

First and second belonged to the Trojans and Sun Devils, who proceeded to put on either the most thrilling or the most disgusting championship slugfest in the history of the College World Series, depending on whom you ask.

"That game gets a bad rap," former USC third baseman Morgan Ensberg said from the clubhouse of Cleveland's Jacobs Field, where he spent the 2008 season as a member of the Cleveland Indians. "When people find out that I was in the 21–14 game they either ask if we thought about going for two after the third touchdown or they tell me that it was the greatest game they ever watched."

The day was hot and it didn't take long for the bats to warm up with the sun. ASU pitcher Ryan Mills, the number-six pick in the MLB Draft, was wrecked by USC's bats and left the game in the second inning, down 6–0. Trojan Robb Gorr already had two home runs. USC went up 8–0, only to see their lead shaved to one run, then they exploded again . . . and again . . . before the final score was posted.

"That game was not just about homers," Ensberg added. "They had cut our lead to one and that's when I stole home in the seventh as part of a triple steal. A triple steal in a one-run game in the seventh inning? If you don't like that, you don't like baseball."

In the end, the NCAA Baseball Committee didn't like what they had seen at all, one member telling the CWS media that he felt "embarrassed for the game of baseball." Someone even figured out that USC had scored more runs in the '98 title game than in their Dedeaux-led five consecutive championship clinchers combined.

So, the sanctioning body sat down with scientists and bat companies and figured out ways to tame the beast. They dumbed down the metal composites and narrowed the diameter of the barrel heads. A study by the *Omaha World-Herald* found that the post–Gorilla Ball bats had sliced off 5 to 8 percent of the average distance. The NCAA also asked CWS of Omaha to do some work on The Blatt, adding height to the outfield wall and moving that wall back to put some length back into power alleys that had been shortened during the field renovations of the early '90s.

In 1998, the eight CWS teams had combined to hit sixty-two dingers. In '99, the duller bats cut that total to thirty-five. In 2002, the stadium renovations trimmed it to thirty-three.

The gorilla had been caged, somewhat. The advantage of one bat over another, not so much.

Somehow, some way, Championship Game Two started only twenty-six minutes late, just as Jesse, Randy, and Bob had promised. Thank God. If Perno had to hear one more person say, "Coach, we're pulling for you guys to win so we can all go home tonight," he was going to punch out someone.

From the first pitch, his Dawgs played like a team that was ready to get it over with. The bangers were banging and the runners were running.

Ryan Peisel led off the game by stroking his ninth hit in the Series and provided his usual spark two batters later, when he went from first to third on Beckham's single to short left field. Conventional baseball wisdom said that was an excellent way to get thrown out, but Peisel had noticed that the outfielders were following the book on hard-hitting Beckham and playing him way deep. The senior also knew that a day of rain would slow down the ball if it landed in wet grass, and rolled to them. As soon as he saw the low trajectory of the hit, he committed to third. As he thundered into the bag the UGA bench erupted, all but Perno, who leaned on his elbow, cracking sunflower seeds and watching Justin Miller's demeanor on the mound. He looked tight. It was time to strike hard and apply pressure to Fresno's wounds.

Runners started sprinting on every pitch and every pitch was turned into contact. Big Rich Poythress, now hitting .429 in the Series, looked terrible on one pitch and brilliant on the next, going the other way with a breaking ball way out of the strike zone, hitting behind Beckham, who was already digging for third, and driving in Peisel. Beckham slid into third so hard he blew apart his belt. Jumpy right fielder Steve Detwiler gunned the ball to third, which allowed Poythress to reach second.

Dawgs 1, Dogs 0, with two men on.

After Bryce Massanari flied out weakly to right, Miller got the signal to intentionally walk Matt Cerione, who'd burned Fresno in Championship Game One, and hopefully set up the inning-ending double play. Then he damn near threw the first lob ball pitch to the screen, which would have scored at least one run. Catcher Ryan Overland leapt to save it.

The next batter was banger number two, Joey Lewis, who sensed Miller's lack of confidence and cranked the first pitch he saw into center field.

Dawgs 3, Dogs 0.

Miller plunked the number-eight hitter Lyle Allen, then bounced back to strike out David Thomas, the last batter in the lineup.

When Nick Montgomery took the mound, he'd been sitting so long during his team's big first inning that he'd been forced to run down to the bullpen and warm back up. The rustiness showed as he walked the leadoff hitter, freshman Danny Muno, but he coerced center fielder Gavin Hedstrom into a groundout and Erik Wetzel into a double play. It wasn't pretty for Montgomery, but it was enough.

The top of the second inning looked a lot like the top of the first. Peisel, the top of the order, was back up and rapped another single. *Let's get this over with.* Again, the team leader was off and running. *Don't let them hang around.* He stole second, advanced to third on a sacrifice fly by Olson, and scored on a deep fly by Poythress. *End this now.*

Dawgs 4, Dogs 0.

Montgomery cruised through the bottom of the second and as the Georgia hitters grabbed their helmets, Perno went to each one individually and shifted his strategy a bit. "Don't jump on the first pitch you see. Be patient. This guy is laboring. Let's let him do the work for us for a little while." In other words, let's beat Fresno with their two-strike game.

Bryce Massanari walked and so did Cerione, which brought the Fresno coaches out to remind Miller to go back to his bread-and-butter, breaking balls on the outside corner. Joey Lewis worked the count to 0–2, but whiffed on—what else?—a breaking ball away.

As David Thoms and his .194 CWS batting average dug in, Mike Batesole was on the stopwatch, timing his pitcher's delivery time to the plate. The kid was starting to slow and that had the potential to open up a whole new bag of problems. A slow delivery to the plate meant opening the door for more aggressiveness from the runners and with Peisel back on deck again, the speed was on its way.

With the count 1-and-0 to Thoms, Batesole shouted to his infielders to remind them that Thoms, the light-hitting second baseman, was bringing a slow bat to the plate and would likely be behind Miller's trademark outside breaking balls. Danny Muno took a step to his right. Unfortunately, he couldn't take a step up into the air. He had the ball played perfectly, but when Thoms smacked it at the shortstop it was a few inches higher than Muno's vertical abilities. RBI single.

Dawgs 5, Dogs 0.

In the press box, writers temporarily stopped banging out their Wednesday morning columns, pausing to call their travel agents or visit their airline's Web site. "It's going to cost me a hundred bucks to change my Thursday morning flight to tomorrow," one Atlanta writer said to a friend. "What do you think, should I do it?"

"Hell yeah, this is over."

Mike Fox could have told them not to pack up. Sitting back in North Carolina, he thought about Fresno State coming back from a game down to send his team home just two nights earlier. He also thought about Oregon State in 2006, a team that Carolina had beaten in the first game of the championship and led 4–0 in the second. One day later it was the Beavers who were celebrating and the Heels who were accepting the dreaded RUNNER-UP trophy.

"Anyone who changes the channel on any College World Series game doesn't know what they're doing," the coach said from his office, forcing himself to laugh. "Trust me on that. Your whole life can change on one pitch."

To understand the potential power and pressure of each and every pitch, you only need to follow the chain of events that every championship throw ignited into action—a series of stats, scribbles, digital signatures, and satellite transmissions that began at The Blatt and ended in homes around the world.

Every time a toss from Miller or Montgomery hit the catcher's mitt, the image was captured by nineteen television cameras and eighty-eight microphones, all racing their data back to the ESPN production compound at the speed of light. In the truck, producer Scott Matthews and director Scott Johnson perused a bank of monitors to decide which angle should be beamed out to the twelve million households tuned in throughout the course of the Series. Each individual camera's unique angle was recorded by a bank of recorders, tape and digital, the best takes reported via headset to the front bench by tape operators and replay producers.

Each pitch was also described and analyzed by four separate broadcast booths—ESPN, Westwood One Radio, and the home networks of Fresno State and Georgia, eight men simultaneously chattering away. In addition, Bill Jensen boomed play-by-play to those sitting in the stands.

In the ESPN compound, two researchers logged each pitch and ran it through an endless set of spreadsheets to recalculate their statistics. An ESPN statistician in the booth also kept score, which was rechecked with another network statistician in the deadline media area of the press box.

He spent the game looking over the shoulder of an all-star team of statisticians, hailing from the NCAA, Creighton, and Universities of Nebraska and Iowa.

Each pitch was logged in a central scoring system that simultaneously compiled the official box score, a running play-by-play, and statistical compilations for each player, team, this 2008 Series, and every College World Series ever played. That box score was fed to monitors throughout the press box, where it was ingested and put to use by live scoring widgets on NCAA.com and CBSSports.com, the official sites of the College World Series, as well as a mountain of blogs, from ESPN.com to Baseball America.com to Yahoo! to individual local newspapers and Web sites you've likely never even heard of.

The sports information directors from the two competing schools also kept their own running score, entering every pitch as it was thrown. So did the operators of each Rosenblatt scoreboard, the massive video screen in left as well as the old-school white light board in right.

In the yellow seats, pro scouts measured each pitch with radar guns and kept a running log of every ball and strike. During the earlier games, they were joined by coaches from future CWS opponents, who weren't allowed to use radar guns during the Series, but always managed to find a seat behind a scout who did.

In the dugouts, every pitch was tracked and charted by an assistant coach or a player, to be discussed and charted for Championship Game Three, should it happen, and used to quickly identify trends during the game: Is he starting to overthrow? When's the last time he threw a curveball? Has he started every batter the same way all night?

All of the above took place in about five seconds. Then, with the next pitch, it happened all over again, usually around three hundred times per game.

But ultimately, no pitch mattered and none became official until seventy-two-year-old Lou Spry had written it down in his scorebook. As the official scorer of the College World Series since 1981, no ball has crossed the plate, been put into play, or sent into the stands without Spry jotting it down and ruling on what exactly it was that the world just witnessed.

For the first four days of the 2008 Series, Spry had been missing and the press box was in overwhelming agreement that life wasn't the same without him. They missed his voice cracking over the in-house public address system to announce his ruling on a hit or error and they missed his sometimes bizarrely random tidbits of trivia that he called "Lou's Clues."

When the first pitch was thrown for Game One, he was standing at a podium outside of San Diego, speaking at the funeral of Joe Axelson, former general manager of the NBA's Kansas City (and eventually Sacramento) Kings and Spry's friend of fifty years. Lou's wife Janice couldn't fly, so the couple set out from their home in Kansas City and drove to the funeral in Coronado, California. By the time they drove from Southern California to Omaha, they had logged more than 3,300 miles for what was usually a three-hour trip up from K.C., but Lou had finally made it for his forty-first Series, taking his press box seat alongside Bill Jensen in time for Game Seven.

The downstairs office he kept back home was college baseball's mini Cooperstown. He'd missed only one College World Series since 1967, serving as media-relations director, tournament director, and ultimately, scorer. Over the decades he's collected photos, plaques, ticket stubs, one very unique needlepoint, and of course, the scorebooks. Every play in every game since Game One of the '81 Series between Mississippi State and Michigan (MSU's Mark Gillaspie, an Omaha native, had the game-winning three-run homer in the fifth) could be found scribbled in those books. Well, almost every play. He lost one of the books a few years back and it'd been driving him crazy.

There are two moments that everyone always asked Lou about. The first was Ron Fraser's Grand Illusion. He loved to talk about it and could describe it right down to the expressions on the Miami batgirls' faces, but from an official scoring perspective the end result was always anticlimactic. What took most sportswriters a thousand words to describe was covered in Lou's '82 scorebook by only two letters—CS.

"Caught stealing," Spry explained, almost apologetically. "Officially, that's all it was. People think there should be more to it because of the idea that the ball was thrown away and all of that, but in reality Stephenson left the bag of his own volition and the pitcher threw to second to catch him. Caught stealing."

The other most-asked-about moment occurred five years later, when Ventura's fifty-eight-game hit streak came to an end in Game Eleven against future Chicago White Sox teammate Jack McDowell and Stanford. He'd come to Omaha tied with Joe DiMaggio's magical number of fifty-six and promptly broke the mark in the opening game of the Series. Six days later, in the top of the ninth, Ventura's Oklahoma State Cowboys were cruising 6–2 and all the crowd cared about was the third baseman's final at-bat. He hit a sharp grounder that ate second baseman Frank Carey alive. Carey knocked it down, dug it back up, dropped it, picked it up a second time, and fired his rushed throw past first and into the dugout. Everyone at The Blatt turned and stared at the scoreboard for Spry's ruling. They waited. And they waited. Finally, a bright white "E" popped up. The streak was over. The crowd was not happy.

"People think it took so long because I was trying to decide if it was a hit or an error, but there was never a question about whether or not it was an error. I was trying to decide if I should charge two errors on the play, one in the field and one on the throw. But ultimately I didn't want to hang the poor kid with two errors, so we just charged the one."

Some folks grilled Spry for his decision while others congratulated him on not caving to the pressure of history. Put Ventura among those who agreed with the call. In 2006, the College Baseball Hall of Fame was founded and Ventura was elected to its inaugural class along with Dave Winfield, Will Clark, Bob Horner, and Texas legend Brooks Kieschnick. To commemorate the occasion, Ventura paid a visit to the 2006 Series, where he was tracked down by Spry to sign a photo from the '87 Series.

"I'm not an autograph guy," the scorer said, though as a semiretired quote-chaser for the Kansas City Royals, he certainly had the opportunity. "But Ventura and I will always be connected by that play so I had to ask. He inscribed it, 'To Lou, Great Call! Best Wishes, Robin Ventura.'"

That photo had been the centerpiece of Lou's office/museum ever since.

In the bottom of the third, Spry and everyone else tracking pitches were coming to a unanimously concurrent conclusion. Georgia starter Nick Montgomery, despite his 5–0 lead, was hitting the wall. He gave up two singles and a walk to load the bases and brought a run in with a wild pitch, the record twenty-fourth errant toss of the Series. Bases loaded again. The Red Wave, which had been lulled to sleep by the early five-run deficit, suddenly started rolling again.

FRES-NO-STATE!

FRES-NO-STATE!

Montgomery labored as sweat dripped off the bill of his cap and every pitch, even the strikes, rode dangerously low. He walked Erik Wetzel to bring up Steve Susdorf, the WAC conference player of the year. Like Peisel, Susdorf was the leader of his team in the clubhouse. But he wasn't a fiery speechwriter; instead he chose to lead by example. Just as Peisel had done for his team in the top of the first and second innings, Susdorf knew that he had to make something, anything, happen.

Before coming to the plate, the left fielder turned to the dugout and announced to his teammates that every pitch Montgomery was throwing was in the dirt, nothing but bad breaking balls. If he saw anything that even dared to come above his knees, anything that came off of the pitcher's fingers even slightly resembling a fastball he was going to drill it.

The first pitch was, of course, a breaking ball in the dirt. Montgomery was assuming that the number-four hitter would be swinging from his ass at the first pitch to try and put a big number on the board, but Susdorf wasn't the typical cleanup hitter. He was an engineering major with a 4.0.

Susdorf got his fastball on the second pitch, a pitch that came off the hand looking like another breaking ball, but held steady and cut the corner. *All right*, the hitter thought, *now I have him timed.*

Another breaking ball low: 2 balls, 1 strike.

Another breaker, high: 3 balls, 1 strike.

All right, Susdorf thought, *give me that fastball I was telling the guys about.*

CRACK.

The ball landed just on the edge of the infield grass and scooted by David Thomas at second, who was playing near to the bag hoping for a double play. As the ball died in the wet grass, the entire Fresno bench played third-base coach, whipping their arms like windmills. Two runs scored and two men were in scoring position with only one out.

Dawgs 5, Dogs 3.

In the next five minutes, David Perno made two decisions that months later still gnawed at his gut. First, he pulled Montgomery off the mound. In retrospect he believed that he pulled that trigger too soon. But the kid that had only walked fifteen batters all season long had already walked three in barely two innings. So he replaced him with Stephen Dodson, who'd been penciled in as a potential starter for Championship Game Three. But the coach needed him now, a solid starting pitcher who could give him a nice long relief appearance. Prior to the game, Dodson's teammates were all over him about his girlfriend, Katie Heenan, a member of UGA's four-time NCAA champion gymnastics squad, shouting, "She's got four rings and you've got zero. You better get going or you'll never catch up!"

The second regrettable decision happened almost instantly. After Dodson got Alan Ahmady to pop up to first, Tommy Mendonca came to the plate with two on and two outs. Perno briefly flirted with the idea of walking the third baseman, but decided that Dodson could get him to chase a breaking pitch and end the inning with a two-run lead.

Dodson threw one pitch. It did not break and Mendonca chased it all the way over the wall into the right-field bleachers. As soon as he hit it, the hot corner son of a dairy farmer eased into a home-run trot that had more than a little swagger mixed in. It wasn't disrespectful, it was a message.

You made your statement last night . . . well, here's ours.

Dogs 6, Dawgs 5.

You can feel it, Garrido thought to himself in Section N. With one swing, the air in The Blatt had changed. Even after Georgia came back and tied the game in the top of the fourth, the greatest coach in the game could see what was happening. The pressure of expectations and the fear of losing were simultaneously setting up camp in the Georgia dugout. He pointed to the hanging heads, the guys leaning on the padded railing of the dugout sulking as if they'd be put in time-out by their parents.

It was actually worse than he knew.

Matt Cerione was called out on a third strike for out two and Ryan

Overland threw down to third to catch Beckham for out three. Perhaps home-plate umpire Mike Conlin had been screened out by Overland, who jumped up to receive the pitch and make the throw, but the call was questionable. Instead of ball four inside and under the knees and two men on, the inning was over.

Like the teams, each umpire had earned his way to Omaha through a lifetime of hard work and an excellent 2008 season. There were eight selected to work all sixteen games, working in four-man crews until the championship, when two additional umpires were added down the baselines. They hailed from six different states and each spent their springs splitting time between at least two different conferences, which put them in direct contact with hundreds of players, dozens of coaches, and tens of thousands of fans, each of whom thought that the man behind the plate was an idiot.

"Abuse is part of the job," admitted Dave Yeast, the NCAA's national coordinator of baseball umpires. Before taking over that post, Yeast had worked the CWS in 1991 and '95, and was behind the plate for the '96 Summer Olympics in Atlanta. From his desk he had organized what was once chaotic at best, implementing testing programs, better evaluation processes, implementing video bulletins to help umpires become better, and developing training camps for aspiring umpires. All Series long he'd hung out in the umpires' locker room with his guys, watching tape, and discussing every close call, especially this year's slew of tight plays at first. But none of that had been enough to replace the feeling of being on the field, interacting with, becoming friends with, and yes, angering coaches and players. So, at the close of the 2008 Series, Yeast was relinquishing his post to return to the action.

"You can't replace the feeling. It's too much fun to call work. Even with the abuse."

Cerione's weapon of choice for Mike Conlin was the glare. He stared, laughed, and then shared some parting words as he went back to the dugout. He had words again as he ran out to take his position in left field. His teammates tried to calm him, but they were pissed, too. The good news for Georgia fans was that the bench was finally showing some passion. Unfortunately, that passion channeled into anger toward the men in blue and not toward defeating the boys in gray.

That anger turned to disbelief as Fresno batted around in the fourth, hanging five runs on the scoreboard. They added four more in the fifth, three in the seventh, and one in the eighth. A bad hop to Beckham . . . a bad hop to Peisel . . . a terrible misjudgment on a lazy fly ball by Lyle Allen . . . a robbing crash-into-the-wall grab of a Cerione drive by Detwiler . . . it just kept getting worse.

"Are you watching this?" Erin Andrews said to a writer from her post at the end of the Georgia dugout. "I've never seen a mood swing like this. Other than Dodson throwing stuff in the clubhouse, no one has made a sound since the fourth inning."

By the time Fresno was finished, every batter in the lineup had at least one hit, compiling nineteen total, including two doubles, two homers, and a triple. The day had started with rain and it was ended with raining baseballs.

Final score: Dogs 19, Dawgs 10.

The two teams left the field to polar opposite atmospheres from the night before. This time it was Fresno coaches and dignitaries who were spilling into the dugout to offer congratulations and Georgia parents who scrambled to the bus to do emotional damage control.

After twelve days, fifteen games, and more than one hundred innings played, the 2008 College World Series championship would come down to one game. Mike Mayne walked in from the bullpen swinging his arms and clapping his hands.

"Let's play one more, what do you say? Hey . . . didn't some crazy old man tell you that it would take a double-digit score to win this game?"

The instant that the last cleat stepped off the field, Jesse Cuevas sent his team into action. They swept the dugouts, cleaned the water coolers, and covered the infield dirt with special-cut tarps. They packed the dirt around home that had been dug up by the night's one hundred batters and repaired the mound from the damage done by nine different pitchers.

Bob Thomas shut down his radio and headed upstairs to recharge it, while Randy Buhr sat in on the postgame press conference in the Hall of

Fame Room. Before leaving for the night, they checked in with one another one more time, discussed the Wednesday weather forecast (hotter
than forty hells) and called it a night.

Together, Jesse, Bob, and Randy had managed to get a game played on
a day when Mother Nature clearly had no intentions of letting anyone in
Omaha play baseball.

As usual, the fans had no idea.

TWELVE

THE GAME

Wednesday, June 25
Championship Game Three: Fresno State vs. Georgia

This was indeed, finally, The Game.

The Game was a culmination of two weeks and a national season of college baseball. A season that began with 286 schools and nearly 9,000 student-athletes was now down to two teams and forty-nine players for nine innings.

The Game was being attended by a crowd that represented every possible corner of the college game. There were local longtime fans, first-time out-of-towners, and every sort in between. They wore the logos of their favorite schools (GO HUSKERS), the two teams on the field (SIC 'EM DAWGS), absent old-time favorites (WE MISS THE HORNS), dead flamingos (GEAUX TIGERS), and schools that had no connection to the Series whatsoever (WINGATE UNIVERSITY BASEBALL).

As the crowd had settled into their seats Fresno State was back in the batting cage one last time. And one last time, Mike Batesole leaned on the padding and hammered the day's mission in the heads of his team.

Two-strike adjustments . . .

What he meant was, "Look for a pitch in the weakest part of your hitting zone . . . choke up on the bat and loosen your grip for more quickness and control . . . be aggressive, don't leave your fate in the hands of the umpire . . . and stay over the ball with your upper body to hit a line drive or slap it up the middle . . ."

But all he had to say was what he'd been saying since fall practice.

Two-strike adjustments . . .

His team was still unbelievably loose. The freshmen, particularly short-stop Danny Muno, were nervous, but the instant Burke and Sprague had gotten on the bus at the Hilton Garden Inn, they'd identified the most uptight targets and as usual, loosened them up with laughter.

"You want to see how nervous these guys are?" Fresno coach Mike Mayne said facetiously as he walked out to the first-base line after his team had gone into the clubhouse and picked up a scattered pile of bats and gloves. "Look at this . . . they didn't even clean their room. It's like they're playing their first game of the year. Loose is not the problem. Here," he said as he handed a writer a couple of bats and motioned toward the dugout. "We might need these tonight. Well, at least one anyway."

Then, with another wink, "It's just another game."

There was nothing loose about the home clubhouse.

This was not just another game, and anyone needing confirmation on that fact only needed to get a look at the post-facelift expressions being worn by the Georgia Bulldogs. The ride to the ballpark had been totally silent. Not even a "Who Let the Dogs Out?" send-off by the barking staff of the Embassy Suites had been enough to rustle up some jocularity.

Coach Perno had finally slept, but only out of exhaustion. He hadn't planned on giving a pregame speech. He knew that his players were well aware of what they had to do and what the reward would be for doing it. But as the home team they had taken batting practice first (curiously, they chose to do it in the indoor cages instead of on the field) and as they sat in the clubhouse waiting on Fresno to finish BP, he had to do something to break the silence.

He told the team that they played in the SEC, that they had already been to the toughest places to play in America and taken everyone's best shot. Sure, this was a big game, but this team had been in plenty of big games and knew how to handle them.

"Just take of care business like you know how to do."

Everything Perno said was true. Their schedule had been brutal. In an effort to cement his school's status among the college baseball elite, he'd taken his team and met those elitists head on. They started the year by hosting number one-ranked Arizona, followed by the game against the

Braves, and road trips to defending national champion Oregon State and then down to see Coach Mike Martin and Buster Posey in Tallahassee. The result was an 8–8 record to start the season, but the scars earned en route to that record had given them the toughness to be here, now, tonight, for The Game.

But the team on the other side of the field hadn't exactly played a church league softball schedule. Sure, the southeast had its giants, but top to bottom no state presented a bigger minefield than Fresno State's homeland of California. As of 2008, no less than 1,893 Major Leaguers had been born in the Golden State, nearly 600 more than the next closest state. From junior colleges to community colleges to schools no one outside of the state would recognize, the game coursed through nearly every Californian's blood. Say you never heard of Cal Poly? Well, it's produced ten big leaguers, including some guy named Ozzie Smith, and in 2008 the Mustangs had nineteen players in pro ball.

Every school in the state has a list like that.

What's more, Fresno had to survive the most ridiculous conference calendar in college sports. To compete with the big-money leagues, the WAC had cobbled together nine schools tossed across four time zones, which added up to the most expensive, diverse, and high-mileage schedule in collegiate baseball.

There was the never-ending wind that blows in over the artificial turf in Hawaii and the never-ending wind that blew out at high-altitude New Mexico State, then the 100-degree temperature/100-percent humidity of Louisiana Tech, and the goofy shifting breezes of Reno, Nevada.

All of that travel and all of those brutal conditions had led the WAC to institute a cost-saving measure that kept their league from having to unnecessarily double up on frequent flyer miles. As it turned out, it was also a helluva way to teach a team and a coaching staff how to navigate a debilitated pitching staff.

"They play four-game weekend series, don't they?" As Orel Hershiser said it out loud, you could almost hear the *ding* of the I-just-figured-something-out bell going off in his head. "That explains a lot. Every other conference plays three-game series. It certainly explains why they haven't seemed nearly as worried about their arms as we have. They'd fought this battle every week every year."

And for this battle, the final battle of the 2008 season, the Fresno State coaching staff finally saw everything break their way. The list of no-name pitchers with their blimp-sized ERAs had managed to completely hit the reset button on the mound. Justin Wilson, the one Fresno fans thought they would need rain to see again, was ready to go on three days' rest (though there had been some disagreement among the coaches about whether or not he should go) and Brandon Burke had been given a recharging respite thanks to the nine-run blowout.

"That's it," Batseole said as he waited impatiently for the first pitch. "Everybody in the stadium knows what my plan is tonight."

The also. knew Georgia's. In Tuesday night's postgame press conference, Perno was asked who would pitch in Championship Game Three. His answer came back in a half-second: "Nathan Moreau, Dean Weaver, Alex McRee, and Josh Fields. You can set your watch by it."

It was the last part that Fresno was worried about.

"We've been saying it all morning," pitcher Clayton Allison said in the hotel lobby as the team loaded the bus. Then, he finished the thought in harmonic unison with dad Buddy Allison.

"Keep Fields off the field."

As the teams lined up along the baselines, the nearly 19,000 in attendance for The Game came to their feet as the color guard strolled in from left field. The sounds of Lambert Bartak's organ rattled off The Blatt's old blue girders, joined by the booming yet gentle voice of public address announcer Bill Jensen: "Ladies and gentlemen, welcome to the championship game of the 2008 NCAA Men's College World Series . . . please rise and, gentlemen, remove your hats . . ."

The Georgia Bulldogs stood shoulder to shoulder down the third-base line, most of the players rocking back and forth nervously as their head coach David Perno stared into the clear blue sky. The Fresno State Bulldogs, as usual, looked like they might explode into hysterical laughter, like someone had just stepped on a whoopee cushion. Their leader,

Mike Batesole, stared at the blades of grass directly beneath his feet, perhaps looking for one last clue that might help his defense.

The national anthem was performed by Amber Matulka, a Nebraska Health and Human Resources employee and karaoke D.J. from Lincoln. The night before, there was no one in the state of Nebraska rooting harder for Fresno State than Amber, who'd survived a cattle-call audition process only to see the dreaded words "If Necessary" beside her game. When the Dawgs jumped out to a five-run lead in Game Two, she became sick to her stomach. Then Fresno came back to save the gig.

When it was finally time to sing, she nailed it, her father holding up his cell phone so that Mom could hear it back home. To generous applause, Matulka finished, waved, and stepped back into the appreciative grandstand.

One of those clapping was a retired schoolteacher named Ann Walters, whom CWS historian W. C. Madden once labeled the "Queen of the College World Series."

During the pregame warm-ups neither team heard her clanking down the stairs behind home plate behind her aluminum walker, but they should have. Walters made her way to her seats—Section J, Row 3, Seats 13 and 14—to more than a little applause of her own. Then, keeping with a custom they had started too many years ago, Bob Thomas popped up through the gate from the field and slipped Ann a piece of candy with a wink. "You think Randy Buhr and I run things around here?" he said as he held Ann's hand. "If this young lady told Dennie Poppe to get rid of us all, he'd do it."

The College World Series arrived at Rosenblatt Stadium in 1950. Walters showed up to watch it in 1951. In the fifty-eight years since there were 845 games played and Walters had missed only seven, six in 1999 for her daughter's wedding, and the seventh the night before because of the rain. Whew, her friends told her when she showed up after being absent, they'd started to panic. There was even a rumor that she was dead.

In 2001, she got a new hip, which made navigating the slick metal stairs of The Blatt a challenge, but she simply left home earlier and made it to all thirteen games, seeing Miami and Jim Morris defeat Stanford and The Mastermind for the title. Every year she ran the Section J pool to see who could correctly guess the attendance. She'd befriended countless numbers of coaches and scouts as they'd surrounded her in the yellow seats, who had quickly realized that, like Miss Marilyn, Miss Walters gave off some seriously good baseball karma. Every year she received letters and cards from coaches and schools all over the United States, some of them still displaying the Kewpie doll that she used to present to the CWS champion to go with their big maple trophy.

From this seat, Ann Walters hadn't merely witnessed some of the greatest moments in college baseball history. She'd seen them all.

She'd seen Dave Winfield, still her all-time favorite CWS athlete, play both ways for Minnesota, watched Stanford's Paul Carey fell LSU with a tenth-inning walk-off grand slam to send the Cardinal to the national title game, and seen Nomar, Barry, Inky, and J. D. Drew all go yard. Ensberg's steal, The Citadel's mad dash, Creighton's heartbreaking final out, and Texas third baseman's Omar Quintanilla's boot-and-throw to home, maybe the greatest defensive play in the history of the Series, all unfolded in front of her behind-the-dish seats.

She'd seen forty-four grand slams and one inside-the-park homer. She'd seen James Street play for Texas and his son Huston do the same thirty-two years later. When the 2008 Major League Baseball season began, seventy-six players across thirty rosters had two things in common: they'd played in the College World Series and they'd played in front of Ann Walters.

Five sections to her left, just past third in Section O, the Walkenhorst family had seen it all, too, only from a different angle. The family patriarch, eighty-two-year-old Dale, attended his first Series in 1951, the same year as Walters, and he'd had his season tickets since '78. He didn't make it to all the games anymore ("damned knee"), but with kids and grandkids scattered all over Nebraska, the seats were never empty. For so many years his June 4 birthday fell squarely in the middle of the Series, and every year the family brought in a birthday cake ("back when they would let you bring food in") and if anyone wanted a slice, "all they had to do was holler."

Across the diamond had long been the domain of Subby Anzaldo, entertainment agent, real estate broker, and, from 1994–95, the acting mayor of Omaha. Long before that he was the mayor of Section 18. Anyone who ever watched a Series on television from Rosenblatt had seen Subby, on his cell phone and waving to friends whenever there was a left-handed batter. Hey, it was never his idea, but rather that of his friends, five kids, and seventeen grandkids who constantly called to say, "Wave! You're on TV!"

Anzaldo ended up with his tickets when City Auditorium Manager Charlie Mancuso (Frankie's brother) tricked him into buying two front-row seats. "I didn't want them," said the seventy-three-year-old, in the midst of managing his son's Frank Sinatra act at the Riviera Hotel and Casino in Vegas. "I said, Charlie, nobody goes to the College World Series. But I paid for them anyway just to get to him to stop talking."

Back then, Subby's seats were at the end of the aisle, hell, the end of the stadium. But as The Blatt expanded, they added one more seat next to his . . . then eventually they added another . . . so he bought them, too. From those seats he watched his kids grow into adults and now, in that same Omaha sunshine, he looked over to see his two great-grandchildren.

He'd become friends with the game's most legendary coaches, Rod Dedeaux and Skip Bertman. He'd befriended all the folks who have always sat around him, from business leaders to out-of-towners who drive in year after year. And what was his favorite moment . . . wait . . . he'll get back to you, his cell phone was ringing . . .

"Everybody wave! We're on TV again!"

From every grandstand section to every dugout to every outside tailgate party, everyone agreed on one fact: Damn, it was hot. Temperatures soared into the nineties and the humidity was right there with it, the sun glaring into the outfield and casting a huge shadow directly between the mound and the plate. One last cruel joke for Mother Nature to play on Dennie Poppe, Jesse Cuevas, and anyone trying to catch a fly ball.

For the first time, the mist-blasting fans in each dugout were turned on, but Dave Perno used the heat as a way to try and get his team to loosen up. "This is Georgia weather!"

Starting pitcher Nathan Moreau—number 13—was exactly the guy that Perno wanted on the mound in this kind of game. He was big, he was a lefty (Fresno had beaten up on every righty they'd seen in Omaha), and he had already come up big in big games, including a start against then-top-ranked Arizona and the SEC championship clincher against Vanderbilt. And all Perno needed out of him was four or five innings, then he could hand it over to the set-up men and, ultimately, Josh Fields.

The first inning was what it should have been for both teams: one single each, some grounders, some pop-ups, and one runner caught stealing. The fielders adjusted their glasses and eye black as they figured out the sun. The hitters watched Moreau and Justin Wilson to see what they were bringing to the table.

"It's no different than two boxers in the first round," explained Louis Spry from his scorer's box over home plate. "Who has what? Who looks quick and who looks slow? Where's my opponent's weakness? Everyone is looking for an edge."

And the coaches?

"They are looking for a hero."

Everyone loves a hero. From Walters to Walkenhorst to Subby to any other longtime Rosenblatt resident, there is a uniform and solitary answer to the question, "What's your favorite College World Series moment?" No one gives you a date, a game, or even a team. They only give you a name.

Warren Morris.

The two greatest programs in the six-decade history of the CWS are Southern California and Texas. But its two greatest programs since 1982 have been Miami and LSU. In 1996, those two schools met at the corner of Thirteenth Street and World Series Boulevard to settle once and for all who truly was the Program of the '90s. To this day, Jim Morris can barely talk about it. Skip Bertman can't shut up about it.

Warren Morris was a twenty-two-year-old senior second baseman and, like Michael Hollander ten years later, was living out his childhood dream of playing baseball in an LSU uniform, having grown up in Alexandria, Louisiana, two hours north of Baton Rouge. His entire life had been a surprise, born to a mother who'd been told she couldn't have any more kids.

Morris became the kind of student-athlete that the NCAA likes to put on the front of promotional pamphlets. He got into LSU on an academic scholarship and made Bertman's team as a third-team, way-too-skinny walk-on, but waited patiently for All-American Todd Walker to trade in second base at The Box for second base with the Minnesota Twins.

When Warren finally took over the position in '95, he exploded with a Walker-ish .369 batting average and eight homers, though the season itself was a disappointment with no trip to Omaha. In '96, amid a bayou's worth of preseason hype, he couldn't shake what was thought to be a simple right wrist injury. The pain became so sharp he couldn't even take notes in class.

Dumbfounded doctors ordered a bone scan, found a broken hamate bone, and sent him for a surgical procedure that caused him to miss twenty-eight days. He was actually supposed to wait a little longer, but dude, it was the NCAA Regionals. Still, the hurting continued.

He trudged through the golden anniversary edition of the College World Series, largely as an involved spectator as the team came from behind to beat SEC rival Florida twice to meet the Canes in the final game. As hard as LSU had worked to get there, Miami had breezed in, averaging twelve runs a game.

The morning of the championship, for the first time all the season, Morris's hand didn't hurt. "As corny as it sounds," he said from his financial adviser's office in Alexandria, "the first time I felt like I could take my full cut at the plate was during batting practice the day before the championship game. It was like the season had lasted just long enough to wait until my hand felt better."

The game itself was a boxing match. LSU made mistakes early and fell behind 7–3. They came back with two runs each in the seventh and eighth, but gave up a run in the top of the ninth to fall behind 8–7. With a runner on third and two outs, Warren Morris dug in at the plate to face All-American reliever Robbie Morrison. Back in Louisiana, all his mother could think was, "Oh no, poor Warren. Please don't let him make the last out."

He was sitting first-pitch curveball and that's exactly what he got. As he swung, he whipped his entire body to the right, flinging the ball toward the right-field wall, which it cleared by only a couple of feet. He thought it was going to be a game-tying base hit into the corner, maybe even a double.

Then he saw first-base coach Daniel Tomlin leaping into the air, and as he turned for second he saw the Miami players falling to their knees. Poor Joey Cora, who had given his team the lead with an RBI single in the top of the ninth, fell to the ground at shortstop as if he'd been shot.

In the fiftieth College World Series, Warren Morris, the unlikeliest of heroes, had provided the event, the city, and The Blatt, with what will likely always be its defining moment. The first, and through 2008, the only walk-off championship-winning home run.

It was also his only home run of the season.

"In 2008, I came back to Rosenblatt for the first time since that day," Morris said, recalling his newfound role as the inspiration for the 2008 comeback Tigers, the hero of those videotapes that Michael Hollander had pulled out of mothballs. Before their Omaha-clinching win at The Box, Bertman and Mainieri had even arranged for Morris to walk into the clubhouse just as the team watched his '96 homer for the umpteenth time. It was as if John Wayne had walked into the room.

"As soon as I walked into the stadium this year I was mad at myself for not coming back sooner. The people were unbelievable. Not just the LSU fans, but the people who lived in Omaha, all the ones who were there that day. They thanked me for the moment. It was just so special. To be such a part of that place and their lives, it's a blessing. It's a little overwhelming."

As the '96 Tigers team rode to Rosenblatt that morning, the very moment that the 2008 team had relived over and over, Morris indeed felt something special. He certainly couldn't have foreseen that the day he was beginning would forever change his life, but there was a special electricity that he felt coursing through his body that morning. And he wasn't the only one to recognize it.

"You could see it on his face," Skip Bertman recalled. "Not magic or anything like that, but that level of concentration and determination that only a handful of athletes can achieve. I hesitate to use the phrase 'in the zone,' but that's where Warren was."

One year earlier, Augie Garrido had recognized that same look in the eye of Mark Kotsay. What the coach also described as "a level of concentration" that led the outfielder to one of the greatest individual championship games in CWS history—two home runs, five RBIs, and eight total bases in Fullerton's 11–5 win over USC.

In 1956, Minnesota coach Dick Siebert told the local Minneapolis papers that on the morning of the title game between his Golden Gophers and the Arizona Wildcats he expected something big out of someone unexpected. Most had their eyes on Kindall, whose cycle had come three days earlier, and ace hurler Jerry Thomas, but the hero of the 12–1 rout was right fielder and team captain Bill Horning, who was moved to the leadoff spot for the championship game. He responded with a 4-for-5 day, setting title game records with ten total bases and two homers. "I needed to have a big game," the longtime schoolteacher recalled during a 2003 visit to The Blatt, "because I was getting married two days later."

Just as Louis Spry had suspected, the two head coaches had spent their mornings before the 2008 title game searching the faces of their teams for The Look. They tried to see past the overwhelmed eyes, the sweaty faces, and even the smiles lined up in their dugouts. They needed a leader, a Morris, a Kotsay, or a Horning.

Mike Batesole found two—his starting pitcher and, of all people, the right fielder with a thumb that didn't work.

Justin Wilson's face was not one that should have belonged to a tough guy. In the press box, one sportswriter Googled images of the Cabbage Patch Kids in his search for an accurate comparison. But if there was any question about what the lefty was made of—not to mention the effects of only three days of rest—they were answered in the bottom of the first. He froze Peisel with a wicked 90-mph pitch and coerced Matt "I'm going to hit it to the zoo" Olson into an easy grounder to second. He gave up a hit to Beckham (who hadn't?), then followed it up by getting Poythress to sky out to center.

As the criminology student walked off the mound and into the dugout, he looked Batesole in the eye for all of one second, never saying a word. And there it was. The Look. "I know it sounds crazy," Bates admitted, "but as soon as I saw the look in his eye I knew it was over."

In the top of the second, Fresno's Steve Susdorf launched a shot to first and sent UGA first baseman Rich Poythress into the air. The big man made contact with his glove, but the ball deflected off into the grass. Error. One on, no outs.

All at once, Perno felt sick and Batesole felt emboldened. The Fresno State coach, already much more animated than normal, tossed his gum aside, and addressed his team. "Let's make them pay for their mistakes! It's not a mistake until we cross home plate!"

Steve Detwiler heard his coach and came to the plate with punishment in mind. When he swung, he did it so hard it resembled former Arizona State outfielder Reggie Jackson, his body contorted and twisted like a corkscrew after every miss, only his looked even worse than Reggie's, thanks to the winces. His left hand still hurt from the torn thumb ligament, but for whatever reason it hadn't hurt him as badly this morning as it had throughout the postseason. Maybe it was the pain medicine, maybe it was adrenaline, or maybe it was the healing powers of the Warren Morris bus ride to the ballpark.

Regardless, he worked the count full and looked to the dugout for a sign from Batesole. *Hit and run*. With a glance to Susdorf at first, the player they called Rottweiler fouled off two pitches, his mind occupied by only one thought. *Get a pitch you can drive.*

What he got was a 90-mph meatball, dead center across the plate but well above his chest. He flung the ball into the right-field corner. Like Warren Morris, he thought it would be an RBI double. But like Morris's ball, it lifted . . . lifted . . . and cleared the yellow line in right by inches, just over the outstretched glove of Olson.

Two-run homer. Fresno 2, Georgia 0.

Again, Garrido felt a shift. The body language he'd seen during the pregame told him that it wouldn't take much to tilt the psychological field. He'd seen a team that was there to win and a team that was there hoping not to lose. The relaxed way of The Underdog versus the pressure of being The Favorite.

In the bottom of the second, that field nearly tilted back.

Georgia showed signs of finally shaking the tightness off when they put two on with no outs in the bottom of the second. Joey Lewis whiffed on a big slow hook from Justin Wilson, and Lyle Allen did the same on a curve in the dirt, but Brandon Burke and Holden Sprague's attempts to loosen up their freshman shortstop hadn't worked. Danny Muno and his giant ball cap committed two errors in the inning, loading the bases with two outs, and bringing the top of the order back up.

Ryan Peisel centered the second pitch he saw, a ball that could have very easily been a grand slam. The ball left the bat like a smash, but arced too soon and fell ten feet shy. Inning over, no runs. In the UGA dugout, everyone immediately thought the same thing at the same time. *Damn Nike bats.*

Though the college baseball bat wars had cooled off over the years, there was still a definite advantage to using one model over the other. Like a growing majority of big-time college athletic departments, Georgia was a Nike school. The world's largest sporting goods company provided everything that every Dawg team used, from uniforms to footballs to shoes to, yes, baseball bats.

But the company hadn't been in the bat business nearly as long as baseball-only companies such as Louisville Slugger and Easton. As a result, most baseball powerhouses agreed to do apparel-only deals with the Oregon-based company and got their bats from somewhere else. That's what Miami did, that's what Florida State did, and that's what Fresno did.

Georgia was an all-or-nothing Nike school. Even if that meant crappy bats.

Even Gordon Beckham, who had put on the greatest offensive years in recent memory, was politely critical of the bats he swung, happily showing anyone that stopped by Foley Field in Athens the pile of more than two dozen black-and-white Nike Torque bats that had shredded, split, or simply exploded upon contact. It didn't take a rocket scientist to figure out that a bat that was in the process of coming apart at the seams probably wasn't going to help the ball go over the fence.

Peisel's shot came up short in the second. Beckham had one die on him in the third. Joey Lewis missed a homer by inches in the fourth. But Detwiler's homer had cleared the fence by inches. And he swung an Easton. Garrido's hunch had been right. The Georgia bench was grumbling. But, much to Perno's helpless chagrin, the Dawgs had found an excuse and a distraction, and they seized upon it. At one point a text message came from inside the Georgia clubhouse to an Easton sales rep in town for the Series bemoaning the Nike bats.

When center fielder Matt Cerione was punched out on a called strike by home-plate umpire David Wiley in the fourth (this time, an excellent call), he mouthed at the official all the way back to the dugout. From the bench he screamed obscenities at the plate and slammed his bat against the green concrete wall. Georgia A.D. Damon Evans saw it, as did the rest of America, via the robotic camera that ESPN had mounted at the entrance to the dugout. Evans descended to the field to see if he couldn't do something to help rally the troops, to come to the aid of his friend Dave Perno and his unraveling morale.

Evans arrived just in time to see the second stanza of Cerione's explosion, the part where he repeatedly ripped the Nike bats, attaching an f-bomb to every mention.

The wheels weren't off the bus, but they were sure as hell wobbling.

No one sensed that weakness quicker than Batesole, who had suddenly turned in his stoic chin-on-his-arm approach for the Mark Marquess Stanford Cardinal pace-and-teach. He pulled his coaches together and motioned frantically with his hands, pushing to the left to say, "Go with those pitches."

In the bottom of the sixth, he grabbed his leader, Steve Susdorf, and counted with his fingers to remind him to work the count. *Two-strike plan . . . take it to the opposite field . . . the game may be bigger, but the plan remains the same.* He recognized that the new pitcher, Dean Weaver, was overthrowing. The urgency of the moment was causing him to push himself too hard. He was going to make mistakes. *Make them pay for their mistakes.*

Susdorf worked the count full and sent a high ball to the opposite field in left. *Two-strike plan, take it to the opposite field.* Left fielder Lyle Allen drifted over toward the corner, battling sun then shade then sun then shade. He had a read on it, but the ball was so high that a gust of wind from the Missouri River grabbed it and caused the ball to lurch suddenly, snapping farther toward the corner. Allen picked up his pace, but it was too late and the ball caromed off the wall and rolled past him back into the outfield grass. Susdorf cruised into second for the stand-up double.

When first baseman Alan Ahmady worked his own two-strike count, Batesole came to the top step of the dugout and shouted to both Ahmady and Steve Detwiler, who was standing on deck. He said it loud enough that Ann Walters, the scouts, and everyone else in the yellow seats could hear him.

"Make him pitch!"

Ahmady took four pitches out of the strike zone to draw the walk.

With two on and two outs in the top of the sixth inning, Steve Detwiler walked to the plate once again. For a split second, Dave Perno again thought about an intentional walk to load the bases. But he glanced over at Tommy Mendonca on deck. The third baseman was having a terrible night at the plate but was still the hottest player in the Series, so Perno opted to pitch to Detwiler. There was no way the kid with the damaged hand was going to do it again.

Batesole couldn't believe it.

The coach came to the top step, where he'd never stood for more than a second or two all Series long, and dug in. The inning nearly ended when catcher Joey Lewis threw down to first and barely missed an out-three pick-off. The count went to 1–0, 2–0, 2–1 . . . *Make him pitch!*

When Weaver missed on a high fastball the count hit three balls and a strike. Detwiler looked into his dugout for a sign. What he saw was his head coach standing two steps out onto the grass, unable to contain himself any longer. He cupped his hands around his mouth and shouted to his injured, dirty, scrappy right fielder:

"This is it!"

The 91-mph fastball rode in chest high. Joey Lewis snapped his glove shut but the ball wasn't there. It was two sections deep in the left-field bleachers.

Fresno 6, Georgia 0.

As the team spilled out and mobbed Detwiler at home plate, Mike Batesole stayed in the dugout. He walked down to the far end, drew a cup of water from the big blue cooler, and sucked it down. When the Bulldogs exploded back onto the bench they shouted and danced and enveloped their very own Warren Morris in a Red Wave of jerseys.

Batesole returned to his perch in the corner of the dugout, behind the fan, his elbow propped on the ledge. For the first time, he tried to suppress a smile.

What he had assumed, but hadn't known for sure, was the desperation that had permeated the Georgia dugout. Playing from behind, the Dawg batters helped Justin Wilson's cause by overswinging at bad pitches, searching in vain for a banger homer that would get them back in the game score-wise and mind-wise. By the time Gordon Beckham smashed his NCAA lead-tying twenty-eighth homer in the eighth—a solo homer—everyone in the old ballpark knew it was nothing more than a fitting farewell to the University of Gordon is Awesome.

The only hiccup in Fresno's march to the final out came in the ninth, when Batesole sent Clayton Allison to the mound to close out the game. Allison had pleaded with the coach not to pitch, but Bates wanted to reward the senior by having him on the mound for the out that clinched the 2008 College World Series championship. The Blatt grandstand openly wondered why Brandon Burke wasn't the coach's choice. Some within the team speculated that it was because the coach and his closer hadn't seen eye-to-eye on, well, much of anything during their four years together. Others assumed that it was because Burke was simply worn out.

As it turned out, Allison's hunch about his dead arm was dead on, as he gave up a single and a walk, and had Ryan Peisel and the top of the Dawg order back on deck. So, however reluctantly, Batesole sent Burke to the mound.

Just as Coach Mike Mayne had promised him after the Championship Game One loss, when Fresno won the championship, they would do so with Brandon Burke on the mound. *You're our guy.*

The tunnels that led from The Blatt's concourse to its dugouts were made of the same concrete and were still the same prisonlike dimensions as they were when they were first constructed in 1947. Electrical wires and TV cables snaked across the roof and the walls, all painted green to try and blend them in with the dugout.

Here, behind the third-base clubhouse in the bottom of the ninth, there were way too many people crammed into way too tight of a space.

The Cuevas Crew shuffled in and out of their tiny office/storage space, preparing to rope off the field and keep the postgame celebration from ruining the grass that the Omaha Royals were going to need two days later. The Fresno State trainers and Eddie Brewer the equipment manager zipped in and out of the clubhouse tending to their regular in-game duties. But there was nothing regular about this. Above everyone's heads was the *boom-boom-boom* of feet and hands stomping and slapping on Rosenblatt's seats, complimented by a muffled *Fres-no-State . . . Fres-no-State.*

At the bottom of the stairs, screened from the team by one humongous member of the Rosenblatt Security Team, Peter Davis and Erica Austin sifted through two very large cardboard boxes. One contained blue baseball caps, the other gray T-shirts, each embroidered or screen printed with the words 2008 NCAA DIVISION I BASEBALL NATIONAL CHAMPIONS along with a red logo of and interlocking "F" and "S."

"Can anyone see how many outs there are?" Davis shouted as he threw a stack of T-shirts over his shoulder. This kind of last-second confusion was old hat to both he and Austin. At every major NCAA championship game, no matter what sport, this is what they did. Distribute the goodies.

Just in case Georgia was to pull off the comeback, there were identical boxes of UGA championship apparel at the top of the stairs, tucked away in the Hall of Fame Room. If all went as planned, those boxes would never be opened and instead shipped off to a Third-World country as part of a disaster relief effort. It wasn't uncommon for Pete and Erica to see the logos of would-be champions during tsunami relief coverage on CNN.

Just two months earlier they had experienced a nightmare scenario at the Final Four. Memphis was carrying a double-digit lead into the final minutes of the game, so they gathered up their Tiger championship stuff and headed to the floor of San Antonio's Alamodome. They arrived courtside just in time to see Kansas send the game into overtime and go on to win. One problem. The Jayhawk gear was half an arena away.

"We barely got it there in time," Davis said, still leaning to grab a glimpse of the scoreboard through bobbing heads and the tiny entrance to the Rosenblatt tunnel. "Then we had to run past these crushed Memphis players with all of this 'Kansas National Champions' apparel. You don't know what to say. It's like, 'Sorry, dude.'"

As he finished his story, the bench up ahead erupted and emptied. The game was over. The Fresno State Bulldogs, the lowest seed in CWS history, had won the national championship. Here in the tunnel, the celebration couldn't be seen, only heard.

No one remembers exactly when the first dog pile took place on the field at Rosenblatt, but the vision of college-baseball players leaping into a big stack of humanity next to the pitching mound had become the single most recognizable image associated with the College World Series. It's the image that accompanies every ESPN telecast and served as the inspiration for the iconic statue at the stadium's entrance.

Fresno's dog pile, as it should have been, was the ugliest ever. Wilson, who pitched eight shutout innings with nine strikeouts and only one walk, was pinned at the bottom and wrenched his arm. Kris Tomlinson dove in so hard that Mr. Skullett caught an elbow with his skull, resulting in a black eye and a bag of ice on his face for all the postgame photos.

As Jack Diesing Jr. and Dennie Poppe, The Insurance Man and The Pope, took their customary places by the mound, the pride and joy of Midwest Trophy Manufacturing was brought out and placed on the table in front of them. In an instant, Randy Buhr, Bob Thomas, and Jesse Cuevas had the area roped off for the postgame awards ceremony. Ann Walters, the Walkenhorsts, and Subby Anzaldo all came to their feet, as did the Matulkas, and, yes, Dave and Linda Burns, still in town and still celebrating the greatest anniversary of all time.

They watched as each team was called out to accept their congratulations. Dave Perno, his face glazed over, held it together with his typical class, even as he accepted another non-champions award to take back to the trophy case in Athens. He kept back the tears until it was time for the individual players to be called up. That's when Ryan Peisel—as if it were on behalf of himself, Michael Hollander, Chad Flack, even Yonder Alonso and Buster Posey, those who would never have the chance to return to Rosenblatt—stood at the third-base line to take over for the coach and greet his team.

Each UGA player was called up by name to accept his own individual version of the runner-up trophy, and as they did Peisel called them by their clubhouse name, grabbed their hand, and pulled them in for a hug. This wasn't some cheesy Hollywood sports moment. This was real. This team would never be the same again. There would be other teams, one day even a championship team, but this was the last time that *this* team would ever stand on a field in uniform together.

"Some people will roll their eyes when I say these are my brothers," he said as the team sat on the bench to watch Fresno's awards ceremony. A few minutes later, at the table in the Hall of Fame Room, he would take a swipe at those damn Nike bats, but for now he was focused on the men who swung them. "Well, they are my brothers. Always will be. Even when we're old."

Around the team bus in Lot A, Mike Mayne worked the crowd, grandson Noah in tow, and repeated his mantra, this time with an addendum.

"It's just another game . . . until you win it all!"

Fresno had been met by their usual army of friends and family, but now those loved ones were joined by several hundred new fans. Some had come in from Fresno as part of the Red Wave, but most were local Omahans. They waited to greet the team in person, to thank them for energizing what had been a sometimes too-long Series. They had once fallen in love with Holy Cross, with Pepperdine, and with Oregon State. But this year their hearts belonged to the Wonderdogs. Their host from the Kiwanis Club, Jim Costello, said good-bye to his team, helping them onto the bus for a final time, each player graciously thanking him and his kids for their help. "Heck of a job, Jimmy," a friend shouted over. "You're the only guy that pulled his team through!"

Once again, Mike Batesole was the last person on the bus. Throughout the celebration he had remained low-key, missing out on the dog pile when he kneeled in the dugout and slapped the floor to thank the holy ground and the baseball gods. He had hugged a few folks and given a couple of interviews, but mostly he watched his team and soaked in the rewards of a too-tough season.

On the bus, he took his usual front seat on the right side of the aisle, paused, and then jumped back up.

"Who has the trophy?"

"It's in the back, Coach."

"Well, I want to hold it." And he went to the back of Chris Clark's Arrow motor coach and grabbed it. He returned to his seat, held it in his lap like a baby and then out at arm's length to read the inscription. Damn if it wasn't true. They *were* the champions.

With three toots of the horn, the Fresno State bus, the one that had driven to The Blatt on Father's Day with less than zero expectations, pulled away at 10:22 P.M.

Over the next hour, The Blatt and The Neighborhood began their joint transformations from center of the baseball universe to just another minor-league ballpark and just another South Omaha neighborhood.

At 10:30, the scoreboard was reset, wiping away the line score from Championship Game Three, and replacing it with the logo of the Omaha Royals. The concessionaires counted cups, and the cleaning crew began their long clockwise crawl around the grandstands with increasingly stuffed garbage bags. ESPN's road crew began taking down cameras and rolling up multiple miles worth of cables. Jesse, Randy, and Bob shook hands and said they'd do it again next year.

Lambert Bartak powered down his Hammond, Lou Spry closed up his scorebook, and the Sobczyks tallied up their final ticket numbers for the two weeks.

Over at the Hilton Garden Inn, Buddy Allison, Ray Mendonca, and the other parents celebrated with cake and beer, a combination Allison claimed, "Probably only works if you've just won a national championship." A random hotel guest, some guy who had nothing to do with the team, couldn't pass up a party and set up an impromptu bar on a restaurant table where he mixed some sort of crazy vodka, rum, and whatever else he could find drinks, which he served in Dixie cups.

Meanwhile, Mike Batesole and his family told their oldest daughter to be careful as she headed out for the Old Market and went back to their room on the third floor.

What did you do with the trophy, Coach?

"It's in a very safe place."

At the Embassy Suites, the Georgia players were nowhere to be found, except for Matt Cerione, who was in the lobby bar with his family, apologizing for his embarrassing tirade, but still cursing those Nike bats.

Perno stood by the bank of elevators in the lobby, trying his best to ignore all the voice mails and text messages that had constantly buzzed into his phone since the end of the game. "How do you respond to them?" he said as he contemplated a late dinner with Matt Woods, the Ryan Peisel of his 2004 College World Series squad. "We were in the hole that year, too. I went to Matt and he told me, 'Don't worry, Coach, I've got this,' and he led us to Omaha. You have to have guys like this or you don't win. They even make the hurting worth it because you have these relationships that you'll keep for the rest of your life."

Thirteenth Street was dark, but alive with the sounds of hammering and tent deconstruction as the vendors tore down like a circus crew heading out to the next town. Only the endless rock-and-roll from behind Starsky's kept the pulse of the party beating weakly. The parking lots were empty, save for a couple of boys playing catch in the north lot as their parents sat around a card table, watching the highlights of the game on *SportsCenter*, and waiting on the grill to cool down enough to load into their minivan. The Boudreaux Thibodeaux boys were long gone, hitting the sack for one more night over at the Council Bluffs Super 8 before hauling their empty coolers back toward Louisiana and into the sunrise.

Over at the zoo, Daniel Morris made one last stroll to make sure all the wild things were set for the night. It had been a wild two weeks. The crowds and even the requests from LSU fans to "borrow a tiger" were just part of the routine. The emergence of a new queen bee in the insect pavilion had been a curveball, but the hive was successfully saved. He was excited about the eventual expansion onto what would soon be the "former site of Rosenblatt Stadium," but like everyone else in Omaha he'd grown up going to Series games and he was going to miss seeing his friends from ESPN when they showed up every June to mount a robotic camera on the roof of his Desert Dome. "It's hard to imagine life without your best neighbor."

Greg Pivovar hadn't had a customer at Stadium View for nearly an hour, but had managed to find some excuse to keep hanging around. He had to empty the register. He had to clean the glass display-case tops. He had to collect the money from the Harper Lee College Fund boxes, and had to bring in the folding tables from outside and put them away. Now he was out of things to do.

At 11:34 P.M., Piv turned off the lights, walked out onto the curb and locked the door. Then he paused, looked across the street at the big blue dark stadium, took a deep breath, and disappeared down the hill toward Fourteenth Street.

See you next year, but for a limited time only.

THIRTEEN

THE LONG GOOD-BYE

Thursday, June 26

The morning after the sixty-second College World Series, everyone who had worked together, lived together, and competed against one another for half a month said good-bye and made their way north to Eppley Airfield to catch their flights home.

As they traveled up Tenth Street in rental cars, shuttle vans, and Arrow buses, everyone looked to their right and saw the Qwest Center, where the U.S. Olympic Committee was putting the final touches on the one-million-gallon swimming pool that would launch Michael Phelps into legend.

To their left was Lot C, the barren asphalt parking space that was now less than three years away from playing host to the sixty-fifth—and its first edition of the College World Series.

Two weeks earlier, this was the spot where Mayor Mike Fahey had braved the boos one final time to announce the longest championship agreement in NCAA history. This was where Jack Diesing and Dennie Poppe, The Insurance Man and The Pope, had officially pushed Omaha and its signature event forward into the future, for better or for worse. But on this morning, the morning after, there was nothing futuristic about it. It was just something to stare at as it rolled by on the horizon, an asphalt flatland in need of some weed killer.

The Georgia Bulldogs and the 2008 National Champion Fresno State Bulldogs drove past that lot, arrived at the airport at exactly the same time, and watched their planes taxi out onto the runway in unison. With a massive thundercloud bearing down on the airstrip, Georgia got the nod to go first and hustled up the runway skyward for home.

By the end of summer, Gordon Beckham and Ryan Peisel would be signed and playing minor-league ball while Josh Fields (and uberagent Scott Boras) held out through the fall to try and squeeze a better deal out of the Seattle Mariners, the only first-round pick not to sign by the August 15 deadline.

When Peisel reported for duty with the Colorado Rockies' Class A Tri-City Dust Devils, he met his new teammate, Fresno's Eric Wetzel. "Wetzel promised not to bring it up too much," Peisel said two months after the Series, joking but admittedly still heartbroken.

The day after Georgia returned to Athens, Uga VI died of a heart attack. The bulldog was buried at Sanford Stadium the following Monday, his body driven across the football field to the strains of "The Battle Hymn of the Republic." He was 82–27 at football games but never made it to Omaha.

In mid-September, Coach Dave Perno opened fall practice with eighteen returning members of his 2008 runner-up squad, joined by a group of incoming freshman that was ranked by *Baseball America* as the nation's number-two recruiting class. Once he'd seen his new team in action and knew that his 2009 roster was in good shape, Perno finally made himself sit down and watch the tapes of the 2008 Series.

His reaction, still, was, "I just don't get it. But I do."

Fresno's Nebraska send-off was very much like their welcome. They were sacked in by a storm and forced to sit on the runway. No one seemed to mind. They read the morning edition of the *Omaha World-Herald* over and over again, marveling at the headlines that screamed, "Best in Show" and "Fresno's First," and soaked up the coverage of their historic accomplishment in *USA Today* and the *Wall Street Journal*. They laughed as they saw their team compared to Joe Namath's 1968 Jets, Jimmy Valvano's 1983 N.C. State Wolfpack, and Rollie Massimino's 1985 Villanova Wildcats. And they fell on the floor when they saw a photo of Steve Detwiler's final-out catch next to Mike Eruzione and the 1980 U.S. Olympic Hockey Team.

While waiting on the tarmac, the athletic department brass were constantly on their phones, either helping organize the waiting celebration at Beiden Field, a parade and party that would draw more than 20,000 Red Wave fans, or figuring out how to get all the newly minted championship merchandise in the hands of those fans.

Soon the players were asleep. It'd been a long post-title night and there was going to be another long night back home on Barstow Avenue.

It would be even longer for the 2008 Most Outstanding Player. In the midst of the Championship Series, Tommy Mendonca received a call from the headquarters of USA Baseball in Cary, North Carolina. They loved what they'd seen and they wanted him to be the starting third baseman on their collegiate team, dislocated fingers and all. If he wanted in he would have to come straight to Cary after the Fresno parade and then head across the Atlantic for the European Championships. He never considered saying no and came away with a gold medal.

Three months later he and the rest of his Fresno teammates were shaking hands with President Bush at the White House.

Not bad for the son of a dairy farmer.

Jesse Cuevas and his grounds crew had The Blatt turned around in plenty of time for the Omaha Royals' game on Friday night. Mother Nature had other plans. A vicious storm blew through The Neighborhood that afternoon, knocking out power to the ballpark. The game was moved to Saturday morning, using emergency generators for only the bare essentials while city crews worked to restore power for a second game later that night.

Without a public address system or a scoreboard, O Royals marketing director Rob Crain sat in the stands and made announcements using a megaphone. Big leftover billboard numbers were hung on the wall to show the score, and the radio broadcast team did the game over the telephone. There was no music, not from Lambert Bartak or anyone else. About 2,000 people showed up.

Somewhere Frankie Mancuso was laughing his ass off.

As the teams and most of his NCAA employees departed, Dennie Poppe stayed in Omaha for a few more days. He met with construction companies and contractors, combing through the first details of the new CWS ballpark. He also met with potential naming-rights suitors, big-money corporations willing to fork over likely tens of millions of dollars to have their name splashed across the entrance to the downtown stadium.

It was a precarious tightrope to walk and no one knew that better than Poppe. The right corporate title would help tie the stadium to its Omaha roots, at least make it seem like the Series was working hard not to undo its family-friendly, last-of-the-great-amateur-events charm. The wrong logo on the front door would be pointed to, fairly or unfairly, as proof that some people's fears of a greedy to-hell-with-the-people era were indeed founded.

"We'll do the right thing," Poppe said with that famous disarming smile. "The event will survive and so will the atmosphere. No one wants that to happen more than I do. A lot of people are counting on that."

No one more than an Omaha-born businessman now living in Scottsdale, Arizona, who watched Poppe's every move with both a civic and emotional interest.

Steve Rosenblatt was there the day that his daddy's new ballpark was christened on October 17, 1949. He was a preteen batboy, sitting in the third-base dugout to watch his childhood heroes suit up and play ball. He held down that same job when the Omaha Cardinals came to town the following spring and when the College World Series came to Municipal Stadium in 1950. Later, he suited up and played ball on that very field.

He was there the day they renamed the place Johnny Rosenblatt Stadium, and he cried the day he realized that Parkinson's disease was finally going to prevent his father from being able to go over and see his ballpark one more time.

Rosenblatt returned to Omaha several times a year to visit old friends and to share steakhouse stories of his time on the city and county councils, when he was at the table for so many of those Omaha versus NCAA throwdown/love-ins. Every year he came back for the first weekend of the College World Series, where he constantly worked handshakes from the parking lots to the grandstand, inevitably shocking unsuspecting revelers whom he met for the first time.

"Did you say Steve *Rosenblatt*? Like *the* Rosenblatts?"

And he always came back to see the Omaha Royals. He remembered that his father's first dream was to bring professional baseball to O Town. The College World Series was the afterthought that unexpectedly became the city's signature event. But Johnny always came out for Opening Day of every minor-league season, no matter what team called his stadium home, eager to hit out the first pitch and spread the sunshine of that infectious smile.

As the O Royals closed out the 2008 season, Steve came back to town for their final home game, an 11–5 loss to the New Orleans Zephyrs. Like the College World Series, they would be forced to leave The Blatt after 2010. Unlike the Series, they didn't yet know where they would be playing in 2011. Maybe in the new ballpark, but probably not.

As Steve threw out the final first pitch of the season, he looked up at his father's name in those big red letters on the roof of the press box. The ones you could see clear across the Missouri River into Council Bluffs. Like everyone else, he'd heard the rumors that his father's name would still be incorporated into the new downtown ballpark, maybe with a statue or a plaque or perhaps even his name on the playing field. Whatever the powers-that-be decided to do would be an honor, but for the Rosenblatt family it would always be an honor with an asterisk.

"My dad loved baseball. I mean, he really, deeply loved the game. And to see it bring the same kind of joy that it did to his life to the lives of so many people in Omaha and beyond, that's just a magical experience for me. I've had plenty of time to come to grips with the fact that Johnny Rosenblatt Stadium is going to be gone soon, more time than most because I could see it coming so many years ago during my years in Omaha politics. I have no doubts that the new facility will be something special, just as I have no doubts that the College World Series will be just as special and as memorable to the people of Omaha as it always has been."

Then he paused and sighed.

"But it won't be the same. Everyone knows that. I tell people all the time that they'd better go and they'd better go now. The future might be better or it might be worse, but it won't be the same."

POSTSCRIPT

THE RETURN

June 12–24, 2009
63rd NCAA Men's College World Series

"The Road to Omaha, huh?"

As Augie Garrido said the words with a laugh, he rose from the bench in Rosenblatt Stadium's first-base dugout. One year earlier he'd sat in the grandstands above that dugout as a fan, cheering along with his fellow Fresno State alums and supporters. He had looked down onto the field, taken the temperatures of the teams below, and had correctly predicted the outcome of the 2008 Championship Series simply by gauging drooped shoulders and confident strides. His guys had won.

Even so, this year's seat was considerably better. This year, Garrido hadn't had to buy a ticket to get in. He was in uniform and his Texas Longhorns were back at The Blatt for their record thirty-third College World Series appearance.

"Let me tell you about that damn road," the now-seventy-year-old head coach said, instinctively placing one foot on the top step of the dugout, the same dugout where he'd stood as either a player or a coach during thirteen previous editions of the Series. "When you come back here to Omaha, to this stadium, this very dugout, as many times as I have or as many times as this team has, you start thinking you'd be able to drive that road with your eyes closed. You'd think it would become easier to get back here after you've made the trip so often."

Then the old ball coach looked up to his left, into the sun and up to the towering blue press box above, squinting and pointing to the bright red lettering: JOHNNY ROSENBLATT STADIUM. "But here's the thing about Ol' Johnny here, he's a baseball man. And he doesn't care what you've done before. He doesn't read résumés. He makes you earn back your invitation. And damn if he doesn't change the way that the Road to Omaha is laid out every single year."

This year marked the sixtieth time that Johnny's ballpark had hosted the College World Series. And just to prove Garrido's point, only two of the eight teams from the 2008 series found their way back in 2009.

On June 11, 350 days after Fresno and Georgia had taken off for home, the new field of eight touched down throughout the day at Eppley Airfield. One by one, their buses rolled south on Abbott Drive, bound for the hotels of downtown Omaha. Just as Fresno had done one year earlier, the players leapt to their feet when they spotted the first clues that the stadium was nearby.

Only this was a different stadium.

As LSU's motorcoach took the familiar lefthander onto Tenth Street, several members of the Tiger baseball squad shouted to get the attention of head coach Paul Mainieri. "Look, Coach! It's the new stadium!"

Several hundred yards away, an eight-foot-high chain-link fence was wrapped around the perimeter of an entire city block. When the team had driven by that same spot one year earlier, it was a parking lot. Now it was a high-energy construction zone. Behind the barrier, bulldozers and earthmovers scooped, hauled, dumped, and graded. The machinery billowed diesel smoke from deep within an infield-shaped hole. From the street, all that could be seen was a series of prerequisite signs advertising all of the contractors at work on the other side of that fence. The largest touted: FUTURE HOME OF OMAHA BASEBALL STADIUM. By the time the teams and fans would roll back by two weeks later, it would be replaced by a new sign: FUTURE HOME OF TD AMERITRADE PARK OMAHA.

Outside of Omaha, CWS fans scoffed at the name, dismissing it as a corporate, antiseptic symbol of a future without the charm of Johnny Rosenblatt Stadium. But those who actually lived in the Big O knew better. They knew that the story behind the $3 billion company was a classic

Omaha tale, no different than Warren Buffett, Cascio's, or those first entrepreneurs who'd wandered over from Council Bluffs in 1854.

In the 1960s, just as Jack Diesing Sr. was getting CWS of Omaha, Inc., up and running, a handful of local businessmen started a small investment banking firm: Rahel, Knack, and Company. In 1975, the company was bought by another three-man team of local partners, including J. Joseph Ricketts, who in 2009 became the new owner of the Chicago Cubs (Ricketts is a graduate of Creighton, former employer of Cubs general manager Leo Hendry). They renamed the company First Omaha Securities. By the mid-1980s, Ricketts owned it outright and it became AMERITRADE. When the Internet exploded in the late 1990s AMERITRADE—eventually TD AMERITRADE—grabbed the leading edge of the digital wave and quickly became the largest online brokerage in the world.

"This is a statement to the city of Omaha," CEO Fred Tomczyk said, hard hat in hand, at the naming rights announcement, which had taken place the day before the teams of the 2009 College World Series arrived. Tomczyk shook hands with the mayor, Jim Suttle, who had succeeded the embattled Mike Fahey, then talked very directly to the people of the city. "Omaha is our home. We have more than two thousand employees living in Omaha. Joe Ricketts built this company in Omaha. This is the greatest sports event in America, and it is Omaha's. We are proud to make sure it is staying here." (For those you scoring at home, that's five mentions of Omaha in one twenty-second sound bite.)

Still, to so many longtime residents, just driving by the site was indigestion-inducing. The "Save Rosenblatt" cries still echoed down from The Neighborhood, though they were becoming harder to hear over the jackhammers and concrete mixers.

To others, the idea of a new ballpark was becoming exciting. They'd seen what the sparkling Qwest Center arena had done for downtown and perhaps TD AMERITRADE Park would bring more of the same. They'd pored over the Web site, picked up the brochures, and privately loved the idea of the wider, taller concourses instead of the cramped hallways of The Blatt. They coveted better parking, better access to concessions, and no one objected to replacing the world's slowest press-box elevator.

But they would never dare to admit any of that in public.

Now, in fact, the city would be opening not one, but two new ballparks in 2011. The Omaha Royals, long ago tired of playing their games in cavernous Rosenblatt, did not want to be subjected to the same second-citizen status in the new downtown stadium, no matter how nice the $128-million facility was going to be. So they elected to build their own cozier 6,000-seat park in the southern Omaha suburb of Papillion. "For a football town," local sportscaster Travis Justice said while explaining the new plans, "we sure are going to have a lot of nice baseball stadiums."

"I'm not worried about the new ballpark," Garrido admitted as he stepped back and reclaimed his spot on the bench at Rosenblatt Stadium. He pushed his sunglasses back onto his face with one hand and used the other to motion toward his Longhorns, who were going through their pregame routines on the field. "I only have two more chances to enjoy this stadium. Maybe one more. The last time we were on this field was 2005. We walked off it as national champions. That seems like a hundred years ago, doesn't it? Like I just told you, that's the thing about that Road to Omaha. There's no guarantee that they'll have me back for the last dance in 2010. Even if we win it all."

Fresno State's now legendary group of seven seniors, the Class of 2008 that orchestrated the greatest upset in CWS history, was graduated and gone. Tommy Mendonca's Omaha momentum continued well into the next season, clubbing twenty-seven homers, hitting .339, and most important, slashing his strikeout total by nearly one-third. But the freshman-heavy Bulldogs found it hard to rediscover their bite. And with assistant coach Mike Mayne now retired and living in Montana, there was no buffer zone and mediator to ease the annual midseason tensions between the youngsters and Mike Batesole.

Like 2008, Fresno got off to a horrible start. Like 2008, they rallied from nowhere to make the postseason. They had to sweep their final regular season series just to qualify for the WAC conference tournament. So they did. Like 2008, they had to win that tournament to earn an NCAA tournament bid. They did that, too. Like 2008, they were sent to an impossible regional, this time hosted by Cal-Irvine and featuring San Diego State and fireball pitcher Stephen Strasburg. But unlike 2008, they were swept in two games and sent home early. Two-and-'cue. "We just ran out of magic," Mendonca admitted two months later, now a member of the Spokane Indians, Class A affiliate of the Texas Rangers, who drafted the third baseman in the second round of the MLB First-Year Draft.

The Georgia Bulldogs, who had come within a handful of innings from winning the 2008 title, were done in by a season that was nearly the total opposite of Fresno's year, though the root of their eventual demise was the same. They started the year hot behind bangers Rich Poythress and Bryce Massanari, spending most of the spring near the top of their conference and the national standings. But when the season started to nose south, the clubhouse captains of 2008 weren't there to help head coach David Perno construct a rally.

Spiritual leader Ryan Peisel was now in the Colorado Rockies organization, struggling with the wooden bats of pro ball. Statistical leader Gordon Beckham had no such problems. The number-eight overall pick of the 2008 draft began the 2009 season in the minors, but by June 4 was the starting third baseman for the Chicago White Sox. On June 20, he hit his first big-league home run. On July 23, he was on the field for pitcher Mark Buehrle's perfect game, just the eighteenth in Major League history, receiving a ribbing from his teammates for acting so nervous on the bench between innings. At season's end, Beckham was named American League Rookie of the Year by *The Sporting News*. When New York Yankees captain Derek Jeter was asked to identify who he thought was the next great MLB infielder, he replied without hesitation, "Beckham in Chicago."

The University of Gordon is awesome.

The Dogs and Dawgs were not alone in their plight. Florida State once again put up gaudy numbers, breezing through their first-round NCAA regional matchups with Marist, Georgia, and Ohio State. The Seminoles averaged twenty runs per game and in the contest that eliminated the Buckeyes, the Seminoles scored thirty-seven runs. However, they were upset in the next round by Arkansas, including a heartbreaking one-run loss to the Razorbacks in the elimination game. As one FSU fan trudged out of Tallahassee's Dick Howser Stadium, he shouted skyward to the hardball gods, "Where are you, Buster Posey?!" The Pick was 2,600 miles away, cruising his way up the San Francisco Giants minor league ladder. He was invited to join the big club in September.

Florida State's archenemy, the Miami Hurricanes, publicly bemoaned the losses of leaders Yonder Alonso and Jemile Weeks as the University of Miami failed to make their twenty-fourth CWS appearance. "The players that I believed were ready to step and lead us have not done that," head coach Jim Morris said as the Canes packed up after an inexplicable early exit from the ACC Tournament as the hands of (gulp) Boston College. "Do me a favor and tell Miss Marilyn hello for me. I'm not going to get to do that in person this year."

Stanford was equally lost without the bat of Jason Castro. As the catcher worked his way through the Houston Astros organization, the Cardinal failed to qualify for the sixty-four-year NCAA postseason field. Closer Drew Storen, who passed up a shot at playing for the Yankees to go to college, was the number-ten pick in the 2009 MLB Draft and came within a whisker of making the Washington Nationals roster in barely half a season. Outfielder Toby Gerhart was also drafted, but chose to come back and play one more year of running back for the Stanford football squad. Good move. He finished second in the Heisman Trophy voting, only twenty-eight points behind Alabama's Mark Ingram. It was the closest margin in the seventy-five-year history of college football's most coveted award.

"Gerhart's the only one here who really understands me," head coach Mark Marquess still loved to say to his baseball team, his arm thrown around the muscle-ripped shoulders of his fellow two-sport Stanford star. "We're the only real athletes here, aren't we, Toby?"

But perhaps the most surprising CWS nonreturnee was Rice. Wayne Graham's Owls had done what they did best, riding big pitching arms all the way to a Conference-USA tournament title and another NCAA postseason berth. They easily swept their first-round regional at home in Houston. "Then," Graham said with his patented gruffness, "we were afforded the privilege of traveling to Baton Rouge to play LSU." Still smarting from their Game Seven collapse against the Tigers in the 2008 CWS, the Owls blew a three-run lead to lose the first game of the Super Regional and saw a tie game slip away in the second. Season over.

Still, the eight teams of the 2009 College World Series did what every CWS bracket always manages to do. They fit nicely into the roles that are seemingly filled each and every year.

Playing the part of The Pick was North Carolina junior Dustin Ackley. Shortly after the Tarheels finished their marathon 2008 visit to Omaha, the long, lean first baseman underwent ligament replacement, or Tommy John, surgery. Some worried that the new elbow would affect his smooth, swishy swing. It did not. For the second consecutive season, he hit a mind-bending .417, bringing his three-year college batting average to .412. When the Heels traveled to Boston College for a late-season series, Carolina alum and Hall of Fame baseball writer Peter Gammons came out to see his alma mater. In reality, he confessed, he came to see Ackley's swing. The next say he filed a column to ESPN.com under the headline: DUSTIN ACKLEY HAS "IT".

On June 9, one day after UNC earned its fourth consecutive trip to Omaha, Ackley was taken by the Seattle Mariners as the second overall pick of the MLB Draft. Like Buster Posey one year earlier or Ben McDonald in 1989 or Jackie Jensen in 1947, Ackley arrived at the CWS with the big-league can't-miss buzz and the pressure that came with it.

But North Carolina came up short once again. And like Posey in 2008, Ackley had a chance to help his team but came up empty. In a ferocious first game against Arizona State, he came to the plate in the bottom of the ninth with a man on base in a 1–1 tie. He struck out looking, his legendary bat sitting on his legendary shoulders. The Heels lost in ten innings, slipping into the deadly 0–1 hole to start the Series. "If Dusty didn't swing at it then it wasn't a strike," head coach Mike Fox said matter-of-factly weeks later from his sparkling office in Chapel Hill's all-new Boshamer Stadium. "It couldn't be."

The Underdog of 2008 was Southern Mississippi. The Golden Eagles were led by head coach Corky Palmer, a folksy USM alum who had aw-shucked his team to its first College World Series appearance. He came into the pre-Series coaches' press conference with the same strategy as

Mike Batesole in 2008, playing up the what-the-hell-are-we-even-doing-here chatter. But his opponents knew better, especially after his team had taken Texas to the mat in the opening weekend's Game Four.

As extra motivation, Palmer had informed his team that he would be retiring at season's end after thirty-one seasons on the benches of two high schools, a community college, and his alma mater. It worked. They won twelve of their final fifteen games, including a sweep of the University of Florida in Gainesville. In the second game, they'd been down five runs before rallying to eliminate the Gators. But the one-run loss to Texas and a five-hit game by Ackley ended the Eagles' season, and Corky's career, with a teary-eyed press conference in The Blatt's Hall of Fame Room.

The Favorite was a familiar face, the blue and orange capital F of the Cal State Fullerton Titans. When the college baseball media was asked to vote for their pre-Series favorite, the Rosenblatt press box was filled with spirited debate, but in the end the Titans were the overwhelming choice. Dave Serrano was in his second year as head coach, heir to the empire that was first built by Augie Garrido and then maintained by Serrano's mentor, George Horton. But on just the third day of the Series, they, too, were gone. Two-and-'cue.

The teams that joined forces to eliminate Fullerton were relative newcomers to Rosenblatt, but their ties to the old blue ballpark ran deep. During the 1980s, the Arkansas Razorbacks were Omaha regulars thanks to future big leaguers like Jeff King and Kevin McReynolds. They hadn't been back since 1989 when head coach Dave Van Horn was hired away from Nebraska in 2003. The previous two seasons he'd packed The Blatt with record crowds eager to support the home state Cornhuskers. During his second year with the Razorbacks they made it to Omaha and now they were back. "I have plenty of fans shouting 'Go Big Red!'" the coached joked. "I'm still wearing red. It's a little darker, but it still works."

Making its first CWS appearance were the Virginia Cavaliers, a 120-year-old program that once had been so terrible that school administrators actually took a vote on whether or not to shut it down. "That's not ancient history, either," reminded UVA head coach Brian O'Connor.

"That was in 2001. They hired me two years later." To most baseball fans, O'Connor was just another head coach happy to be on Johnny Rosenblatt's field. But to the more observant CWS fans, his face . . . hmmm . . . why did his face look so familiar?

"Which one of these guys is Coach O'Connor?" As Jarrett Parker approached the iconic Road to Omaha sculpture outside the entrance to the stadium, the sophomore outfielder and his teammates scanned the faces of the four athletes, forever celebrating in bronze. The lefty locked in on the shouting face on the far right side of the statue, the one without a cap on, his hand grasped firmly around the leg of his leaping helmeted teammate. "Wait . . . there he is! That has to be him."

"Yeah," the coach said, clearly having answered the question a thousand times before. "That's me."

O'Connor grew up just across the Missouri River from Rosenblatt, where his family still lives, and was a member of the area's greatest college baseball team, the '91 Creighton University Blue Jay squad that electrified the ballpark with their near-championship run. Six years later, sculptor John Lajba was commissioned by the city to create a piece commemorating the fiftieth anniversary of the College World Series, to be unveiled at the entrance of the stadium in 1999. As a longtime Omaha resident who'd long ago fallen in love with the CWS, Lajba took the assignment to heart. He visited local schools, including Creighton, to try and get a feel for the emotions involved in putting together a truly great baseball team.

While sitting in the office of a friend, Lajba couldn't stop staring at a photo on his friend's desk. It was of a young, confident college kid dressed in a Creighton baseball uniform. With one glance, the artist knew that he wanted to capture that image of twinkle-in-the-eye youthful exuberance and work it into his new project. He asked his friend to borrow the picture and his friend obliged.

The friend was John O'Connor. His son, the one in the photo, was Brian.

In a classic game of connect-the-coach, Brian O'Connor played for Jim Hendry at Creighton, who helped his apprentice land an assistant coaching job at Notre Dame under Hendry's old friend, Paul Mainieri.

When they led Notre Dame to a CWS berth in 2002, just its second in school history, O'Connor became the nation's most sought-after young coach. The following season he was the head coach in Charlottesville. In 2009, the local kid whose face was on the statue was coaching in the College World Series. When his Virginia Cavaliers arrived for their first Series game, they had to walk right past that statue to get to their clubhouse.

"It's magical," Lajba said when talking about the story. "It's like a storybook."

Unfortunately, O'Connor's storybook opened with a matchup against his mentor. Virginia was welcomed to Rosenblatt with a 9–5 loss to Mainieri and LSU in Game Two. The bounced back to eliminate Fullerton two days later, and then lost to Arkansas in an extra-inning spirit-crusher in Game Nine.

"We agreed before our opening game that we wouldn't look at each other," Mainieri admitted afterward. "That was tough for me. To shake Brian's hand and hug him before the game was so gratifying. It's like one of my sons going out and doing so well. At first, you want to celebrate the win and then you want to go console your friend on his loss. It's very hard."

For the rest of the CWS field, Mainieri refused to show such mercy.

"You know, I really feel sorry for whoever we end up playing in the championship."

As the head coach leaned against the batting cage at Bellevue East High School, he addressed every hitter who stepped to the plate and every player who stood by his side as they waited their turn. Mainieri had already greeted Marilyn Ralston, gotten his hug and a bottle of Gatorade. Now he was chattering, in full-on "we are so much better than everyone else" confidence-building mode. The skipper eased from player to player in his deep purple jersey emblazoned with a gold number one. Here, knocking on the door of LSU's sixth CWS Championship Series, he didn't talk about swing adjustments or fielding strategies. He was focused solely on attitude.

"I'm serious," he said to outfielder Jared Mitchell, one of a staggering nineteen Tigers who were back from the 2008 squad. "To win championships you have to have everyone locked in. I've only had a few teams that were just locked in, where everyone had found the zone. I feel that with this team. When you have that confidence, no one can beat you."

For a season and half, since that magical April 2008 at-bat by D. J. LeMahieu versus Tulane, no one had beaten the Bayou Bengals with any regularity. They had ended the 2008 season with a record of 26–3 and that momentum had carried forward into 2009. The season began with a nine-game win streak and ended by winning ten in a row. In the postseason they were a perfect 5–0 before getting to Omaha and 3–0 since arriving. Over a year and a half they'd lost two games in a row only once.

Throughout 2009, Mainieri had tinkered with the Tiger lineup, sometimes to the great frustration of his 9,000-plus supporters in the grandstand of the all new $36 million Alex Box Stadium. Only three weeks before the end of the regular season he moved LeMahieu from shortstop, the only position that the twenty-year old had ever played, to second base. Freshman Austin Nola took over in the six-hole. Some fans grumbled that the team was being overmanaged. That complaining didn't last long. After the move, the team went 23–4, sweeping the SEC tournament, NCAA regional, NCAA Super Regional, and their first three games of the College World Series.

The Tigers were indeed "locked in."

As they walked off the Rosenblatt field after crushing SEC rival Arkansas 14–5 in the CWS semifinals, one press-box scribe pointed to the two remaining teams as they walked into the stadium to see who would face LSU in the championship. He shouted to his colleagues, "You can have these other two. I'll take the guys in purple."

The statement was weightier because of the two teams he was speaking of. The Texas Longhorns and Arizona State Sun Devils, like LSU, were easily among the top five greatest versions of The Program to ever stride into the hills of South Omaha. Texas's six CWS titles were second only to Southern Cal's twelve. LSU and ASU were right behind with five each.

"I know we're not supposed to root for teams," said CWS scorekeeper Lou Spry as the Horns and Devils took infield on the field below. "But here in the last stanzas for the old ballpark, there is something very fitting about seeing these classic college baseball programs slugging it out for the next-to-last title here at Rosenblatt. You see that purple and gold, or the burnt orange and white, or the maroon and gold . . . and you realize that this could be 1990, or 1980, or even 1960, and these uniforms were out here on this field. It's classic Rosenblatt Stadium."

So was the game.

ASU ace Mike Leake, the number-eight pick of the MLB Draft, started the game opposite Texas righty Cole Green. The two juggernauts slugged their way into the ninth inning with Arizona State clinging to a one-run lead. The mighty Texas bats had swung at the air all night, registering a dozen strikeouts. Closer Michael Lambson had relieved Leake and retired the first seven batters he faced.

Then, in the words of Augie Garrido, "We woke up the Texas baseball ghosts in this building."

Cameron Rupp, the number-seven hitter, came to the plate with one out and down three runs to two. He launched a homer over the twenty-two-foot wall in centerfield. Tie game.

When catcher Preston Clark fouled out weakly to the catcher for the second out, ASU head coach Pat Murphy immediately began preaching to his bench about an extra-inning victory. After all, the batter coming to the plate for Texas was light-hitting number-nine batter Connor Rowe. The centerfielder was hitting a solidly generic .278 with only six homers on the year.

Tink.

Make that seven.

With one swing, Texas had advanced to its amazing twelfth CWS Championship Series and its fourth of the decade. And with one swing, Arizona State's seniors and drafted juniors were forced to make that long drive back to the hotel. Their college careers—and in some cases, their baseball lives—were over.

One year after his own college career had ended while sprinting up the first-base line at Rosenblatt, Michael Hollander still involuntarily winced a little when he talked about it. It was his leadership that pushed the LSU Tigers into the 2008 CWS. And if you talked to the members of the 2009 roster, they still pointed to "Holly" as one of the biggest reasons for their Omaha return.

After Omaha, he reported to the Texas Rangers farm system and spent most of the summer in Arizona, rehabbing a couple of nagging injuries. That fall he was back in Baton Rouge for the LSU alumni game. The next February, when the school opened the new ballpark, Hollander and fellow 2008 senior Jared Bradford were invited back to throw out the stadium's first of the ceremonial first pitches.

Throughout spring training, and as he toiled through his first full minor league season with the Class A Hickory Crawdads in North Carolina, Hollander never lost touch with his old team. When LeMahieu, who was being heavily scouted as a shortstop by Major League teams, was told that he was being moved to second base, the first person he called to talk about it was Hollander. He had seen how well Mike had handled the same situation the previous year, when LeMahieu was the freshman hotshot and Hollander was being rooted out of his natural position. "Don't complain and don't resist," LeMahieu remembered Hollander telling him. "You do what's best for the team. Even if that means doing something you've never done before."

In the pros, Hollander was experiencing plenty of newness himself. Gone was the "hold the rope" attitude and atmosphere of the college locker room. The professional clubhouse was full of divisions: age, background, education, language, culture—too many to list. The bridge builder between those divisions became Hollander, who won over his teammates with his dirty-jersey playing style. He even spoke just enough Spanish to earn the respect of the hard-to-crack international side of the dugout. He also had no idea what position he would be playing from day to day. They'd even started prepping the lifelong infielder to play catcher.

"He's a natural born leader," said Crawdads manager Bill Richardson, a longtime high-school coach in California in his third year as a minor-league manager. "Mike was bound to end up as a catcher. And if he doesn't make it as a player he is destined to be a great manager or coach if he wants to be."

Throughout the first week of the Series, he'd carefully staked out his position on the benches of ballparks throughout the South Atlantic League, finding the best spots to keep an eye on any televisions that might be within viewing distance. "I'd be watching the LSU games on TVs all over the stadium. In the stadium sports bar or a sky box . . . whatever I could spot. I couldn't ever hear it and it might be like three hundred feet away. But I could always see just enough to know what was happening. The guys on the team figured out just to leave me alone if LSU was playing."

However, during the three nights of the best-of-three 2009 CWS Championship Series, Hollander was alone in his apartment in the foothills of North Carolina. The title games fell squarely in the middle of the South Atlantic League's three-day All-Star break. Most of the Crawdads had left town and he'd been offered a chance to jet out to Omaha with some of his old friends from Section L2 at The Box. But instead he chose solitude.

"We jumped out to an early lead in Game One," Hollander described two months later, sitting in a Hickory barbecue joint. "I could just hear Coach saying, 'Attack early!' Then we trailed by two runs two different times. Louis (Coleman) was having a hard night. Texas just kept blasting solo home runs. Remember, Coleman was the one who gave up that big bomb to North Carolina the year before and I knew that if I was there I could have come to the mound and calmed him down. But I was in Hickory. I was a mess. People were calling me and texting me, and finally I just told everyone to leave me alone. I was all sweating. I felt like I was playing in the damn game."

Down two runs in the ninth, their ace pitcher having been chased from the mound, the team answered the chants of L-S-U and the strange bayou voodoo calls coming from all corners of the Rosenblatt grandstand. The atmosphere became eerily reminiscent of their Hollander-led rally versus Rice in 2008. LeMahieu stroked a two-out, two-run double in the bottom of the ninth to force extra innings. In the top of the eleventh, LeMahieu led off with a walk, stole second, and advanced to third when Texas catcher Cameron Rupp's throwdown ended up in centerfield. When freshman Mikie Mahtook, who'd required intravenous fluids in the sixth inning to keep playing, singled in LeMahieu for the winning run, the celebration at The Blatt was second only to the one in a near-empty apartment in Hickory, North Carolina.

As Hollander talked about it, you would have never known that it had been well over a year since his last night in an LSU uniform. He paused, looked up, and then stared out of the window as he continued on. "Pro ball is just different. It's my job. But those guys, that's my team. And now they were one win away from the national championship. It drove me nuts not being there."

Hollander watched the entire Championship Series from the same bunkerlike location. For Championship Game Two, he was especially glad to be alone. "Texas bounced back big time," he recalled with a shake of the head. "They romped us 5–1 to force a third game. It was the first time an LSU team had ever lost a game during the championship round. If anyone had been with me I might have punched them out."

The next night he would have kissed them.

For the second consecutive year the College World Series came down to one game.

The Game.

Thirteenth Street was supercharged with even more pregame electricity than usual. Starsky's was rocking the '80s hair metal tunes. Zesto was grilling burgers fifty at a time. The jigsaw puzzle of Vicky's Valley was completely put together a full two hours before the first pitch. The two best traveling, hardest partying teams in CWS history were playing for the title, and the spirits of the Wild Bunch and Dingerville swirled over The Neighborhood to create the perfect Rosenblatt storm.

Down on Bob Gibson Boulevard, the Boudreaux Thibodeaux boys were in their full purple-and-gold regalia. These two weeks had been even more fun than usual, due in equal parts to LSU's run to the finals and the marriage of one of the Nebraska's contingent's daughters, a wedding that was planned on a Series off-day so that their dear friends from Louisiana would be in town to attend. Just across the street sat the Mobile Intensive Tailgating Unit. No, the lettering on the side of the ambulance wasn't fixed, still reading "Mobile Intensive Care Unit." But this year it was parked a little farther north, adjacent to the Omaha Police and EMT units, so the owners could simply direct the weak and wounded to the professionals instead of having to come up with their own on-the-fly first-aid methods.

In the south parking lot, the Dale family had also moved their location, sliding a few hundred feet to the left and squarely into the bend of the road to join forces with Mark Samstad's Professional Tailgaters. It was a truly glorious union of two of The Blatt's great parking-lot superpowers. The result was Hooding Ceremony crowds that were much larger than anyone could remember. Samstad was already talking about organizing a charity golf tournament in 2010 to commemorate the final year of Rosenblatt Stadium, and inquired on how to get in touch with the Thibodeaux outfit on the north side about teeing it up.

Would there be enough charcoal and beer in the city of Omaha to support such a merger?

Squarely in the heart of it all, Stadium View Sportscards was packed out. Fans sipped free beer, sifted through the clearance racks of souvenirs from CWS of the past, and snatched up T-shirts that read TWO MORE YEARS OF COLLEGE BASEBALL, FREE BEER AND GREAT MEMORIES. As the cash registers and laughter rang out around him, Greg Pivovar took it all in, perched on his stool alongside the main display case and grinning ear to ear. This year, however, his face and hair were noticeably thinner.

"What did I tell you last year? We love LSU. And you know who we love just as much as we love LSU? Texas. No two teams bring more people. No two groups of people stay longer. And no one, I mean no one, spends money like these two schools spend money. They love it here. They're like part of the family. And we've only got this year and next to have our annual family reunion."

Throughout the winter and early spring, Piv had used that reunion as a target, his motivation to come back as quickly as possible from an unexpectedly difficult bout with throat cancer. The energy- and spirit-sapping procedures and treatments had left him laid up in bed, but he always kept one eye on the calendar, aimed directly at mid-June.

"Yeah, it was no fun. And I wear out a lot quicker than I'm used to. I have to sit down a lot, make the kids here do the legwork. But I wouldn't miss this. Besides, people would have just come to my house and dragged my ass out here if I'd stayed home complaining about not feeling good."

Then he winked, smiled, and pointed to his daughter, Harper Lee, now eight years old. The donation cans of the Harper Lee College Fund were lined up once again, emblazoned with the insignia of all eight teams of the 2009 Series. Two of the receptacles were filled to the brim. The ones that belonged to Texas and LSU.

Inside The Blatt, everyone took their places as naturally as if they were putting on an old pair of bedroom slippers. Ann Walters was with her daughter behind home (she hadn't missed any games this year), the Walkenhorsts were down the third-base line, the Anzaldos behind first. The Insurance Man and The Pope had been busy all week, already working their plans to send Rosenblatt off in style in 2010. There would be special ceremonies honoring the legendary players, coaches, fans, and even the behind-the-scenes legends, from the box office to the organist's booth.

But first, there was a champion to crown. And it didn't take long for that champion to stand up and be identified.

Jared Mitchell, LSU's two-sport star and recent first-round draft pick of the Chicago White Sox, blasted a three-run homer in the top of the first inning. Already the chants had started from the blue seats of The Blatt to the bars of The Neighborhood. *L-S-U!* They added another run in the second. *L-S-U!* Texas came back to tie it up in the fifth. *Hook 'em Horns!* But in the sixth, the purple-and-gold machine got going again. Mitchell, who would be named the Series' Most Outstanding Player, led off with a walk. He moved to second on a passed ball and then scored on a double by the suddenly scorching-hot Mahtook. 5–4, *L-S-U!* An error and two sacrifices later, Mahtook scored. 6–4, *L-S-U!*

Suddenly, as he would admit weeks later, Augie Garrido began to feel the air escaping from the same dugout that had become so desolate for the Georgia Bulldogs one year earlier. As he had once described the feeling when talking about the virus that destroyed his heavily favored 2004 Texas squad: "The fear of failure swept through the team and we never recovered."

By inning's end, Texas had committed a passed ball, an error, a wild pitch, had hit two batters and walked two, and had given up two hits. The Tigers scored five runs and led 9–4. They won by a final score of 11-4, clinching their sixth College World Series title.

On the field, Paul Mainieri brought down his father, his mother, his children, and everyone else in attendance who was included in his legendary speed-dial list. Some of the players had already texted Hollander to congratulate him, sitting in his apartment half a continent away, but still a part of the team. (So much so that when the team was invited to visit the White House later that summer, he was accidentally included on the e-mail list when the itinerary was sent out.)

In the craziness of it all, Mainieri accepted a handshake and hug from a devastated Garrido. To his credit, the Texas coach hung around for the postgame ceremonies, which he had controversially ditched after losing the title in 2004. And on the way out of the stadium that night he made one more flyby around the curb where he'd cried his eyes out as a college kid, just to make sure it was still there. And to swear to it that he would be back for one more round in 2010.

"There is no one who loves this old place more than I do," the coach confessed. "Even though it has broken my heart as many times as it has embraced me. There will be an extra sense of urgency to make it back here for the last dance in 2010. It will be that way for every coach in the country, but especially for the coach at the University of Texas. I can't imagine closing this place going down without letting the Longhorns on the field one last time."

Then he laughed and quoted himself from the start of the 2009 Series nearly two weeks earlier: "But they give the map to only eight teams. And that Road to Omaha can be one hellaciously unpredictable ride."

Later that night, shortly before midnight and long after LSU and Texas had both boarded their buses and roared away, the only sounds from Rosenblatt Stadium were the motors and shouts from the Cuevas Crew as they started the stadium-flipping process, once again making the switch from "Home of the College World Series" to "Home of the Omaha Royals."

Gathered just inside the concourse was a group of ridiculously polite adults, three women and two men, trying to decide if it was too late to go grab a bite to eat and if not, where they might go.

Bob Thomas, having turned in his radio and successfully put on yet another Series, stood with his wife. Lou Spry, who had marked the final play "ROWE: K" in his twenty-ninth consecutive official CWS scorebook, stood with his wife. With them was Donna Mancuso, widow of Frankie, the longtime stadium manager and groundskeeper who had nurtured the six-decade-old facility from a little municipal ballpark into a national sports cathedral, making sure that every blade of grass was as green and every inch of the grandstand as blue as it always was in every young ballplayer's dreams.

"As sad as this is," she said, watching the The Blatt's lights shut down one tower at a time, "it is so exciting to hear people talk about their memories of the place. Their favorite games, their favorite moments, their favorite people. As sad as it has been coming here and knowing that they are tearing it down, it has been worth it to hear people talking again about my Frank. His work . . . the work of so many people that no one knew about until now, has really meant a lot to people's lives. Too many to count—it's . . . it's amazing. . . ."

She stopped to catch herself, perhaps to catch the knot in her throat. So Lou Spry finished the thought for her.

"I think that's exactly what Johnny Rosenblatt had in mind."

BIBLIOGRAPHY

Books

Baseball America Directory 2008. Durham, NC: Baseball America, 2008.

The Baseball Encyclopedia. New York: Macmillan, 1993.

Bertman, Skip, with Bruce Hunter. *Skip: The Man and The System*. Baton Rouge: Victory Publishing, 1992

Bristow, David L. *A Dirty, Wicked Town: Tales of 19th Century Omaha*. Caldell, Idaho: Caxton Press, 2006.

Brock, Jim, and Joe Gilmartin. *The Devils' Coach*. Fullerton, CA: David C. Cook Publishing, 1977.

Burns, Ken, and Geoffrey C. Ward. *Baseball: An Illustrated History*. New York: Alfred A. Knopf, 1994.

Clark, William, and Meriwether Lewis. *The Journals of Lewis and Clark*. Washington: National Geographic Adventure Classics, 2002.

Fraser, Ron. *Championship Baseball*. North Palm Beach, FL: Athletic Institute, 1983.

Gibson, Bob, with Lonnie Wheeler. *Stranger to the Game*. New York: Penguin Books, 1994.

Hyde, Thomas, and Devon M. Niebling. *Baseball in Omaha*. Charleston, SC: Arcadia Publishing, 2004.

Johnson, Richard and Glenn Stout. *Red Sox Century*. New York: Houghton Mifflin, 2004.

Kindall, Jerry, and John Winkin, ed. *The Baseball Coaching Bible*. Champaign, IL: Human Kinetics, 2000.

Madden, W. C., and John E. Peterson. *College World Series*. Charleston, SC: Arcadia Publishing, 2005.

Madden, W. C. and Patrick J. Stewart. *The College World Series: A Baseball History, 1947–2003*. Jefferson, NC: MacFarland & Company, 2004.

Montville, Leigh. *The Big Bam*. New York: Broadway Books, 2006.

Okrent, Daniel, and Steve Wulf. *Baseball Anecdotes*. New York: Oxford Press, 1989.

Pearlman, Jeff. *Love Me, Hate Me: Barry Bonds and the Making of an Antihero*. New York: HarperCollins, 2006.

Peter, Father Val J. *I Think of My Homelessness: Stories from Boys Town*. Boys Town, NE: Boys Town Press, 1992.

2008 Media Guides

NCAA Men's College World Series, College of the Holy Cross, University of California Berkeley, Florida State University, Fresno State University, University of Georgia, Louisiana State University, University of Miami, University of North Carolina, University of Oklahoma, Rice University, University of Southern California, Stanford University, University of Texas, ACC, Conference USA, PAC-10, SEC, WAC

Periodicals

The Baton Rouge Advocate, Athens Banner-Herald, Atlanta Journal-Constitution, Baseball America, The Charlotte Observer, Collegiate Baseball, Dallas Morning News, Durham Herald-Sun, Fresno Bee, Houston Chronicle, Miami Herald, NCAA Champions Magazine, New Orleans Times-Picayune, New York Times, Nebraska Life, Omaha City Weekly,

Omaha Magazine, Omaha World-Herald, Palo Alto Daily News, Pittsburgh Post Gazette, Raleigh News & Observer, Sports Business Journal, The Sporting News, The State, Sun-Sentinel, Tarheel Monthly, USA Today, Worcester Telegram & Gazette

Web sites

Baseball-Alamanac.com, BaseballAmerica.com, BaseballHall.org, CBSCollegeSports.com, CWSofOmaha.com, CollegeBaseballFoundation.org, CollegeBaseballInsider.com, CSTV.com, ESPN.com, IMDB.com, NCAA.org, NOLA.com, Omaha.com, OmahaStadium.com, Rivals.com, SaveRosenblatt.com, TheCollegeBaseballBlog.com, YouTube.com, and the official sites of the eight competing schools.

ACKNOWLEDGMENTS

I have to be honest. Working on this project was like robbing a bank. I've never had so much fun while also on the clock.

Like so many others, I attended my first College World Series with my father. Jerry McGee is one of the world's great baseball fans and was a tremendous help in writing this book, from his endless relationships throughout college sports to his pure, unspoiled love of the game. If he liked what I had written, that's about as solid a test audience as one could hope for. Throughout this great story of fathers and their families, it was hard not to think about Dad, brother Sam, and me settling into stadium seats all over this great land.

To the other members of the McGee Clan of the Old North State, especially my girls at home, Erica and Tara. They endured months of their man being in absentia, both physically and mentally, sometimes ignoring them as I stared at the floor trying to figure out yet another way to describe a curveball.

To my dear late mother Hannah and my grandparents, especially Lib Covington, who passed away shortly before the start of the 2008 Series and who was so thrilled with the idea of this project.

To the great folks at Thomas Dunne Books and St. Martin's Press, especially the endlessly enthusiastic Pete Wolverton, whose one simple sentence of advice—"Remember Omaha"—kept me on track through the summer months; then whose second simple sentence—"Remember Baseball"—got me back on track in the fall. And thanks to Elizabeth Byrne for somehow keeping track of the constantly moving targets of McGee and Wolverton.

To Jud Laghi, Jenny Arch, Larry Kirshbaum, and everyone at LJK Literary Management. It took us a while to finally find the right project, but Mr. Laghi is the one who sold it, even as his heart was being broken by the Mets . . . again.

As always, I am indebted to my coworkers at ESPN The Magazine and ESPN.com, from the Garys to J. B. Morris to Chris Raymond to K. Lee Davis and the Internet wizards of Bristol. Their insistence on perfection when I was way too tired to provide it has managed to convert a TV production refugee into an actual writer. They were also kind enough to let me disappear into a spider hole to finish this book when they certainly could have demanded that I do otherwise.

To my Brothers of The Blatt, who made the longest CWS of all-time even more enjoyable: Eric Sorenson of CBS College Sports, Aaron Fitt of Baseball America, Kendall Rogers of Rivals.com, Andy Gardiner of USA Today, Lauren Reynolds of ESPN.com, and Matt James of the Fresno Bee, among so many others.

Being a sports information director can be a thankless task, especially when some guy you've never seen before is constantly bugging you about a book that won't come out for another year, but thanks to these SIDs for playing ball: Stanford's Aaron Juarez, UNC's John Martin, Fresno's Steve Weakland, LSU's Bill Franques, Miami's Kerwin Lonzo, Georgia's Christopher Lakos, Florida State's Jason Leturmy, and Rice's John Sullivan. Also, thanks to Scott Ball at California, Pacific's Glen Sisk, and Benjamin Harry at the National Baseball Hall of Fame and Museum for quick turnaround on some induction speech questions.

A big thanks as well to my new friend Kyle Peterson, who lived the CWS as a fan, a player, and now as a broadcaster. Now I feel bad for using one of his Milwaukee Brewer baseball cards as a bookmark all those years.

I also owe a huge debt to the works of authors W. C. Madden and David L. Bristow. This book was never meant to be a detailed blow-by-blow history of the College World Series. Anyone looking to get inside every CWS game ever played need look no further than Madden's book, The College World Series: A Baseball History, 1947–2003. His research skills are impeccable and made my job easier than it could have been. I hope that this work is a complement to his. And Bristow's A Dirty, Wicked Town is as entertaining a book on nineteenth-century Wild West life as one could ever hope to find.

I dare anyone to find another nationally televised sport where the coaches of each team are willing to let you follow them around all day the week of the championship, or to grant a writer a ninety-minute interview the day of an elimination game. Nearly every coach in Omaha did exactly that, particularly Mark Marquess, Paul Mainieri, Mike Fox, and Dave Perno, who went even further by inviting me down to Athens later in the fall to go over the games with him after the fact. Augie Garrido also gave me a ridiculous amount of time on a Saturday afternoon, even chatting with my four-year-old daughter for a second.

On the champion's side, it was assistant coach Mike Mayne who opened the doors into the Fresno State clubhouse and psyche, trusting a writer he'd never met to portray accurately the team, kids, and game that he was obviously so passionate about.

The NCAA supported me on this project from day one, particularly Dennie Poppe and his baseball staff, including Randy Buhr, Bob Thomas, and Damani Leech. J. D. Hamilton, and his entire militia of CWS help from multiple schools were also a greater help than I could have expected; in particular, Hamilton patiently waded through a couple of dozen random middle-of-the-night questions that started in April and lasted until October. He was nice even when I made an exhausted smart-ass remark about the postgame coverage plans on the day of the title game. If I'd been he I would have punched me in the nose, but he just smiled and said, "We'll see what we can do for you."

A similar nod has to be made to Jack Diesing, Jr. (whom I nearly stood up by accident), CWS of Omaha, Inc., and Tom Giitter at Bozell, who wrote up the greatest pre-championship media contact list of all time. Thanks as well to Mayor Mike Fahey's office, especially communications director Joe Gudenrath, who found time for me in the midst of one of the most tumultuous weeks of the Fahey era.

To the superb staff of the Omaha World-Herald—if there is an American newspaper that does a better job of covering its city's signature event, I haven't seen it. No matter where I went or how big of a scoop I thought I had, I inevitably picked up that morning's edition of the OWH and, dammit, there it was. To my new friend Mitch Sherman, who sent more than a few enthusiastic locals in my direction with stories and opinions, as well as the tireless efforts of Tom Shatel, Steven Pivovar, and their coworkers.

Thanks to my old friend Scott Matthews and his entire ESPN production team. It was good to see a guy I used to work with when we were both starting out in the TV business.

Dawn Ream at the Henry Doorly Zoo and Shawna Forsberg at the Durham Western Heritage Museum were a tremendous help, as was Gary Kastrick of Omaha South High and his Omaha Project and South Omaha History Museum. I also received some serious history lessons from the staff at the Western Historic Trails Center in Council Bluffs, a museum that was sandwiched between the Missouri River levee to the west and endless youth baseball games tinking away to the east. God bless America indeed.

And to Mary and the good folks at the Sleep Inn by the airport. They'd never seen a guy set up a whole library of reference books in a hotel room and then never ever be around to use them.

I interviewed more than two hundred people for this book, from big leaguers and long-forgotten CWS players to Hollywood directors and regular Omaha citizens. The list is far too long to tally for you here, but I thank each and every one of them for his and her cooperation and enthusiasm.

It is their passion about the College World Series that makes the event what it is. I can only hope that I was able to do them justice.

INDEX

CPSIA information can be obtained
at www.ICGtesting.com
Printed in the USA
LVHW102130200623
750327LV00023B/107

9 780312 628024